The
EVERYTHING
Quick and Easy 30-Minute, 5-Ingredient Cookbook

Dear Reader,

When developing these recipes, I worked as hard as I could to make sure they could be made in 30 minutes or less. Depending on your skill in the kitchen, they may take a little more or less time, but you can be assured they are all quick and easy. It can be difficult to create new recipes using so few ingredients, but several trips to the supermarket gave me many new wonderful convenience or "value-added" foods to work with. When you are shopping, keep your eyes open for new products. Home economists in food companies work hard every day to introduce new foods that will help you get in and out of the kitchen in a flash. A list of my favorite convenience foods appears in Appendix A at the end of the book.

Of course, you can add more ingredients to these recipes! Chop up some red or orange bell peppers to toss into a salad, add more frozen vegetables to a stew, and frost cakes and cookies using your own frosting recipe or by jazzing up canned frosting with sour cream or chocolate. These additions take no more time at all, so add (or subtract!) according to your family's tastes.

When a recipe uses canned ingredients, sodium content can become a concern. You can usually find low-sodium or no-sodium products, if not in the regular grocery store, then online or in health food stores. Low-fat products can be used in most of these recipes; just be careful in baking recipes because low-fat products can affect texture and flavor.

Enjoy these recipes. I hope that they inspire you to "make over" some of your more complicated recipes and that they become part of your permanent repertoire. Let's get cooking!

The EVERYTHING® Series

Editorial

Publishing Director	Gary M. Krebs
Director of Product Development	Paula Munier
Associate Managing Editor	Laura M. Daly
Associate Copy Chief	Brett Palana-Shanhan
Acquisitions Editor	Kate Burgo
Development Editor	Jessica LaPointe
Associate Production Editor	Casey Ebert

Production

Director of Manufacturing	Susan Beale
Associate Director of Production	Michelle Roy Kelly
Series Designer	Colleen Cunningham
Cover Design	Paul Beatrice
	Erick DaCosta
	Matt LeBlanc
Interior Layout	Heather Barrett
	Brewster Brownville
	Colleen Cunningham
	Jennifer Oliveira
Series Cover Artist	Barry Littmann

THE
EVERYTHING®
QUICK AND EASY
30-MINUTE, 5-INGREDIENT
COOKBOOK

300 delicious recipes for busy cooks

Linda Larsen
The About.com Guide for Busy Cooks

Adams Media
Avon, Massachusetts

This book is dedicated to
Grace, Maddie, and Michael, my sweethearts.

An Everything® Series Book.
Everything® and everything.com® are registered trademarks of F+W Publications, Inc.

Published by Adams Media, an F+W Publications Company
57 Littlefield Street, Avon, MA 02322 U.S.A.
www.adamsmedia.com

ISBN 10: 1-59337-692-8
ISBN 13: 978-1-59337-692-5

Printed in the United States of America.

J I H G F E D C B A

Library of Congress Cataloging-in-Publication Data
Larsen, Linda.
The everything quick and easy 30-minute, 5-ingredient cookbook / Linda Larsen.
p.   cm.
Includes index.
ISBN-13: 978-1-59337-692-5
ISBN-10: 1-59337-692-8
1. Quick and easy cookery. I. Title.
TX833.5.L37 2006
641.5'55--dc22

2006028213

This book is available at quantity discounts for bulk purchases.
For information, please call 1-800-289-0963.

Contents

Acknowledgments

So many people took part in the creation of this book, even if indirectly. First of all, I have to thank my parents, Duane and Marlene, for their unconditional love, help, and support. As always, my agent Barb Doyen has to be thanked for her faith in me. And my editor, Kate Burgo, is always there to help and offer advice and suggestions. My cooking life and life in general has been greatly enhanced by family members Laura, Lisa, Rod, Grace, Maddie, Michael, Ted and Dagmar, Nancy, Bill, Andy, Zach, Richard, Daryl, Bryce, and Trent, and friends Steve and Kris, John and Cheryl, Kevin and Wendy, Bob and Nancy, and Lee and Kathy. And of course, to my dear husband, Doug, for his support during the creation process and all other times. He'll happily eat anything I make!

Introduction

With our busy lifestyles today, cooking often gets relegated to the bottom of the list. But your life doesn't have to be filled with takeout, frozen TV dinners, expensive restaurant meals, and junk food. With some planning and organization, plus a few new cooking skills, you can make meals using recipes that take 30 minutes or less, using 5 ingredients or fewer.

Cooking and baking your own food means that you will spend less money, offer more nutritious meals to your family, and you'll certainly spend less time in the kitchen than ever before. With the judicious use of convenience and value-added foods, making delicious recipes is easier than ever.

New recipes that start with deli ingredients means you can make complicated recipes in just minutes. For instance, use a deli fruit salad as an ingredient in creamy fruit parfaits, or buy a rotisserie chicken to use for grilled cheese and chicken sandwiches. Planning what I call "overlapping meals," where leftovers from one day are used as ingredients in meals later in the week, also expands your recipe repertoire exponentially while staying within the five-ingredient limit. Have Spicy Vegetarian Chili (page 144) and Corn Bread (page 39) on the menu Monday, and Tuesday toast the corn bread and use it to make Southern Corn Bread Salad (page 56). Thursday, Taco Salad (page 64) is on the menu, using the leftover chili.

Preparing recipes in 30 minutes or less means you'll need to learn some special skills. Efficient shopping, organizing your kitchen and your cooking habits, and planning meals for the week are at the top of the list. You'll learn streamlined preparation techniques and how to follow simple rules like starting the longest-cooking ingredients first to create a pocket of time while you work on others. And you'll find an extensive ingredient substitution list, for those times when you run out of a key ingredient in the middle of a recipe. I'll also include a primer on different cooking techniques so you will become an expert in grilling, microwaving, broiling, and stir-frying.

Of course, staying within that 30-minute time limit will depend on your kitchen expertise, the number of distractions (kids, pets, ringing telephones and doorbells) in your home, and any help you may have. With a little bit of concentration, you should be able to prepare these recipes in 30 minutes or less.

You'll also learn how to enjoy food preparation. I'll remind you to listen to the sounds of foods, enjoy the aromas, and relish the feeling of coziness as you revive the family table.

Once you build a repertoire of quick and easy 30-minute, 5-ingredient dishes, you'll learn how to stock your pantry, fridge, and freezer with enough ingredients so you'll never again be caught without the means of preparing an excellent meal for your friends and family. So join me and learn how you can feed your family delicious, nutritious, and super-easy quick meals ready in 30 minutes or less, using 5 ingredients. And enjoy imagining what you'll do with all your extra time!

Chapter 1

Starting Out

Learning how to prepare food as a chef does, organizing your techniques and your kitchen, instinctive measuring, and planning a cooking schedule as you read a recipe are all key to preparing food in under 30 minutes. With some practice, these techniques and methods will become second nature. All of your kitchen work will be streamlined, and you will be able to prepare every recipe more quickly and efficiently.

The Game Plan

Let's start by learning how to read a recipe. The ingredient list is organized in order of use, stating amounts in package sizes, cups, tablespoons, and weights. Be sure you have all of the ingredients on hand. Read through the recipe twice so you understand all of the preparation steps. Make sure you have all of the necessary utensils and equipment. Use a food glossary to look up terms you may not understand. The directions are written with time saving in mind, starting with the preparation that takes the longest. It may help you to add notes to the recipe to mark the jobs you can "multitask" and those that require constant attention.

Learn how to visualize a recipe as you read through it. Literally try to see yourself collecting the ingredients; pulling out pots, pans, and utensils you will need; prepping ingredients; and cooking the food. This "dress rehearsal" in your head will teach you how to streamline preparation techniques and will help ensure that you understand the recipe.

When you start learning new methods of cooking, measuring, and preparing food, go slow. It will take some experience before you can peel and chop an onion in less than a minute. Learn how to prepare foods properly and your speed will increase as you become more comfortable with new techniques.

The Basics

These recipes all require five ingredients or less, not counting flour, sugar, cornstarch, oil, water, baking powder and soda, and seasonings like salt, pepper, vanilla, and dried herbs and spices. Those are basic, inexpensive ingredients everyone should have on hand. Fresh herbs are counted as an ingredient. Many recipes use different parts of the same food to decrease the ingredient list. For instance, Ambrosia (page 212) uses canned mandarin oranges in the salad and the juice from the oranges in the dressing.

FACT

These basic ingredients do have expiration dates even if they aren't marked on the package. Dried herbs and spices lose potency after a year. Baking powder becomes less effective after about six months. And flour, especially whole wheat flour, can become rancid in a few months. Mark the dates you buy these products on the cans and packages and discard them after these time periods.

Since these recipes use so few ingredients, the ingredients must be top quality. You won't be able to disguise limp broccoli or soft apples in these recipes. And the short cooking time, too, requires that the ingredients be premium. Fruits and vegetables should be heavy for their size and bright colored, with no discoloration, wrinkling, or soft spots. Fish should smell sweet and the flesh should be firm. Meats should be bright red, with even marbling and little juice in the package. And chicken should be firm and pink, again with little juice in the package.

Cook Once, Eat Twice

Leftovers are not only desirable when quick cooking, they will save you time tomorrow. When you're making rice to go with Sweet and Sour Pork Stew (page 249), cook twice as much as you need. Then tomorrow night you can make Chicken Fried Rice (page 109) in about 10 minutes since the rice is already cooked and chilled. And it doesn't take any more time to cook more food, unless you are microwaving. Be sure to cover and chill or store the extra food you're saving before you get dinner on the table. Label it so you know what's in the container. Use the leftover foods within two to three days for food-safety reasons.

Organizing

Every kitchen is planned and arranged differently, but there are key principles to follow when organizing your work area. Whether you have a small galley kitchen or a huge gourmet space with restaurant-quality appliances, any kitchen will benefit from some scrutiny and planning.

Kitchen organizers focus on the "work triangle." This is the shape formed when you walk from the sink to the fridge to the stove. For best efficiency, the length of each leg should be no more than nine feet and no less than four feet. If your kitchen isn't laid out this way, you can create your own triangle, or triangles, for different tasks. Many kitchen designers now think that having two or three smaller work triangles is more efficient than one large one. Put a cutting board between the stove and sink and you've created a small work triangle. Place a rolling butcher-block counter near the refrigerator and you can create a small work triangle with the pantry.

E
ALERT!

Every piece of equipment should have a home it returns to after being used. You'll always be able to find your kitchen shears and your can opener if they have a specially designated area in a designated drawer and if they are returned to that spot every time after they are used and cleaned.

Be sure your equipment and measuring utensils are kept in an accessible place. Keep pots and pans near the stove, towels and dishwashing materials near the sink, flour and sugar near your baking center, and can openers and spoons near the pantry and work surfaces.

Professional organizers recommend that you literally plot out the steps you take and the movements you make when working in your kitchen. This takes only about an hour to do while you're making a recipe. It may help to have someone watch you cook to make suggestions about streamlining your methods. If you find, for instance, that you walk between the pantry and the drawer containing your measuring spoons many times, it will help to move those spoons closer to the pantry.

Paper management can be just as important as equipment management in a kitchen. Keep all your loose recipes together, keep similar cookbooks together on your bookshelves, and have a place specifically set aside for bill filing and paying.

Shopping

Grocery shopping is one of the most time-consuming aspects of cooking. To streamline your shopping trips and use the time most efficiently, there are several things you can do.

Try to plan meals at least a week in advance. By doing this, not only will you be able to better balance your family's nutritional intake, but you can take advantage of sales and specials at the grocery store. You can include some of your family's favorite recipes and try a new recipe or two each week.

Always keep a running list of staples along with another list of foods specific to recipes you will be making each week. The staples list keeps track of foods that are currently in your pantry that you use regularly. For instance, olive oil, flour, sugar, baking powder, eggs, milk, butter, and bread may be on your staples list. Whenever you use up a staple food, add it to your list so you won't run out of these items when you're cooking.

ESSENTIAL

Organize your coupons in a small expandable folder. You can organize them by type of food and arrange the folder so it follows the pattern of your supermarket. Be sure to go through the folder twice a month to use coupons before their expiration dates and discard any past that date.

Use the menus you have planned for the week along with grocery fliers and your collection of coupons to plan out your weekly list. Try to arrange it according to the layout of your favorite supermarket. Go shopping at less crowded times of the day, like early in the morning or later at night. Clean out your pantry, fridge, and freezer before your weekly shopping trip. Discard products past their use-by dates, wipe down the shelves, and organize food items so they're easy to find. After your shopping trip, think about prepping some foods after you unpack.

Shopping Do's

- Use a cooler to store frozen foods if you live some distance from the store.
- Divide hamburger into patties, wrap, and freeze.
- Cut larger pieces of meat into serving-size pieces, rewrap, and label.
- Wash herbs, shake dry, wrap in paper towels, and place in plastic bags.
- Wash, peel, and chop hard vegetables like carrots, cauliflower, and broccoli.
- Wash salad greens, dry thoroughly, and store in plastic bags.

Shopping Don'ts

- Go shopping with kids in tow, if at all possible.
- Shop when you are tired, hungry, or ill.
- Take the long way home. Perishable food should be refrigerated promptly.
- Rinse delicate fruits like strawberries and raspberries.
- Prepare fresh mushrooms or any fruit that can turn brown after cutting.
- Let perishable food sit on your counter for more than an hour; refrigerate or freeze these products immediately.

Convenience Foods

One of the best ways to limit the total number of ingredients used in a recipe is to use convenience foods that combine several ingredients in one product. For instance, frozen bell peppers and onions are packaged together and sold as a stir-fry ingredient. And cooked ground beef in a spicy tomato sauce is available in the meat department of your supermarket; this one product substitutes for eight or nine ingredients needed if it was made from scratch. See Appendix A (page 294) for a list of good convenience foods that will help you fill your pantry, fridge, and freezer.

FACT

Most convenience foods were introduced to the American public after World War II. Companies had developed many products like canned meats and freeze-dried foods to feed armies, and they now wanted to sell those products to the consumer.

Make sure that your family likes the convenience food before you stock up. When you find a winner, buy multiples and fill your freezer and pantry. With these foods and the recipes in this book, you'll be prepared for any occasion.

Equipment

Have multiple sets of utensils that you use frequently. Every kitchen should have at least two sets of nested measuring cups and spoons. Glass measuring cups that are angled so you can accurately measure by looking straight down into the cup will help shave minutes off prep time. Have more than one whisk, several heat-resistant spatulas, wooden and metal spoons, forks, knives, slotted spoons, and hot pads.

You may want to invest in a food processor, a convection oven, or a stand mixer with attachments, depending on the food you cook most often. A rice cooker needs no attention and cooks rice to perfection very quickly. Steaming food is faster than simmering or boiling it, so a few bamboo or stainless steel steamers may be a good addition to your kitchen. Immersion blenders and countertop rotisserie cookers are other appliances that may be put to good use in your kitchen. Egg slicers and apple corers make quick work of preparation chores, and mini food processors are great for quickly chopping and mincing ingredients.

How do I keep track of the timing when more than one food is cooking at a time?
Purchase a multiuse timer. These electronic gadgets allow you to keep track of at least three different cooking times at once. Write down on the recipe which task is number one, two, and three so you don't get confused. And practice using the timer before you begin cooking.

Then there are garlic presses, bottle and jar openers, grill pans, dual-contact grills, strawberry stemmers, and shrimp deveiners. Think carefully before purchasing new equipment. If you really think you'll use it often, buy it. But if it isn't used several times in a month, have a garage sale and use the money to go out to dinner!

Cooking Methods

These quick-cooking methods are simple and they don't require special equipment, pots, or pans. When you learn how to use all of these cooking techniques, you'll be able to make any recipe in this book in 30 minutes or less.

Grilling

Grilling is cooking food quickly over high heat. This method adds flavor and, when using an outdoor grill, helps keep your kitchen cool on hot days. Make sure the grill is ready to use before you begin cooking: charcoal should be gray, with no apparent flames. Gas grills usually have a readiness indicator.

Whether you use a gas grill, charcoal grill, or an indoor dual-contact grill, keep it clean! Indoor grills will wipe clean with a damp paper towel. Outdoor grills can be cleaned using a wire brush or special compounds that will dissolve hardened grease.

Watch food carefully when it's on the grill. Follow the instructions. Many recipes call for cooking the food covered to create an ovenlike environment. Be sure to use a set of tongs, not a fork, to turn food. And keep kids and pets away from the hot grill until it's completely cool.

Microwaving

Microwave ovens cook by generating electromagnetic waves that react with water and sugar molecules in foods. The molecules begin to vibrate and twist, creating friction that heats up the food and cooks it.

Read your microwave user manual carefully. Many new microwave ovens come complete with preprogrammed cooking times for commonly used foods. You simply choose the food you want to cook, put it in the oven in a microwave-safe container, and then select the cooking code for that food.

FACT

Microwave ovens are a good choice for quickly defrosting frozen foods. The magnetron shuts off and turns back on in a cycle when the thawing option is chosen, letting the energy travel through the food slowly, gradually melting the ice crystals.

Be sure to use only microwave-safe bowls, cups, plates, plastic wrap, and waxed paper in the oven. Arrange food with the thickest parts toward the outside of the bowl or plate. Carefully observe stirring and rearranging instructions and standing times. And follow the safety recommendations in the manual to the letter!

Stir-Frying

Stir-frying quickly cooks small pieces of foods over high heat in a small amount of oil. For best results, the food should be about the same size, shape, and thickness. This increases the time you'll spend preparing the foods, but the cooking time will be only a few minutes. And you really do have to stir constantly while the food is cooking.

Heat the pan before you add the oil for best results. And if you have a wok, use it! The rounded shape helps you toss the food as it cooks and provides higher heat on the bottom of the pan and less intense heat on the sides, letting you control cooking temps and speed.

Steaming

Steaming is a moist-heat method of cooking food that's quick and very healthy, too. Once the water underneath the steamer comes to a simmer, you're ready to cook. You can buy stainless steel steamers, collapsible basket steamers, or stackable bamboo steamers; all work equally well. Make sure the simmering water in the bottom pan doesn't touch the steamer for best results.

Fish and more delicate vegetables are the best choices for steaming because they cook quickly. If you have stackable steamers, pay careful attention to rotating and layering the steamers so all the food cooks evenly.

Cooking in paper, or *en papillote*, is also a steaming method. Parchment paper or foil is used to enclose the food and holds in the steam the food produces as it cooks. Chicken, fish, vegetables, and fruit are great choices for cooking *en papillote*.

Pan Frying or Sautéing

Preheat your pans for pan frying and sautéing before you add the oil or butter and the food won't stick. When pan-frying meats, season the meat well, place it in the pan, then leave it alone for a few minutes. If you move the meat before it has formed a crust and has seared, it will tear and be less juicy and tender.

Don't crowd the pan when cooking with this method or the temperature will lower and the food will boil or steam rather than sear and cook through. The recipe will let you know when to stir or turn the food.

Once you remove the cooked meat, deglaze the pan by adding a small amount of liquid—broth, water, or juice. Scrape up the browned bits and the drippings left in the pan to add lots of flavor to your gravy. And this step cleans the pan, too!

Deep-Frying

This is a dry-heat method because no liquid is used. Special deep fryers can be purchased to make the job easier if you use this cooking method often. Again, don't overcrowd the pan when deep-frying or the food will steam, absorb oil, and turn out soggy.

When deep-frying, choose oils with the highest smoke point. This is the temperature at which the oil will begin to break down and smoke, releasing fumes into the air. Oils with high smoke points that are flavorless include peanut oil, canola oil, and safflower oil.

Be sure to leave at least one to two inches of headspace at the top of the pan to allow space for the oil to bubble up when the food is added. Use tongs to slide the food into the fryer, stand back to avoid splattering, and drain foods well on paper towels before serving.

Broiling

This dry-heat method is similar to grilling. Preheat the broiler before you begin prepping the foods. Most broilers work best when the oven door is ajar. Spray the broiling pan with nonstick cooking spray for easy cleanup. Arrange the racks so the food is the correct distance from the heat source, and be sure to watch the foods carefully and turn when the recipe directs.

Broiling is used for tender or marinated meats and vegetables. This is also a good way to roast chilies and tomatoes for Southwest-style cooking. This cooking method is controlled by timing and by rearranging the oven racks to move the food closer to or farther away from the heat source.

Pressure Cooking

There are new pressure cookers on the market that are totally self-contained, with digital controls and excellent safety features. Most of these cookers have a quick-release feature that makes it possible for you to cook using this appliance in less than 30 minutes.

Pressure cookers work by increasing pressure in a closed and locked container, which allows the food to boil at a higher temperature than 212°F. Be sure to carefully read the instructions of your pressure cooker. The type that sit on the stovetop are still available; you must watch them carefully to regulate the heat and cooking times.

Quick Chilling

There are several methods you can use to quickly chill foods. Spread the food in a shallow pan and place in the freezer for 20 minutes. You can also place the pan or bowl into a larger pan or bowl that you have filled with ice cubes and cold water; stir occasionally so the food cools evenly. Fill a glass or plastic bottle with ice and water, seal it, and use to stir soups or sauces that you want to cool down quickly.

Or you can combine these methods. Place the pan or bowl of food into the pan full of ice water and use a bottle filled with ice to stir. Some freezers have a "quick freeze" shelf, usually located at the top of the freezer, that will cool and freeze foods more quickly. Read the manual to see if your freezer has this capability.

Shortcuts and Techniques

There's a reason that chefs all prepare food in the same way; they save energy and make the most of every second when they can consistently peel and chop an onion in under a minute or julienne a green pepper in two. Other shortcuts include learning to estimate quantities when cooking, preheating appliances and pans, and cleaning as you go.

Prep Once

As you read through the recipe, note ingredients that are used more than once and prepare the entire amount needed at one time. For instance, if salad recipes use 2 tablespoons of grated Parmesan cheese in the dressing and 2 tablespoons sprinkled on top of the completed salad, grate ¼ cup of cheese while preparing ingredients.

For easiest cleanup, store ingredients used more than once on waxed paper or parchment paper rather than in little dishes or plates. A very large cutting board can also be very efficient for storing ingredients before you are ready to use them.

Since these ingredients will be used so quickly, there's no need to cover them or return them to the fridge or freezer while they are waiting to be used. If there is a delay of more than an hour in your cooking schedule, cover and chill all prepared foods to keep them at the peak of freshness and whole-someness.

Chop Like a Pro

Use a well-sharpened, balanced chef's knife. Hold the knife in your domi-nant hand and keep the tip of the knife on the work surface or cutting board. Move the handle up and down to slice through the food. Hold the food, with the flat- or cut-side down, in your nondominant hand, and curl your fingers under to protect them as the knife blade cuts next to the knuckle. Start slow; as you gain experience, you'll be able to chop and slice faster.

When chopping fruits and vegetables, start by creating a solid base. Trim a small piece off one side of the food so it will sit securely on your cutting board and not rock back and forth. You won't notice the cut in the prepared food and you'll reduce the chances of cutting yourself.

When mincing foods like herbs and garlic, rock the knife back and forth on the food, using your dominant hand to hold the handle and the other on top of the knife to guide the blade. Occasionally, stop and scrape the material together into a small pile, then continue mincing.

You can use a scissors for many of the ingredients that need to be trimmed, sliced, or chopped: top and tail green beans; mince herbs; and chop toma-toes, pears, and peaches still in the can. Be sure to label the scissors (or hide them) so they're only used on food.

Instinctive Measuring

Cooking recipes (soups, salads, most meats) do not require the precise measurements that baking recipes do. So take a few minutes and train your eye to recognize common measurements. Measure out 1 teaspoon, 1 table-spoon, ¼ cup, ⅓ cup, ½ cup, and 1 cup of flour or cornstarch and line them up on a piece of waxed paper. Scoop them into your hand, one at a time, and notice how high the flour is piled up and how it looks on your palm. Now practice pouring out the different amounts onto your hand and measure your guesses. If you go through this two or three times, you'll be able to cut minutes off your cooking time and still measure accurately.

For liquid ingredients, generally one "turn" around a bowl or pot will measure 2 to 3 tablespoons of that liquid, whether it's oil or buttermilk. Meat stocks and broths are usually 1¾ cups per can or 4 cups per shelf-stable box.

E ALERT!

When using measuring spoons and cups, do not hold the spoon or cup over the bowl containing the rest of your ingredients. It's very easy to slip and add too much of the ingredient, especially when you're measuring liquid flavorings and ingredients like baking powder or soda.

Baking recipes require that you always measure ingredients because they are precise chemical formulas developed for narrowly defined results. If you add more flour than the recipe calls for, your baked product will be heavy and dry. If you add too much liquid, a cake or bread will fall. So take the time when baking to measure precisely. Using mixes is a great baking shortcut, because mixes are just a mixture of the premeasured dry ingredients.

Clean as You Work

Keep a dishpan or one sink full of hot, soapy water. As you work, drop utensils, bowls, pots, and pans into the water to soak. Cleaning as you go is more efficient than trying to tackle a big mess at the end. Have a bag or bowl on hand to hold vegetable trimmings if you have a compost pile. Prepare ingredients near the sink so it's easy to rinse vegetables and fruits before chopping or slicing them. And keep a garbage bag nearby so you can quickly discard packages and wrappings.

When measuring sticky ingredients, coat the cup or spoon with non-stick cooking spray and the ingredient will slide right out after it's measured. Your measuring will be more accurate, and it's easier to clean oil from metal or glass surfaces than the sticky food.

Wipe up spills on cooking surfaces as soon as the appliance cools down. This will save many minutes of scrubbing and is easier on you and the appliance. And wipe spills from your counters and floors when they occur. Keep a damp sponge or kitchen towel on hand in a designated place so it is readily available to clean and mop.

If you have a dishwasher, rinse and load dishes as you work. This is far easier to do as you go along, rather than waiting and facing a big job when you're done cooking. Read your dishwasher manual and follow instructions about prerinsing dishes and how to stack dishes for maximum efficiency.

Timing and Cooking

Remember this term: *mise en place*. This French phrase means that before you start cooking, you have all of the ingredients and equipment you will need on hand so you don't have to stop in the middle of the process and search for something. Before you begin, get all of your ingredients out of the fridge, freezer, pantry, and garden. It may help to remove the lids of the ingredients, then as you add them to the pot or bowl, put the lid or cover back on the bottle or can.

Timing is critical when cooking foods quickly. You must usually do two tasks at once (the word *meanwhile* in recipes is a clue to multitasking). This isn't difficult; you can chop vegetables while pasta cooks, stir together a sauce while meatballs cook in the microwave oven, or prepare greens for a salad while the chicken cooks on the grill.

Organize a plan, either on paper or in your mind, for every recipe you make. Note the tasks that will take the longest, and start them first. For instance, in a baking recipe, the oven must be preheated; this can take from 5 to 10 minutes, so the first thing you'll do is turn on the oven. When cooking pasta, a large pot of water has to come to a rolling boil; put this on the stove first, and cover the pot so the water boils faster. Preheat heavy-duty pans so they are waiting for you. A hot pan will cook foods better, searing the outside immediately and developing great flavors.

ALERT!

Don't preheat older nonstick pans for more than a minute! Studies vary on how long the coating can maintain its integrity under high heat. Some studies have shown the coating can release toxic chemicals if the pan is heated when empty. Other studies have shown it's perfectly safe. It's best not to take a chance, especially if your nonstick cookware is more than a few years old.

Once your pots and oven are preheating, start prepping the ingredients. Begin with the foods that take longest to cook. For instance, most sauces start by sautéing onions or garlic in olive oil. Prepare those ingredients and get them cooking while you prep other foods.

Don't forget to watch the foods that are cooking while you're prepping others. Every 2 to 3 minutes, you should stir sautéing vegetables, check on foods that are thawing or cooking in the microwave oven, stir pasta boiling in the pot, and check on anything under the broiler or on the grill.

Keep distractions to a minimum. Pets and kids underfoot in the kitchen will not only slow you down, they can present a safety hazard. If someone is helping you, have them work on tasks that are out of the main work triangle so you aren't tripping over each other as the meal progresses.

When baking, think about measuring out all of your ingredients, in order, on a large sheet of waxed paper or parchment paper. And when the batter or dough is complete, read over the recipe again to make sure that you have added all of the ingredients. For instance, it's very easy to omit the baking powder or soda from a cake recipe; then you'll have a flop on your hands.

When you start cooking, keep the overall plan of recipe preparation in mind. Pay careful attention to each step and follow the schedule you created carefully. And enjoy watching the recipe come together in the alchemy of cooking and baking.

Chapter 2

Appetizers and Beverages

½ cup apricot preserves
⅓ cup finely chopped dried
    apricots
2 tablespoons water
1 tablespoon honey
½ teaspoon chopped fresh
    thyme leaves
2 cups grated Parmigiano-
    Reggiano cheese

Parmesan Wafers with Apricots

Your guests will never believe that this recipe uses just five ingredients and is ready in less than 30 minutes. The crisp and savory wafers are the perfect accompaniment to the sweet and tart apricot topping.

1. Preheat oven to 350°F. Line a cookie sheet with parchment paper.

2. In a heavy saucepan, combine preserves, apricots, water, honey, and thyme leaves and bring to a simmer. Simmer for 5 to 8 minutes, stirring frequently, until dried apricots are softened and mixture is thickened. Remove from heat and let cool slightly.

3. Meanwhile, using a tablespoon, place mounds of cheese 4 inches apart on prepared cookie sheet and gently pat to form 2-inch rounds. Bake at 350°F for 4 to 6 minutes or until cheese is melted and turns light golden brown.

4. Let crisps cool for 5 minutes on baking sheet, then remove to a paper towel to cool. Serve with warm apricot mixture as a dip.

Why Parmigiano-Reggiano Cheese?
You must use the expensive authentic Italian Parmigiano-Reggiano cheese because it is of such high quality and, as such, has the most density and a lower fat content. When the wafers bake in the oven, there will be little fat rendered, and the wafers will become crisp and delicate as they cool.

Pesto Dip

*This easy dip has wonderful crunch from the toasted pine nuts.
Pine nuts are usually used when making pesto; they are
ground along with the basil leaves and olive oil.*

Serves 8–10

⅓ cup pine nuts
1⅓ cups sour cream
¼ cup plain yogurt
½ cup prepared pesto
¼ cup grated Parmesan
    cheese

1. To toast nuts, spread on small cookie sheet and bake in preheated 350°F oven for 5 to 8 minutes; watch carefully, shaking pan once during baking. Let nuts cool completely.

2. Combine all ingredients in medium bowl and mix well. Serve immediately with dippers like carrot sticks, celery sticks, breadsticks, crackers, and tortilla chips.

Dill Dip

*If you can find fresh dill, by all means use it in this easy and savory dip.
Good choices for dippers include baby carrots, bell pepper strips,
small sticks of celery hearts, and cauliflower florets.*

Serves 8

1 8-ounce package cream
    cheese, softened
½ cup mayonnaise
½ cup plain yogurt
2 teaspoons dried dill weed
2 cloves garlic, finely minced
½ teaspoon salt

In medium bowl, beat cream cheese until soft and fluffy. Add mayonnaise and yogurt and mix well. Stir in dill weed, garlic, and salt until combined. Serve immediately, or cover and refrigerate for 20 minutes to 2 hours before serving.

Fresh Herbs, Dried Herbs

When substituting fresh herbs for dried herbs, multiply the amount by three. So, if a recipe calls for ½ teaspoon of dried thyme, you would use 1½ teaspoons of fresh thyme. The same proportion applies if you are substituting dried herbs for fresh. When a recipe calls for 1 tablespoon of fresh dill, use 1 teaspoon dried dill weed.

Serves 6–8

¼ cup olive oil

3 tablespoons raspberry vinegar, divided

1 tablespoon honey

¼ teaspoon ground ginger

¼ teaspoon salt

2 avocados, peeled

1 cantaloupe, peeled and seeded

Melon and Avocado Cocktail

This elegant recipe is the perfect starter for a fancy dinner party. If the event is formal, use a melon baller to create balls from the avocado flesh for a fancier presentation. Serve it in parfait or sherbet glasses with small silver spoons.

1. In medium bowl, combine olive oil, 2 tablespoons vinegar, honey, ginger, and salt, and mix well with wire whisk. Cut avocados into chunks, or make balls using a melon baller. Sprinkle remaining tablespoon vinegar over prepared avocado.

2. Use a melon baller on cantaloupe to make small balls. Place cantaloupe and avocado in serving bowl and drizzle raspberry vinegar dressing over all. Serve immediately.

How to Ripen Avocados
The avocados you buy in the store are almost always rock hard, so purchase them a few days in advance. To ripen, store them together in a closed paper bag on the kitchen counter, checking every day to see if the flesh gives when gently pressed.

Cheese Puffs

These little puffs will melt in your mouth. The dough you are making is a cream puff dough, or choux pastry, flavored with thyme and two kinds of cheese.

Makes 24 puffs

½ cup milk
¼ cup butter
⅛ teaspoon salt
¼ teaspoon dried thyme
    leaves
½ cup plus 1 tablespoon flour
1 egg
⅓ cup mascarpone cheese
¼ cup cold-pack processed
    cheese food

1. Preheat oven to 425°F. In medium saucepan, combine milk and butter and bring to a rolling boil over high heat. Add salt, thyme leaves, and flour and cook over high heat, stirring constantly, until mixture forms a ball and cleans the sides of the pan.

2. Remove from heat and stir in egg, beating well to incorporate. Add mascarpone cheese along with the cheese food and beat until mixture is well blended.

3. Drop by teaspoonfuls onto parchment paper- or Silpat-lined baking sheets and bake at 425°F for 12 to 18 minutes or until puffed and golden brown. Serve immediately.

Mascarpone Cheese

Mascarpone cheese is a soft Italian cheese that's known as a triple crème cheese. This means it has a very high fat content, about 50 percent, and a rich and smooth texture. Substitutions include ricotta cheese and cottage cheese that has been blended to smoothness in a food processor.

Serves 6–8

3 tablespoons lemon juice
½ teaspoon salt
2 ripe avocados
¼ cup finely chopped red
    onion
1 tomato, chopped
¼ cup sour cream
⅛ teaspoon pepper

Guacamole

*Avocados turn brown, or oxidize, rapidly when the flesh is
exposed to air. To prevent this, drizzle lemon juice or lime juice
over the avocados as soon as you cut them open.*

1. In medium bowl, combine lemon juice and salt and stir to dissolve
   salt. Cut avocados in half, remove pit, then peel and place in bowl with
   lemon-juice mixture; toss to coat. Mash avocados using a fork; make
   the mixture as smooth or chunky as you like.

2. Stir in red onion, tomato, sour cream, and pepper and mix well. Serve
   immediately or cover by placing plastic wrap directly on the surface of
   the guacamole and refrigerate for 20 to 25 minutes.

Burying the Pit?
*Burying the pit in a bowl of guacamole does nothing to stop the mixture
from browning. The browning occurs when cells of certain fruits and
vegetables are exposed to air. The only way to stop it is to add an acid
ingredient, like lime juice, or limit the exposure to air by placing plastic
wrap directly on the surface of the guacamole.*

Spicy Meatballs

Peach jam and chili sauce sound like an unlikely combination, but the flavors blend perfectly. This sweet and sour recipe is very delicious and so easy to make.

───────

Serves 8–10
───────

1 16-ounce package frozen mini meatballs
1 tablespoon olive oil
1 onion, chopped
¼ teaspoon salt
Dash white pepper
¾ cup chili sauce
½ cup peach jam
¼ cup water

Bake meatballs as directed on package. Meanwhile, heat olive oil in a heavy saucepan and add onion, salt, and pepper. Cook and stir until onion is starting to turn brown and caramelize. Add chili sauce, peach jam, and water; stir; and bring to a boil. Add the cooked meatballs and stir to coat. Serve in a chafing dish or Crock-Pot.

Holding Appetizer Dips
Most hot appetizer dips like Spicy Meatballs can be held in a Crock-Pot during a party. Place the hot food into the Crock-Pot and turn it to low. Stir the food every 10 to 15 minutes so it doesn't scorch. The Crock-Pot will keep the dip warm for up to 2 hours.

Yields 24

24 frozen mini filo shells
8 ounces Brie cheese
12 strawberries
½ cup blueberries
2 tablespoons apple jelly
½ teaspoon dried thyme
    leaves
¼ teaspoon salt

Berry Filo Shells

*These beautiful little shells are filled with melted Brie cheese, then topped
with a mixture of fresh cool berries and thyme. This unusual appetizer
has a wonderful combination of textures, temperature, and flavors.*

1. Preheat oven to 350°F. Unwrap the mini filo shells and place on a baking sheet. Let stand at room temperature for 10 minutes until thawed. Meanwhile, cut Brie into 24 pieces. Fill each filo shell with a piece of Brie. Bake at 350°F for 4 to 5 minutes or until Brie melts.

2. While shells are baking, chop strawberries and combine with blueberries, apple jelly, thyme leaves, and salt in small bowl. When shells are deep golden brown and Brie is melted and bubbly, remove from oven and top each with a spoonful of the berry mixture. Serve immediately.

Mini Filo Shells

If you can't find mini filo shells, make your own. Layer four sheets of filo dough with butter and cut into 3" × 3" squares. Place in a buttered mini muffin tin, press down, and bake at 375°F for 4 to 6 minutes until lightly browned and crisp. They can be stored at room temperature for a couple of days.

Coconut Fruit Dip

This sweet and rich fruit dip is the perfect accent for strawberries, slices of kiwi fruit, apples, mandarin oranges, peach or mango slices, and pear slices. For a dessert, offer fruit plus some slices of pound and angel food cake.

Makes 2 cups

1 cup mascarpone cheese
1 cup marshmallow crème
3 tablespoons frozen orange
    juice concentrate
¼ teaspoon salt
2 tablespoons honey
½ cup toasted flaked coconut

In medium bowl, beat mascarpone cheese until light and fluffy. Add marshmallow crème, orange juice concentrate, salt, and honey and beat well. Fold in coconut and serve with fruit dippers.

Toasting Coconut

To toast coconut, spread into a thin, even layer on a cookie sheet and bake in a preheated 325°F oven for 4 to 6 minutes, stirring once during cooking time, until coconut is lightly browned and fragrant. Cool on paper towels; store at room temperature for up to 3 days.

Yields 2 cups

4 cloves garlic

2 tablespoons extra-virgin
  olive oil

1 15-ounce can garbanzo
  beans, drained

¼ cup tahini

2 tablespoons lemon juice

¼ cup sour cream

½ teaspoon salt

⅛ teaspoon crushed red
  pepper flakes

Hummus

*Roasting garlic usually takes about 35–40 minutes in a hot oven.
But you can sauté the cloves in oil on the stovetop for just about
10 minutes. The cloves will become sweet and nutty tasting.*

1. Peel garlic cloves but leave whole. Place in a small heavy saucepan along with olive oil over medium heat. Cook the garlic until it turns light brown, stirring frequently, for about 5 to 8 minutes; watch carefully. Remove from heat and let cool for 10 minutes.

2. Combine the garlic and oil with all remaining ingredients in blender or food processor and blend or process until smooth. Spread on serving plate, drizzle with a bit more olive oil, and serve immediately with pita chips.

About Tahini

True hummus is made with tahini, which is a peanut-butter-like paste made of ground sesame seeds. It adds a rich flavor and smooth, creamy texture to any recipe. You can make hummus without it, but do try it with tahini at least once.

Crab Cakes

Crab cakes are a wonderful appetizer to start a dinner party on the porch. These little cakes are light, creamy, and crunchy. Serve them with more of the Dijon mustard/mayonnaise combo, with a few lemon wedges on the side.

Serves 8

1 egg
3 tablespoons Dijon mustard and mayonnaise combination
½ teaspoon salt
½ teaspoon Old Bay seasoning
⅛ teaspoon white pepper
8 round buttery crackers, crushed
1 pound lump crabmeat, picked over
4 tablespoons olive oil

1. In medium bowl, combine egg, mustard/mayonnaise combo, salt, Old Bay seasoning, pepper, and cracker crumbs; mix well. Let stand for 5 minutes. Meanwhile, carefully pick over the crabmeat, removing any cartilage or bits of shell. Add crabmeat to cracker-crumb mixture and mix gently but thoroughly.

2. Using a ¼-cup measure, scoop out some crab mixture and press into a small cake on waxed paper. When crab cakes are all formed, place in freezer for 5 minutes. Heat olive oil in nonstick skillet and sauté crab cakes, turning once, until they are golden brown, about 3 to 4 minutes per side. Serve immediately.

Using Canned Crabmeat
You can substitute canned crabmeat for the lump crabmeat. Two 8-ounce cans, well drained, will equal about a pound of lump crabmeat. Taste a bit of the crabmeat; if it tastes salty, rinse it briefly under cold water and drain well again before using in the recipe.

12 Parmesan Crescents (page
43)
⅓ cup mayonnaise
⅓ cup grated Parmesan
cheese
¼ cup chopped grape
tomatoes
¼ cup chopped green onion

Parmesan Cups with Cheesy Filling

*Form the Parmesan Crescents into mini muffin cups when hot, then fill
with a savory cheese and tomato filling for a fabulous appetizer.*

1. Bake Parmesan Crescents as directed in recipe; except when just out
   of oven, wait for 1 minute, then remove the still-pliable crisps from the
   cookie sheet and press each into a greased mini muffin cup. Let cool.

2. Meanwhile, in small bowl, combine remaining ingredients. When cups
   are cool, fill each with a spoonful of the mayonnaise mixture. Serve
   immediately or cover and chill for 1 to 2 hours before serving.

Layered Reuben Dip

Mixing the cream cheese with the Thousand Island dressing in the base of this dip ensures the flavor of the dressing will be in every bite. Serve it warm with pretzel sticks, toasted rye crackers, and pita chips.

Serves 8

1 8-ounce package cream cheese, softened
½ cup Thousand Island dressing, divided
2 cups shredded Swiss cheese, divided
¼ pound thinly sliced corned beef, chopped
1 cup sauerkraut, drained

1. In medium bowl, beat cream cheese until fluffy. Stir in ¼ cup Thousand Island dressing and 1 cup Swiss cheese and mix well to combine. Spread in bottom of 9" microwave-safe glass pie plate.

2. Top cream cheese mixture with corned beef and sauerkraut, spreading evenly to cover. Drizzle with remaining ¼ cup Thousand Island dressing, and top with remaining 1 cup Swiss cheese.

3. Microwave dip on high for 3 to 5 minutes, turning once during cooking time, until cheese melts and mixture is hot. Let stand on a flat surface for 3 to 4 minutes and serve.

Sauerkraut
You can buy sauerkraut packaged in cans, in jars, fresh in the produce section of the supermarket, and frozen. Fresh sauerkraut usually has less sodium. Taste the sauerkraut before using it to check the salt content. If it tastes especially salty, rinse it briefly under cold running water and press between paper towels to drain.

Yields 30

30 cherry tomatoes
3 ounces cream cheese,
  softened
¼ cup whipped salad
  dressing
2 tablespoons roasted garlic
  paste
⅓ cup grated Parmesan
  cheese

Garlic Stuffed Cherry Tomatoes

These little appetizers are a bit fussy to make, but they are so delicious.
Serve with some chilled white wine to begin your dinner party.

1. Cut off the tops of the cherry tomatoes and, using a small teaspoon, scoop out the flesh, leaving the shell intact. Drain upside down on paper towels.

2. In small bowl, beat cream cheese until soft and fluffy. Add salad dressing, roasted garlic paste, and Parmesan cheese and beat well. Stuff a teaspoon of this mixture into each cherry tomato. Serve immediately or cover and refrigerate up to 4 hours.

Roasted Garlic Paste
You can buy roasted garlic paste in gourmet shops and often in the produce or baking aisle of your supermarket. If you can't find it, roast a head of garlic at 350°F for 1 hour, then cool and press out the flesh; mix well and store in refrigerator for up to 1 week or in the freezer up to 1 month.

Spicy Mixed Nuts

This simple sweet and hot glaze brings plain mixed nuts to life. You can increase the amount of cayenne and white pepper if you like your food really spicy.

Yields 2 cups

¼ cup butter
2 tablespoons brown sugar
1 teaspoon salt
¼ teaspoon cayenne pepper
⅛ teaspoon white pepper
2 tablespoons Worcestershire
   sauce
2 cups mixed nuts

1. In heavy saucepan, melt butter with brown sugar, salt, peppers, and Worcestershire sauce. Cook mixture over low heat until blended, stirring frequently. Place nuts in single layer on microwave-safe baking sheet and drizzle the butter mixture over them. Toss gently but thoroughly.

2. Microwave the mixture on high power for 5 to 9 minutes, stirring three times during cooking, until nuts are darkened and crisp and butter is absorbed. Cool on paper towels, then store in airtight container.

Mixed Nuts
Be sure to carefully read the labels of the mixed nuts you purchase for baking and cooking. The best buys are usually generic brands of cashews, almonds, and pecans, without peanuts. You can purchase them in bulk or buy the nuts separately and mix your own blend.

Yields 2 cups

2 cups large pitted green
 olives
¼ cup olive oil
3 cloves garlic, minced
3 tablespoons lemon juice
½ teaspoon paprika
⅛ teaspoon pepper
1 teaspoon dried oregano
 leaves

Marinated Olives

*Heating the marinade and the olives helps the olives absorb the
flavors very quickly, so they can be served almost immediately.*

Drain olives well and discard brine. In small saucepan, heat olive
oil and garlic over medium heat until garlic sizzles, about 3 minutes.
Remove from heat and add lemon juice and seasonings and stir well.
Add olives and stir well. Cook over medium heat, stirring frequently,
until olives are hot, about 2 to 4 minutes. Remove to serving bowl and
let cool for 10 to 15 minutes, tossing gently from time to time. Serve
warm. Refrigerate leftovers.

Olive Sizes
*Olive sizes have some funny names. From smallest to largest, they are:
bullets, fine, brilliant, superior, large, extra large, jumbo, extra jumbo,
giants, colossal, super colossal, mammoth, and super mammoth. For
comparison, super mammoth contain about 42 per pound, giants are
70 per pound, large are 110 per pound, and bullets are 160 per pound.*

Sparkling Punch

You can make this easy punch using lots of different combinations of frozen juice concentrates. Browse through your supermarket's frozen juice section and try several flavors.

Serves 24

1 12-ounce can frozen
    tangerine juice
    concentrate
1 6-ounce can frozen orange
    juice concentrate
2 cups water
¼ cup lime juice
2 28-ounce bottles ginger ale,
    chilled if desired
2 sprigs fresh mint

In large pitcher or punch bowl, combine tangerine juice concentrate and orange juice concentrate with water and lime juice; mix well until concentrates dissolve. Add ginger ale and mint; mix gently and serve.

Be Party-Ready
Keep a couple of bottles of ginger ale, plain or flavored sparkling water, or juice chilled in the refrigerator and you'll be ready to whip up a punch, smoothie, or frosty at a moment's notice. Having crushed ice ready to use in your freezer is also a good idea.

Pineapple Orange Frosty

Whipped topping mix can be found in the baking aisle of the supermarket, near the gelatin and pudding mixes. It's the secret ingredient in this easy drink recipe.

Serves 6

2 6-ounce cans pineapple-
    orange juice
1 6-ounce can frozen orange
    juice concentrate
2 envelopes whipped topping
    mix
2 cups crushed ice
6 sprigs fresh mint

In a blender or food processor, combine the pineapple-orange juice, the orange juice concentrate, the whipped topping mix, and the crushed ice. Cover and blend or process at medium speed until mixture is thick, blended, and smooth. Serve immediately, garnished with mint sprigs.

1 cantaloupe
1 12-ounce can frozen
    lemonade concentrate
½ cup water
½ cup orange juice
⅛ teaspoon ground ginger
1 28-ounce bottle ginger ale,
    chilled

Melon Ginger Punch

Cantaloupes are ripe when they give slightly to gentle pressure.
You can ripen cantaloupes by placing them in a paper bag
with a banana or apple; check once a day.

1. Peel cantaloupe, remove seeds, and cut into 1" chunks. Place in blender or food processor along with lemonade concentrate, water, orange juice, and ginger. Cover and blend or process until mixture is smooth.

2. Place mixture in large pitcher or punch bowl and stir in ginger ale. Serve immediately.

Specialty Melons

Most melons can easily be substituted for each other. The newer varieties of specialty melons include Santa Claus, Crenshaw, Persian, and orange-fleshed honeydew. These melons are ripe when they smell sweet and the skin gives gently when pushed with a finger.

Hot Cocoa

Preparing hot chocolate mix with milk instead of water makes a wonderfully creamy, rich drink, perfect to sip after an afternoon of ice skating.

Serves 4

½ cup whipping cream
1 tablespoon powdered sugar
¼ cup marshmallow crème
4 1-ounce envelopes hot
    chocolate mix
4 cups milk

1. In small bowl, combine cream, powdered sugar, and marshmallow crème. Beat on high speed until stiff peaks form; set aside.

2. Divide hot chocolate mix among 4 mugs. In medium saucepan, heat milk until bubbles form around edge and steam rises. Pour a bit of milk into each mug and stir briskly until hot chocolate mix dissolves. Add remaining milk to mugs, stirring as the milk is added. Top each serving with a spoonful of the whipped-cream mixture.

Make Your Own Hot Chocolate Mix

To make your own hot chocolate mix, in medium bowl, combine 4 cups dry milk powder, 1 cup chocolate-flavored nondairy creamer powder, 1 cup powdered sugar, ¼ cup cocoa, and 2 cups instant chocolate drink mix. Blend well, then store in airtight container. Substitute ¼ cup of this mix for a 1-ounce envelope.

Serves 8

1½ cups water

1 cup superfine sugar

² cups crushed ice

⅛ teaspoon salt

2 6-ounce cans pineapple-
orange juice

½ cup freshly squeezed
lemon juice

Lemonade

Pineapple-orange juice adds a more complex flavor to plain lemonade.
Keep a batch in the fridge during the hot summer months.

1. In medium saucepan, combine water and superfine sugar. Bring to a boil; cook and stir until sugar is dissolved, about 2 minutes.

2. Place crushed ice in large bowl and pour sugar water over ice. Stir until most of the ice is dissolved and mixture is cold. Pour into a pitcher and add salt, pineapple-orange juice, and lemon juice. Mix thoroughly and serve over ice.

Chapter 3

Bread and Breakfast

Yields 1 loaf

1 cup flour
¼ cup whole wheat flour
¾ cup sugar
½ teaspoon ground
   cinnamon
1 3-ounce package instant
   butterscotch pudding
   mix
½ teaspoon baking soda
½ teaspoon baking powder
½ cup butter, melted
2 eggs
1 cup canned pumpkin pie
   filling

Pumpkin Bread

It's important to use pumpkin pie filling, not canned pumpkin puree, in this easy recipe, because it contains spices and emulsifiers that flavor the bread and add to its texture.

1. Spray a glass 9" × 5" loaf pan with baking spray and set aside.

2. In a large bowl, combine flour, whole wheat flour, sugar, cinnamon, pudding mix, baking soda, and baking powder, and stir to blend. Add melted butter, eggs, and pumpkin pie filling and stir just until blended. Pour into prepared pan.

3. Microwave the pan on 75 percent power for 8 minutes, then rotate the pan one-half turn and continue microwaving for 8 to 10 minutes on 75 percent power or until a toothpick inserted in the center comes out clean. Let stand on a flat surface for 5 minutes, then remove from pan and cool completely on wire rack.

Quick Breads

Quick breads use baking soda or baking powder for leavening; they are quick to stir up and quick to bake. For best results, measure all ingredients carefully and be sure to mix the wet and dry ingredients just until combined. Overmixing will make the bread tough, with large tunnels running through it.

Corn Bread

Corn bread is best served hot, with some softened or whipped butter and honey or butter and salsa, depending on whether you want it sweet or spicy!

Serves 9

1¼ cups pancake mix
¾ cup yellow cornmeal
½ teaspoon paprika
1 cup buttermilk
⅓ cup frozen corn kernels, thawed
¼ cup vegetable oil
1 egg

1. Preheat oven to 400°F. Grease a 9" square baking pan and set aside.

2. In medium bowl, combine pancake mix, cornmeal, and paprika and mix well. In another medium bowl, combine buttermilk, corn kernels, oil, and egg and beat with wire whisk. Stir into dry ingredients just until combined. Pour into prepared pan.

3. Bake for 17 to 23 minutes or until edges are golden brown and top springs back when touched with finger. Serve warm.

Make Your Own Pancake Mix
You can make your own mix: combine 1 cup dry buttermilk powder, 3 cups flour, 1 cup whole wheat flour, ¾ cup sugar, 2 tablespoons baking powder, 1 tablespoon baking soda, and 1 teaspoon salt. To make pancakes, combine 1½ cups mix, 1 egg, 2 tablespoons melted butter, and 1 cup water and mix well; cook on greased griddle.

½ cup butter, softened
1½ cups shredded Swiss
cheese
½ cup grated Parmesan
cheese
1½ cups flour
½ teaspoon cayenne pepper
2 tablespoons water, if
needed
½ cup ground pine nuts

Cheese Crackers

*The two kinds of cheese and the pine nuts give these wonderful
little crackers perfect flavor and crunch. You can change the amount
of cayenne pepper if you'd like; more or less, it's up to you!*

⁓

1. Preheat oven to 375°F. In large bowl, combine butter and cheeses and mix well. Add flour along with cayenne pepper and mix until a crumbly dough forms. You may need to add a bit of water to make the dough workable.

2. Add pine nuts to the dough and mix well. Form 1-inch balls, place on ungreased cookie sheets, and flatten with the bottom of a glass until the crackers are ¼ inch thick. Bake for 15 to 18 minutes until crisp and golden. Cool on wire rack.

Freezing Dough
Most doughs can be frozen and thawed and baked later. To freeze cookie or cracker dough, divide into balls as recipe directs and freeze in single layer on a baking sheet. When frozen solid, remove from sheet and package in freezer bags. Bake as directed, adding one-third to one-half of the baking time to allow dough to thaw.

Pineapple Puff Pastries

This recipe sounds a lot harder to make than it is. Follow the directions carefully and you should be able to shape all of the pastries in about 5 minutes.

Yields 8 rolls

1 sheet frozen puff pastry dough, thawed
5 tablespoons plus 1 teaspoon pineapple-flavored cream cheese, softened
3 tablespoons pineapple preserves
2 tablespoons butter, melted
2 tablespoons sugar
½ teaspoon cinnamon

1. Preheat oven to 375°F. Roll out puff pastry dough on lightly floured surface to 12" × 12" rectangle. Cut into four 6" × 6" squares. Cut each square in half diagonally to make 8 triangles.

2. Arrange triangles on work surface so the long edge is away from you and the right angle is toward you. Spread each with 2 teaspoons of the cream cheese to within ½" of edges, and top with about 1 teaspoon pineapple preserves.

3. Bring the upper left-hand corner of each triangle down to the bottom right-angle point and press to seal. Then bring the upper right hand corner of each triangle down to the bottom point and press to seal, forming a square. Press outer edges to seal, leaving the center line open. Brush each with butter. Combine sugar and cinnamon in a small bowl and sprinkle over dough.

4. Bake for 9 to 14 minutes or until rolls are golden brown. Serve warm.

12 eggs, beaten
¼ cup light cream
¼ cup mascarpone cheese
½ teaspoon salt
⅛ teaspoon white pepper
¼ teaspoon dried marjoram
    leaves
3 tablespoons butter
1 cup shredded Havarti or
    Swiss cheese

Scrambled Eggs with Cheese

*Scrambled eggs are best served hot, right from the saucepan,
so have your family waiting for the eggs rather than holding the eggs
for them. Serve along with hot, crisp bacon and buttered toast.*

1. In a large bowl, combine eggs with cream, mascarpone cheese, salt, pepper, and marjoram. Beat with egg beater or hand mixer until smooth.

2. Heat butter in large skillet over medium heat. Add egg mixture. Cook eggs, stirring occasionally, until they are set, about 10 to 12 minutes. Add Havarti cheese, cover pan, and remove from heat. Let stand for 2 to 3 minutes, then remove lid, stir cheese gently into eggs, and serve.

Cheese Substitutions

Most cheeses can be substituted for each other in recipes. Ricotta cheese is a good substitute for mascarpone, as is softened or whipped cream cheese. Gruyère and Swiss are good substitutes for Havarti, and Colby cheese works well in place of Cheddar. Cotija, a Mexican hard cheese, is a great substitute for Parmesan cheese.

Mini Popovers

Popovers "pop" without any leavening in the batter because it contains lots of gluten and liquid. When the popovers are placed in the hot oven, the batter almost explodes with steam, and the gluten keeps the shell together.

‿

1. Preheat oven to 425°F. Spray mini muffin pans with baking spray and set aside.

2. Combine all ingredients in medium bowl and beat well with wire whisk until batter is blended and smooth. Pour 1 tablespoon of batter into each prepared muffin cup. Bake for 15 to 22 minutes or until popovers are deep golden brown and are puffed. Serve immediately.

Yields 24 popovers

2 eggs
⅔ cup milk
⅔ cup flour
1 tablespoon oil
¼ teaspoon salt

Parmesan Crescents

Thaw puff pastry as directed on the package. These little rolls are crisp and tender, nicely flavored with cheese. They are delicious served with hot soup or stew, or alongside a grilled steak.

‿

1. Preheat oven to 375°F. Sprinkle half of cheese on work surface and place pastry on cheese. Roll out puff pastry to a 12" × 12" sheet. Brush surface with egg and sprinkle evenly with remaining Parmesan cheese and the basil leaves.

2. Cut pastry into four 6" × 6" squares, then cut each square in half diagonally to form 8 triangles. Loosely roll up triangles to form a crescent and place on parchment paper-lined cookie sheets; curve ends to form a crescent shape. Bake at 375°F for 10 to 14 minutes or until rolls are puffed and golden brown.

Yields 8 rolls

½ cup grated Parmesan cheese
1 sheet puff pastry, thawed
1 egg, beaten
½ teaspoon dried basil leaves

Yields 44 muffins

1 9-ounce package blueberry
quick-bread mix
5 tablespoons orange juice,
divided
¾ cup milk
¼ cup oil
1 egg
½ cup powdered sugar

Orange-Glazed Blueberry Muffins

These mini muffins are the perfect quick breakfast for families on the run.
They are tender and sweet and very delicate; kids love them.
Serve warm for best flavor.

1. Preheat oven to 375°F. Line 44 mini muffin cups with paper liners and set aside.

2. In large bowl combine quick-bread mix, 4 tablespoons orange juice, milk, oil, and egg and stir just until dry ingredients disappear. Fill prepared muffin cups two-thirds full of batter. Bake for 10 to 15 minutes or until muffins spring back when gently touched with finger. Cool for 3 minutes, then remove to wire rack.

3. In small bowl combine powdered sugar and 1 tablespoon orange juice; drizzle this mixture over the warm muffins and serve.

Reheating Muffins

You can make muffins ahead of time and store in airtight containers, then reheat for best taste and texture. To reheat, place a few muffins on a microwave-safe plate, cover with microwave-safe paper towels, and heat for 10 seconds per muffin, until warm.

Peach Pancakes

Serve these wonderful pancakes on warmed plates with warmed maple syrup, peach jam, and some powdered sugar sprinkled on top, along with Canadian bacon and orange juice.

〜

Serves 4
_____

2 ripe peaches, peeled and
   diced
4 tablespoons sugar, divided
¼ teaspoon cinnamon
¾ cup flour
1 teaspoon baking powder
1 egg, separated
¾ cup milk
1 teaspoon vanilla
2 tablespoons butter

1. In small bowl, toss peaches with 2 tablespoons sugar and cinnamon. In medium bowl, combine flour, remaining 2 tablespoons sugar, baking powder, egg yolk, milk, and vanilla and stir just until combined.

2. Beat egg white until stiff; fold into flour mixture, then fold in peach mixture. Grease a skillet heated to medium with butter and cook pancakes, flipping once, until done.

Cooking Pancakes

Use a ¼-cup measure to scoop out the batter, and pour onto a hot, greased skillet. Cook pancakes until the edges start to look dry and cooked and bubbles form on the surface, about 2 to 4 minutes. Carefully flip the pancakes and cook until the second side is light brown, 1 to 2 minutes longer.

2 cups flour
⅔ cup oatmeal
⅓ cup brown sugar
1½ teaspoons baking powder
¼ teaspoon cinnamon
6 tablespoons butter
2 eggs
6 tablespoons heavy cream,
    divided
1 tablespoon sugar
⅛ teaspoon cinnamon

Oat Scones

*You could add chopped nuts, raisins, dried cranberries, or currants
to these wonderfully tender, crumbly scones. Serve them hot just out
of the oven with butter, honey, and a selection of jams and jellies.*

1. Preheat oven to 400°F. Line a cookie sheet with parchment paper and set aside. In a large bowl combine flour, oatmeal, brown sugar, baking powder, and ¼ teaspoon cinnamon. Cut in butter until particles are fine.

2. In a small bowl combine eggs and 5 tablespoons cream and beat until smooth. Add to oatmeal mixture and mix until a dough forms. Shape into a ball, then press into a 9" circle on prepared cookie sheet. Cut dough into 8 wedges and separate slightly. Brush with remaining 1 tablespoon cream and sprinkle with 1 tablespoon sugar mixed with ⅛ teaspoon cinnamon. Bake for 12 to 15 minutes until edges are golden brown. Serve hot with butter.

Cherry Oat Muffins

Use quick cooking oatmeal for best results in these tender and flavorful muffins. You can use either bing cherries or sour cherries, or use dried cherries to save some more time.

~

Yields 24 muffins

1½ cups oatmeal
1½ cups flour
1 teaspoon baking powder
½ teaspoon baking soda
⅔ cup brown sugar
1 cup buttermilk
½ cup oil
2 eggs
1½ cups halved, pitted cherries or frozen cherries, unthawed

1. Preheat oven to 375°F. Line 24 muffin cups with paper liners and set aside. In a large bowl, combine oatmeal, flour, baking powder, baking soda, and brown sugar. In small bowl, combine buttermilk, oil, and eggs and beat well. Add to oatmeal mixture and stir just until combined. Stir in cherries.

2. Fill prepared muffin cups two-thirds full with batter. Bake for 17 to 22 minutes or until muffins are rounded and tops are golden brown.

Pitting Cherries

There are several ways to pit cherries. You can cut the cherry in half and pry the pit out with your fingers. Cherry pitters work well; be sure that you see the pit come out each time. Or you can push a straw through the center of the cherry, removing the pit and stem at the same time.

Serves 6

1 cup half-and-half or low-fat
    evaporated milk
1 egg, beaten
½ teaspoon vanilla
2 tablespoons powdered
    sugar
3 tablespoons butter
8 slices whole wheat bread

French Toast

Serve this crisp and creamy toast with maple syrup, powdered sugar, and some crisp bacon, cold orange juice, strong hot coffee, and a melon wedge or two.

1. Preheat griddle over medium heat. In a shallow casserole dish, combine half-and-half, egg, vanilla, and powdered sugar and beat until combined.

2. Melt butter on preheated griddle, then dip bread into egg mixture, coating both sides. Let the bread sit in the egg mixture for 1 minute. Immediately place onto sizzling butter on griddle. Cook over medium heat for 6 to 9 minutes, turning once, until golden brown.

French Toast Toppings
You can top French Toast with any pancake or waffle topping. Offer heated maple syrup, several kinds of jam, heated fruit syrups, powdered sugar, cinnamon sugar, and even peanut butter or Nutella spread. Or combine some fresh fruits with apple jelly and heat until warm.

Caramel Rolls

*You could add chopped pecans or dark raisins to this easy recipe
if you'd like. Place them on the topping before adding the rolls.*

Yields 12 rolls

¼ cup caramel fudge ice
   cream topping
2 tablespoons brown sugar
2 tablespoons heavy cream
¼ cup butter, softened
¼ cup brown sugar
½ teaspoon cinnamon
1 8-ounce can refrigerated
   crescent roll dough

1. Preheat oven to 375°F. Spray a 9" round cake pan with nonstick baking spray. In a small bowl combine ice cream topping, 2 tablespoons brown sugar, and heavy cream and mix well. Spread mixture evenly in the prepared cake pan.

2. In another small bowl, combine butter, ¼ cup brown sugar, and cinnamon and mix well. Unroll dough and separate into 4 rectangles. Press seams to seal. Spread butter mixture over rectangles. Roll up dough, starting at short edge, and pinch edges of dough to seal. Cut each roll into 3 slices and arrange the twelve rolls on the topping in cake pan.

3. Bake for 15 to 20 minutes, until dough is deep golden brown. Invert pan onto serving plate and remove pan. If any caramel remains in pan, spread onto rolls. Serve warm.

3 tablespoons butter
2 cloves garlic, minced
½ cup grated Parmesan
    cheese
¼ cup grated Romano cheese
½ teaspoon dried Italian
    seasoning
1 11-ounce can refrigerated
    breadstick dough

Cheese Breadsticks

These delicious breadsticks taste like the famous ones from a national restaurant chain that serves soup and breadsticks to go! Serve with Savory Minestrone (page 239) on a cold winter day.

1. Preheat oven to 375°F. Line cookie sheets with parchment paper and set aside. In a microwave-safe dish, place butter and garlic. Cook on 100 percent power for 1 to 2 minutes, until garlic is fragrant. Pour butter mixture onto a shallow plate and let stand for 5 minutes.

2. Meanwhile, on another shallow plate, combine cheeses and Italian seasoning and mix. Open dough and separate into 8 breadsticks; cut each in half crosswise to make 16 breadsticks. Dip each breadstick into butter mixture, then roll in cheese mixture to coat. Place on prepared cookie sheets, about 2 inches apart.

3. Bake breadsticks for 12 to 16 minutes or until they are puffed and light golden brown. Let cool for a few minutes and serve.

Parmesan or Romano?

Parmesan and Romano are often listed as substitutes for each other, but they are different cheeses. Parmesan cheese is made from cow's milk and has a milder flavor and less salty taste than Romano, which is made from sheep's milk (Pecorino Romano) or goat's milk (Caprino Romano).

Sausage Rolls

Cheese, sausage, thyme, and some puff pastry make delicious little rolls that are perfect for breakfast on the run. Bake them ahead of time, freeze them, then microwave each on high for 1–2 minutes until hot.

Yields 24 rolls

24 pork sausage links
1 17-ounce package frozen puff pastry, thawed
1 cup grated Cheddar cheese
½ cup grated Parmesan cheese
1 teaspoon dried thyme leaves
1 egg, beaten
¼ teaspoon salt

1. Preheat oven to 400°F. Line cookie sheets with parchment paper and set aside. In a heavy skillet, cook pork sausage links over medium heat until golden brown and cooked, about 5 to 7 minutes. Remove to paper towels to drain.

2. Unfold puff pastry sheet and place on a lightly floured surface. In a small bowl, combine cheeses and thyme leaves and toss to combine. Sprinkle this mixture over the puff pastry and gently press cheese mixture into pastry; roll to a 12" × 18" rectangle. Cut into three 12" × 6" rectangles, then cut each rectangle in half to make 6 squares. Cut each square into four 3" × 3" squares. Place a cooked and drained sausage on the edge of each square and roll up to enclose sausage; press pastry to seal.

3. In small bowl, beat egg with salt and brush over sausage rolls. Place on prepared cookie sheets and bake for 12 to 18 minutes until puffed and golden brown. Serve hot.

Puff Pastry
Puff pastry is found frozen near the pie shells and cakes in your supermarket. Follow the directions for thawing and using the pastry. Many brands require thawing overnight in the refrigerator so the butter that is encased in the layers of pastry doesn't melt. Keep a couple of boxes on hand to make easy snacks.

Serves 4

4 tablespoons melted butter, divided
½ cup mascarpone cheese, divided
¼ cup strawberry preserves
8 slices cracked wheat bread
2 eggs
1 teaspoon vanilla
¼ teaspoon cinnamon

Stuffed French Toast

Broiling French Toast helps significantly cut the cooking time and ensures that the bread will be crisp.

1. Preheat broiler. Spread 3 tablespoons melted butter in a 15" × 10" jelly-roll pan and set aside. In a small bowl, combine ¼ cup mascarpone cheese and preserves and mix.

2. Spread preserves mixture on 4 bread slices and top with remaining slices. Cut these sandwiches in half to make triangles.

3. On a shallow plate, beat remaining ¼ cup mascarpone cheese until fluffy, then add eggs, remaining 1 tablespoon melted butter, vanilla, and cinnamon, and beat until smooth. Dip sandwiches in egg mixture, turning to coat. Place coated sandwich triangles in butter on jelly-roll pan. Broil 6 inches from heat source for 4 to 5 minutes, then carefully turn the sandwiches and broil for 3 to 5 minutes longer on second side until golden brown and crunchy. Serve immediately.

Broiling
When broiling foods, be sure to watch the food carefully as it burns easily. Most foods should be placed about 4 to 6 inches away from the heated coils, and most ovens require that the oven door be slightly open when broiling. Use the broiler pan that came with your oven, or a heavy-duty stainless steel pan that won't buckle under the high heat.

Toasted Garlic Bread

This crisp bread is perfect to serve alongside spaghetti and meatballs and a tender baby spinach salad. Make extra pieces and refrigerate; use the leftovers to make Bread-Crumb Frittata (page 55).

Serves 6

1 loaf French bread
1 tablespoon olive oil
4 cloves garlic, minced
½ cup butter
1 teaspoon lemon pepper
½ cup grated Cotija cheese

1. Slice bread about ¼ inch thick. In a heavy skillet, heat olive oil over medium heat and sauté garlic until soft and fragrant, about 2 to 3 minutes. Pour oil and garlic into medium bowl and let stand for 10 minutes. Add butter, lemon pepper, and Cotija cheese and mix well.

2. Preheat broiler. Spread butter mixture onto both sides of each piece of bread. Place on cookie sheet and broil 6 inches from heat source for 3 to 5 minutes, until light brown. Turn and broil for 2 to 3 minutes on second side, until light brown and crisp. Watch carefully, as these can burn easily. Serve hot.

Serves 12

1 tablespoon olive oil
3 cloves garlic, minced
½ cup butter, softened
2 cups shredded provolone
    cheese
1 teaspoon dried Italian
    seasoning
1 1-pound loaf unsliced
    Italian or French bread

Melty Cheese Bread

This bread is a perfect choice to serve alongside any Italian pasta dish.
You can make it ahead of time, then bake it just before serving.

1. Preheat oven to 350°F. In a small saucepan, heat olive oil over medium heat. Add garlic; cook and stir for 2 to 3 minutes, until garlic is fragrant. Remove from heat and pour into a heatproof bowl.

2. Meanwhile, in a medium bowl, combine butter, cheese, and Italian seasoning and mix well until blended. Stir in garlic mixture. Slice bread into 1-inch slices. Spread cheese mixture onto one side of each bread slice. Reassemble loaf, placing coated sides against uncoated sides.

3. Wrap loaf in heavy-duty foil. Bake for 15–22 minutes or until bread is hot and cheese has melted.

Garlic Bread Options

To make crisp garlic bread, slice the bread thinly, spread sparingly with coating, and bake it uncovered on the oven rack or cookie sheets. For soft and chewy garlic bread, slice the bread 1-inch thick, use more cheese, and wrap the bread in foil, then bake it. You can unwrap the bread for the last 3 to 5 minutes to help crisp the crust if you'd like.

Bread-Crumb Frittata

*This excellent and easy recipe is a wonderful way to use up any
leftover bread; simply toast it and crush it by placing in
a plastic food bag and rolling it with a rolling pin.*

Serves 4

5 slices Toasted Garlic Bread
   (page 53)
3 tablespoons butter
1 onion, finely chopped
8 eggs, beaten
½ teaspoon salt
Dash black pepper
1 cup grated Italian-blend
   cheese

1. Preheat broiler. Crush Toasted Garlic Bread into fine crumbs and set
   aside. In a heavy ovenproof skillet, melt butter over medium heat. Add
   onion and cook until tender, about 4 to 5 minutes. Season eggs with
   salt and pepper and add to skillet and stir.

2. Cook eggs for 2 minutes, lifting edges to let uncooked mixture flow
   underneath, until eggs begin to set. Add bread crumbs. Continue cooking, shaking pan occasionally, until eggs are almost set but still moist.
   Top with cheese and place under broiler for 2 to 3 minutes, until cheese
   melts and eggs are set. Cut into wedges and serve immediately.

Baked Eggs

*Dry mustard and Muenster cheese add a bit of a kick to baked eggs. Serve this
easy casserole with cantaloupe wedges and some Caramel Rolls (page 49).*

Serves 4

3 tablespoons butter, melted
8 eggs
½ teaspoon salt
⅛ teaspoon white pepper
½ teaspoon dry mustard
¼ cup heavy cream or
   evaporated milk
1 cup shredded Muenster
   cheese
¼ cup grated Parmesan
   cheese

1. Preheat oven to 350°F. Pour melted butter into a 9" square glass baking
   pan. In a large bowl, beat eggs with salt, pepper, mustard, and cream
   until blended. Pour into butter in pan and sprinkle with cheeses.

2. Bake for 15 to 20 minutes, until eggs are set, puffed, and golden brown
   around the edges. Cut into squares and serve immediately.

4 (3" × 3") squares Corn Bread (page 39)
1 15-ounce can black beans, rinsed and drained
1 pint grape tomatoes
1½ cups cubed Pepper Jack cheese
1 cup spicy ranch salad dressing

Southern Corn Bread Salad

The toasted Corn Bread is crisp on the outside and tender on the inside, providing wonderful texture to this beautiful salad.

1. Preheat oven to 400°F. Cut Corn Bread into 1-inch squares and place on a cookie sheet. Bake for 5 to 8 minutes, until toasted, watching carefully. Remove to wire rack and let stand for 5 minutes to cool slightly. Place bread in serving bowl.

2. Add black beans, tomatoes, and 1 cup of the cheese to the Corn Bread and toss gently. Drizzle with salad dressing, toss again, then top with remaining cheese. Serve immediately, or cover and chill for 2 hours before serving.

Bread Salads

Many cultures use leftover or stale bread in salads. In America, Southern Corn Bread Salad is probably the most well known. Italians make a bread salad called panzanella *with stale bread, and Greeks make* fattoush *with crisp pieces of flatbread or pita bread.*

Cornmeal Pancakes

Crunchy cornmeal adds great taste and flavor to these easy pancakes.
Serve them with warmed maple syrup and fruit preserves.

Serves 6–8

2 cups flour
1 cup yellow cornmeal
3 tablespoons sugar
½ teaspoon salt
1 teaspoon baking powder
1 teaspoon baking soda
2 cups buttermilk
½ cup sour cream
2 eggs
3 tablespoons butter

1. In a large bowl, combine flour, cornmeal, sugar, salt, baking powder, and soda and mix with wire whisk to blend. In a medium bowl, combine buttermilk, sour cream, and eggs and beat with an eggbeater until smooth.

2. Add buttermilk mixture to flour mixture and stir with a wire whisk until combined. Let batter stand while preparing griddle.

3. Heat griddle until a drop of water sizzles as soon as it touches the hot surface. Lightly grease griddle with butter. Pour batter by ¼ cupfuls onto griddle and cook for 3 to 4 minutes until edges look dry and bubbles form. Carefully turn pancakes and cook on second side for 2 to 4 minutes, until golden. Serve immediately.

Serves 6

12 eggs
½ cup cream
½ teaspoon salt
⅛ teaspoon white pepper
3 tablespoons butter
1 cup shredded Monterey
    Jack cheese
½ cup prepared basil pesto

Scrambled Eggs with Pesto

Pesto adds great flavor and color to simple scrambled eggs.
You could call these Green Eggs, especially if you serve them with ham!
Orange juice and pork sausages make a nice accompaniment too.

1. In a large bowl, beat eggs with cream. Season with salt and pepper. In a heavy skillet, melt butter and add eggs. Cook over medium heat, stirring occasionally, until eggs are almost set.

2. Sprinkle eggs with cheese, cover, and remove from heat. Let stand for 2 to 3 minutes, then remove cover, add pesto, and stir gently to mix. Serve immediately.

Flavors of Pesto
Pesto can be made from almost any green herb or edible leaf. Spinach pesto is made by blending thawed frozen spinach with cheese, olive oil, and garlic. Mint pesto can be made with fresh mint leaves, oil, and walnuts. And pesto can include any type of nut, most cheeses, and any combination of herbs and spices.

Chapter 4

Beef Entrées

6 4-ounce beef tenderloin
    steaks
½ cup balsamic and oil
    vinaigrette
1 sweet red onion, chopped
2 cloves garlic, minced
1 tablespoon olive oil
¾ cup crumbled feta cheese
    with herbs

Greek Tenderloin Steak

*Beef tenderloins are also called filet mignon. This method
of preparing steak can be varied with different cheeses.
Serve with a green salad and corn on the cob.*

1. Prepare and preheat grill. Place steaks in baking pan and pour vinaigrette over. Let stand at room temperature for 10 minutes.

2. Meanwhile, in heavy saucepan, cook onion and garlic in olive oil over medium heat until tender and just beginning to brown around the edges, about 6 to 8 minutes. Remove from heat and set aside.

3. Drain steaks and place on grill; cook, covered, 4 to 6 inches from medium heat for 7 minutes. Turn, cover, and cook for 4 to 8 minutes, until desired doneness. Uncover grill and top each steak with some of the feta cheese. Cover grill and cook for 1 minute, until cheese melts. Place steaks on serving plate and top with onion mixture.

Easy Steak Doneness Tests
Put your hand palm up, and touch your thumb and index finger together. Feel the pad at the base of your thumb; that's what rare steaks feel like. Touch your thumb and middle finger together; the pad will feel like a medium-rare steak. Ring finger and thumb is medium, and thumb and pinky feels like a well-done steak.

Beef Stir-Fry

Serve this delicious stir-fry with some hot cooked rice, Grape and Melon Salad (page 200), and Sherbet Roll (page 287) for dessert.

Serves 4

1 pound sirloin steak
2 tablespoons stir-fry sauce
2 tablespoons oil
1 onion, chopped
1½ cups sugar snap peas
1 red bell pepper, thinly sliced
½ cup stir-fry sauce

1. Thinly slice the steak across the grain. Place in medium bowl and toss with 2 tablespoons stir-fry sauce. Set aside.

2. Heat oil in large skillet or wok over medium-high heat. Add onion; stir-fry for 3 to 4 minutes until crisp-tender. Add peas and bell pepper; stir-fry for 2 to 3 minutes. Add beef; stir-fry for 3 to 4 minutes, until browned. Add stir-fry sauce and bring to a simmer; simmer for 3 to 4 minutes, until blended. Serve over hot cooked rice.

Stir-Fry Variations
Once you've learned a stir-fry recipe, you can vary it with many different cuts of meat and lots of vegetables. Just be sure that the veggies are cut to about the same size so they cook in the same amount of time. And experiment with different bottled stir-fry sauces you'll find in the Asian aisle of your supermarket.

4 cube steaks
3 tablespoons flour
1 tablespoon chili powder
1 teaspoon salt
2 tablespoons olive oil
1 14-ounce can diced
    tomatoes with green
    chilies
1 10-ounce can condensed
    nacho cheese soup
1 cup sliced mushrooms

Spicy Cube Steaks

This comforting, old-fashioned recipe is delicious served with refrigerated mashed potatoes, heated with some sour cream and Parmesan cheese.

1. Place cube steaks on waxed paper. In small bowl, combine flour, chili powder, and salt and mix well. Sprinkle half of flour mixture over the steaks and pound into steaks using a rolling pin or the flat side of a meat mallet. Turn steaks, sprinkle with remaining flour mixture, and pound again.

2. Heat olive oil in large saucepan over medium-high heat. Add steaks; sauté for 4 minutes on first side, then turn and sauté for 2 minutes. Remove steaks from saucepan. Pour tomatoes and soup into pan; cook and stir until simmering, scraping up browned bits. Add steaks back to pan along with mushrooms; simmer for 15 to 20 minutes, until tender.

Cube Steaks

Cube steaks are typically round steaks that have been run through a machine that pierces the steak all over to break up connective tissue so the meat is more tender. You can pound your own round steaks using the pointed side of a meat mallet.

Grilled Steak Kabobs

The combination of barbecue sauce and cola beverage adds nice spice and flavor to these easy grilled kabobs. Serve with hot cooked rice, a green salad, and some breadsticks.

Serves 4

1 pound sirloin steak
¾ cup barbecue sauce
2 tablespoons cola beverage
¼ teaspoon garlic pepper
8 ounces cremini mushrooms
2 red bell peppers, cut into
    strips

1. Cut steak into 1-inch cubes and combine with barbecue sauce, cola beverage, and garlic pepper in a medium bowl. Massage the marinade into the meat with your hands; let stand for 10 minutes.

2. Meanwhile, prepare vegetables and prepare and preheat grill. Thread steak cubes, mushrooms, and bell peppers onto metal skewers and place on grill over medium coals. Grill, covered, brushing frequently with remaining marinade, for 7 to 10 minutes, turning frequently, until steak is desired doneness. Discard any remaining marinade.

Grill Temperatures
Check the temperature of them by carefully holding your hand about 6 inches above the coals and counting how many seconds you can hold your hand steady before it gets too hot. If you can hold your hand for 5 seconds, the coals are low; 4 seconds, medium; 3 seconds, medium-high; and 2 seconds, high.

Serves 4
_____

2 tablespoons vegetable oil
1 onion, chopped
2 cloves garlic, minced
1 16-ounce package cooked
    sirloin tips in gravy
1 10-ounce can beef broth
1½ cups water
1 16-ounce package frozen
    mixed vegetables
½ teaspoon dried marjoram
    leaves
⅛ teaspoon pepper

Quick Beef and Vegetable Stew

*Precooked meats in gravy are a fabulous new product you
can find in the meat aisle of your supermarket. You get
the rich taste of a slow-cooked dinner with almost no work!*

In large saucepan, heat vegetable oil over medium heat. Add onion and garlic; cook and stir for 3 to 4 minutes, until crisp-tender. Stir in sirloin tips and gravy along with beef broth and water. Bring to a simmer over medium heat. Add frozen vegetables, marjoram, and pepper and bring back to a simmer. Simmer for 5 to 7 minutes, until vegetables are hot and stew is slightly thickened. Serve immediately.

Serves 4
_____

1 cup leftover beef mixture
    from Beef Tacos (page 70)
1 cup leftover refried bean
    mixture from Beef Tacos
    (page 70)
1 10-ounce bag mixed salad
    greens
2 cups blue corn tortilla chips
2 cups shredded Colby cheese

Taco Salad

*You can use Spicy Vegetarian Chili (page 144) in place of the beef
mixture and refried bean mixture. Top the salad with chopped
tomato and chunky salsa, sour cream, or more tortilla chips.*

In large saucepan, combine beef mixture and refried bean mixture and stir over medium heat until hot. Meanwhile, place salad greens on plates and top with tortilla chips. When beef mixture is hot, spoon over tortilla chips and top with shredded cheese. Serve immediately.

Tortilla Chips
You can make your own tortilla chips. Choose flavored or plain corn or flour tortillas and cut them into wedges using a pizza cutter. Heat 2 cups oil in large pan over medium-high heat and fry tortilla wedges until crisp. Drain on paper towels, sprinkle with salt and seasonings, and serve.

Pesto Steaks

This elegant dish deserves some superb accompaniments.
Make Grilled Asparagus (page 223) and Pasta Pilaf (page 224).
For dessert, Chocolate Toffee Torte (page 278) is perfect.

Serves 4

4 tenderloin steaks
1 teaspoon salt
⅛ teaspoon white pepper
1 cup basil pesto, divided
⅓ cup blue cheese
½ cup fresh basil leaves

1. Prepare and heat grill. Place steaks on a platter; sprinkle both sides with salt and pepper. Using a very sharp knife, cut into the side of each steak, creating a pocket. Be careful not to cut through to the other side. Fill each pocket with about 2 tablespoons pesto.

2. Grill steaks, covered, over medium coals for 5 minutes. Turn steaks, cover again, and cook for 4 minutes. Top each steak with 2 tablespoons of pesto and sprinkle blue cheese on top of the pesto. Cover and grill for 2 to 5 minutes, until desired doneness is reached. Meanwhile, roll basil leaves into a round shape and cut into thin strips, creating a chiffonade. Place steaks on serving platter and sprinkle with basil chiffonade. Let stand 5 minutes, then serve.

Tenderloin Steaks

The tenderloin of beef, or filet mignon, is the most expensive cut of beef available, but it is also economical because there is no waste. The steaks do not need to be trimmed; most of the fat is intramuscular and not visible, but it creates great flavor.

*1 16-ounce package frozen
    meatballs*
3 tablespoons oil
1 onion, chopped
2 cloves garlic, minced
*2 9-ounce boxes frozen Asian
    vegetables in sesame-
    ginger sauce*
½ cup beef broth

Ginger Meatball Stir-Fry

*Serve this excellent quick stir-fry over hot cooked rice, with a
deli fruit salad on the side. The only work you have to perform is
chopping onions and garlic, then cook for a few minutes.*

1. Place meatballs in a 12" × 8" microwave-safe dish and heat on high power for 4 minutes. Rearrange meatballs and heat on high power for 2 minutes longer. Set aside.

2. In heavy skillet or wok, heat oil over high heat. Add onion and garlic; stir-fry for 4 to 5 minutes, until onion is crisp-tender. Add frozen vegetables in sauce and beef broth and bring to a boil over high heat. Cover, reduce heat, and simmer for 5 minutes.

3. Uncover pan and add meatballs. Stir-fry for 3 to 5 minutes longer, until vegetables and meatballs are hot and sauce is slightly thickened. Serve immediately.

Cooking Rice
To cook rice, combine 1 cup long-grain, converted, or Texmati rice in a heavy saucepan with 2 cups water or broth and a pinch of salt. Bring to a boil, reduce heat to low, cover, and simmer for 15 to 20 minutes, until liquid is absorbed. Remove from heat and let stand for a few minutes, then fluff with fork and serve.

Almost-Instant Shepherd's Pie

Shepherd's Pie is an old-fashioned recipe that's a great way to use up leftover mashed potatoes. The premade refrigerated type also works very well.

Serves 6

1 20-ounce package cooked
    ground beef in taco sauce
1 16-ounce package frozen
    broccoli, cauliflower, and
    carrots
¼ cup water
2 9-ounce packages
    refrigerated garlic
    mashed potatoes
1 cup sour cream
½ cup grated Parmesan
    cheese

1. Preheat oven to 400°F. Place ground beef and sauce in a heavy saucepan and heat over medium heat for 5 to 7 minutes, until hot, stirring occasionally.

2. Meanwhile, place frozen vegetables in 2-quart casserole and sprinkle with ¼ cup water. Cover and microwave on high for 5 minutes, stirring once during cooking time; drain well. Then place potatoes in microwave-safe bowl and heat on high for 5 minutes. Remove from microwave, stir, and add ½ cup sour cream; let stand. Add drained vegetables to beef mixture and simmer for 2 to 4 minutes longer.

3. Place hot beef mixture in 2-quart casserole dish. Stir potatoes, add Parmesan cheese, and spread over ground-beef mixture. Bake for 12 to 15 minutes, until casserole is hot and potatoes begin to brown.

Serves 4–6

2 cups sliced cooked Spicy
    Grilled Flank Steak (page
    74)
½ cup salsa
1 4-ounce can diced green
    chilies, drained
2 cups shredded Pepper Jack
    cheese
12 10-inch flour tortillas

Steak Quesadillas

*Serve these spicy little Tex-Mex sandwiches with more salsa, chopped
tomato, sour cream, and guacamole, along with some fresh fruit.*

1. Slice steak across the grain and combine in medium bowl with salsa
   and green chilies. Place six tortillas on work surface and divide steak
   mixture among them. Top with cheese and remaining tortillas.

2. Heat griddle or skillet over medium-high heat. Cook quesadillas, pressing down with spatula and turning once, until tortillas begin to brown
   and cheese melts, about 4 to 7 minutes. Cut into quarters and serve
   immediately.

Guacamole

*To make your own guacamole, combine 2 mashed avocados with
¼ cup mayonnaise, 2 tablespoons fresh lemon or lime juice, ½ teaspoon salt, dash cayenne pepper, a dash of hot sauce, and 1 chopped
tomato. Blend well and put into small bowl. Press plastic wrap onto the
surface and refrigerate for 2 to 4 hours before serving.*

Steak and Bean Enchiladas

These hearty enchiladas are wonderful served with Spanish rice made from a mix and a crisp butter lettuce salad with a garlic ranch dressing.

Serves 4

1 16-ounce flat iron steak
1 teaspoon salt
⅛ teaspoon cayenne pepper
1 tablespoon chili powder
1 teaspoon ground cumin
3 tablespoons oil
2 16-ounce cans pinto beans, drained
1 16-ounce can enchilada sauce
8 10-inch flour tortillas
2 cups shredded Pepper Jack cheese, divided

1. Preheat oven to 400°F. Cut the steak, against the grain, into thin strips. Sprinkle steak with salt, pepper, chili powder, and cumin. Heat a large skillet over medium-high heat and add oil; heat until the oil ripples. Add steak; stir-fry for 2 to 4 minutes, until steak is desired doneness. Remove steak from pan using slotted spoon and place in large mixing bowl.

2. Add drained beans and half of enchilada sauce to steak and stir to mix. Divide mixture among the flour tortillas and top with half of the cheese. Roll up tortillas to enclose filling. Place in 3-quart casserole dish. Drizzle with remaining enchilada sauce and sprinkle with rest of the cheese. Bake for 15 to 18 minutes, until heated through.

About Flat Iron Steak
This cut of meat is actually a brand-new cut! It's the top blade steak that has been cut in half to remove some very tough connective tissue that runs through the center of the meat. This steak is inexpensive, tender, and well flavored, especially when quickly grilled or sautéed.

Serves 4–6

1 16-ounce package cooked
     ground beef in taco sauce
2 tablespoons olive oil
1 onion, chopped
1 15-ounce can seasoned
     refried beans
12 crisp taco shells
2 cups shredded Co-Jack
     cheese

Beef Tacos

Tacos are a kid-friendly supper that's very easy, especially when you start with fully cooked ground beef in taco sauce. Serve with all the traditional toppings: guacamole, sour cream, chopped tomatoes, and more taco sauce.

1. Preheat oven to 400°F. Heat beef and sauce according to package directions. Meanwhile, heat olive oil in large skillet over medium heat. Cook onion, stirring frequently, until tender, about 5 to 6 minutes. Stir in refried beans and cook for 3 to 4 minutes longer, until hot.

2. Place taco shells on a baking sheet and heat at 400°F for 4 to 7 minutes, until crisp. Serve the ground-beef mixture along with the refried-beans mixture, the taco shells, and shredded cheese and let diners make their own tacos.

Tacos: Crisp or Soft?

You can make crisp tacos, usually with preformed shells heated in the oven, or soft tacos, made by heating tortillas until softened, then filling and folding to enclose the filling. Soft tacos are essentially the same as burritos, but they aren't fried or baked after filling. Don't worry too much about the nomenclature—just enjoy the food!

Meaty Spaghetti

Starting with fully cooked meatloaf means this spaghetti is ready in about 20 minutes; it's also perfectly seasoned.

Serves 6

1 16-ounce package cooked meatloaf in tomato sauce
2 tablespoons olive oil
1 onion, chopped
1 28-ounce jar pasta sauce
1 pound spaghetti pasta
1 cup grated Parmesan cheese

1. Bring a large pot of water to a boil over high heat. Remove meatloaf from package and crumble. In heavy saucepan, heat olive oil over medium heat. Cook onion for 4 to 5 minutes, stirring frequently, until crisp-tender. Add crumbled meatloaf, tomato sauce from package, and pasta sauce. Bring to a simmer; cook for 7 to 9 minutes, until sauce is slightly thickened.

2. Meanwhile, add spaghetti to boiling water and cook according to package directions, until al dente. Drain well and place on serving platter. Top with meat mixture and sprinkle with Parmesan cheese. Serve immediately.

Recipe Substitutions
You could use leftover meatloaf in this easy spaghetti recipe, or use frozen precooked meatballs, heated according to the package directions, along with one 8-ounce can of tomato sauce. For more nutrition, add some preshredded carrots to the pan when adding the meatloaf and let simmer in the sauce.

Serves 4–6

1½ pounds ground beef
1 onion, chopped
2 tablespoons flour
1 4-ounce can chopped
   jalapeños, undrained
2 8-ounce cans tomato sauce
   with seasonings
2 14-ounce cans diced
   tomatoes with garlic,
   undrained
1 cup water

Five-Ingredient Chili

*Using tomato products seasoned with spices and
garlic cuts down on the ingredient list. Serve the chili with
sour cream, shredded cheese, and chopped tomato.*

1. In large saucepan, cook ground beef and onion over medium heat, stirring frequently to break up meat, about 4 to 5 minutes. When beef is browned, drain off half of the liquid. Sprinkle flour over beef; cook and stir for 2 minutes.

2. Add remaining ingredients, bring to a simmer, and simmer for 10 to 15 minutes, until flavors are blended and liquid is thickened. Serve immediately.

Five-Way Chili
In Cincinnati, "five-way chili" means chili served with spaghetti, cheddar cheese, beans, and chopped raw onions. If you vary the additions, you'll be serving "two-way" (with spaghetti), "three-way" (spaghetti and cheese), and "four-way" (three-way plus raw onions). "One-way," of course, is plain chili.

Beef and Tortellini

This simple dish is packed full of flavor. Serve it with some grated Parmesan cheese, a green salad with lots of tomatoes, and some sautéed broccoli.

Serves 4
_____

1 pound ground beef
1 onion, chopped
1 16-ounce package frozen
    beef-filled tortellini
1 10-ounce jar four-cheese
    Alfredo sauce
1 9-ounce container
    refrigerated pesto

1. Bring a large pot of water to boil over high heat. Meanwhile, in large saucepan, cook ground beef and onion over medium heat, stirring to break up meat, for 4 to 6 minutes, until beef is browned. Drain well. Cook tortellini in boiling water according to package directions, until tender; drain well.

2. Combine beef mixture, cooked and drained tortellini, and Alfredo sauce in large saucepan and cook over medium heat for 5 minutes, stirring occasionally, until mixture is combined and sauce bubbles. Stir in pesto, cover, remove from heat, let stand for 5 minutes, and serve.

Pressure-Cooker Beef Goulash

The pressure cooker makes beef tender and delicious in minutes. Serve this hearty dish over hot cooked buttered noodles with a spinach salad.

Serves 6
_____

2 pounds beef round steak
3 tablespoons flour
1 teaspoon salt
⅛ teaspoon pepper
1 tablespoon sweet paprika
2 tablespoons olive oil
1 onion, chopped
3 russet potatoes, chopped
½ cup water
2 8-ounce cans tomato sauce
    with roasted garlic
1 cup sour cream

1. Cut steak into 1-inch pieces. In small bowl, combine flour, salt, pepper, and paprika. Sprinkle over beef cubes and rub into meat. Heat olive oil in pressure cooker; add beef and brown on all sides, stirring frequently, about 3 to 5 minutes. Meanwhile, prepare the onion and potatoes.

2. Add onion and potatoes to pressure cooker along with water and tomato sauce. Lock the lid and bring up to high pressure. Cook for 12 minutes, then release pressure using quick-release method. Test to be sure potatoes are tender; if not, lock lid and cook for 2 to 3 minutes longer. Then release pressure, stir in sour cream, and serve over hot cooked noodles or mashed potatoes.

3 garlic cloves
1 teaspoon salt
1 tablespoon grill seasoning
¼ teaspoon dry mustard
¼ teaspoon cayenne pepper
2 tablespoons balsamic
*   vinegar*
1½ pounds flank steak

Spicy Grilled Flank Steak

Grill seasoning contains lots of spices, usually including cumin, oregano, pepper, garlic, and sugar. Use it for hamburgers as well as grilled steaks.

1. Prepare and heat grill. On cutting board, mince garlic cloves, then sprinkle with salt. Using the side of the knife, mash garlic and salt together to create a paste. Place in a small bowl and add remaining ingredients except flank steak; mix well. Prick both sides of the steak with a fork and rub the marinade mixture into the steak. Let stand for 10 minutes.

2. Place steak on grill over medium coals and cover. Grill for 5 minutes, then turn steak, cover, and grill for 3 to 5 minutes longer, until medium-rare or medium. Let steak stand for 5 minutes, then slice across the grain to serve.

It's All in the Slicing

Flank steak is a lean, flavorful cut that is tender only if sliced correctly. Look at the steak: you'll see parallel lines running through it. That's called the grain of the steak. When you cut the steak, cut against, or perpendicular to, those lines and the steak will be tender and juicy.

Herbed Steak

The combination of balsamic vinegar and mustard with fresh thyme seasons these tender steaks to perfection. Cook a few more and you can make Asian Beef Rolls (page 175) or Grilled Steak Sandwiches (page 194) tomorrow.

~~~~

Serves 6
___

6 6-ounce strip steaks
1 teaspoon salt
⅛ teaspoon white pepper
2 tablespoons olive oil
2 tablespoons Worcestershire sauce
2 tablespoons fresh thyme leaves
½ teaspoon dried oregano leaves
¼ cup balsamic vinegar
2 tablespoons mustard

1. Prepare and preheat grill. Place steaks in a glass baking dish; pierce all over with a fork. Sprinkle on both sides with salt and pepper. In small bowl, combine remaining ingredients and mix well. Pour over steaks, turning to coat, rubbing marinade into steaks with hands. Let stand for 10 minutes.

2. Place steaks on grill over medium coals and drizzle with any remaining marinade. Cover grill and cook for 5 minutes. Turn steaks and cook for 4 to 6 minutes longer, until desired doneness. Let stand 5 minutes, then serve.

Steak Grilling Temps

An instant-read meat thermometer is always a good utensil to have on hand. When grilling steaks, 140°F is rare, 145°F is medium-rare, 160°F is medium, and 170°F is well done. Be sure to let the steak stand for a few minutes before carving and serving to let the juices redistribute.

2 eggs
½ teaspoon dried Italian
    seasoning
½ teaspoon onion salt
⅛ teaspoon garlic pepper
¾ cup soft bread crumbs
¾ cup ketchup, divided
1½ pounds meatloaf mix
1 cup shredded Co-Jack
    cheese, divided

Mini Meatloaf

Meatloaves made in muffin tins are cute, fun to make, and fun to eat. Serve with some ketchup and frozen French fries to give your kids a treat.

1. Preheat oven to 350°F. In large bowl, combine eggs, Italian seasoning, onion salt, garlic pepper, bread crumbs, and ½ cup ketchup and mix well. Add meatloaf mix and ½ cup cheese and mix gently but thoroughly to combine.

2. Press meat mixture, ⅓ cup at a time, into 12 muffin cups. Top each with a bit of ketchup and remaining cheese. Bake at 350°F for 15 to 18 minutes, until meat is thoroughly cooked. Remove from muffin tins, drain if necessary, place on serving platter, cover with foil, and let stand 5 minutes before serving.

About Meatloaf Mix

Meatloaf mix is found in the meat aisle of the supermarket. It usually consists of one-third beef, one-third pork, and one-third veal, but read the label to find out what the blend is in your area. The veal lightens the mixture, and the pork adds a slightly different flavor and texture, because meatloaf made with all beef tends to be heavy.

Quick Beef Stroganoff

Beef Stroganoff is an elegant dish that usually takes a while to make, but using precooked meat products means the dish is ready in about 20 minutes.

∼

Serves 4

2 tablespoons olive oil
1 onion, chopped
1 16-ounce package fully
    cooked beef tips with
    gravy
1 16-ounce package frozen
    cut green beans, thawed
    and drained
4 cups egg noodles
1 cup sour cream

1. Bring a large pot of water to a boil. Meanwhile, heat olive oil in large saucepan over medium heat. Add onion; cook and stir for 3 to 4 minutes, until crisp-tender. Add contents of beef package along with green beans. Bring to a simmer; cook for 6 to 7 minutes, until beef and green beans are heated.

2. When water is boiling, add egg noodles. Cook according to package directions, until al dente, about 4 to 5 minutes. Meanwhile, stir sour cream into beef mixture, cover, and remove from heat. When noodles are done, drain well, place on serving platter, and spoon beef mixture over.

Menu Suggestions
Serve this rich entrée recipe with Simple Spinach Salad (page 207) and Braised Carrots (page 228). Some heated bakery rolls or Parmesan Crescents (page 43) would be a nice addition, and for dessert, make Raspberry Continental (page 276).

Serves 4

1 pound strip steak
2 tablespoons oil
1 onion, sliced
3 tablespoons flour
½ teaspoon salt
1 tablespoon curry powder
⅛ teaspoon white pepper
1 12-ounce jar baby corn on
    the cob, drained
½ cup frozen orange juice
    concentrate
1 15-ounce can evaporated
    milk

Curried Beef Stir-Fry

Serve this richly seasoned curry on hot cooked rice, with mango chutney and chopped cashews, toasted coconut, and raisins or currants for condiments.

1. Cut steak into ½-inch pieces across the grain and set aside. Heat oil in a large skillet over medium-high heat. Add onion; stir-fry for 3 to 4 minutes, until crisp-tender. Add steak; stir-fry for 3 to 4 minutes, until steak is browned. Sprinkle with flour, salt, curry powder, and pepper. Stir-fry for 2 to 3 minutes longer.

2. Stir in remaining ingredients; stir-fry over medium heat for 5 to 6 minutes, until liquid is thickened and corn is hot. Serve over hot cooked rice.

Recipe Substitutions
If you can't find baby corn on the cob, you can substitute frozen asparagus cuts, frozen stir-fry vegetables, frozen green beans, frozen sweet corn, or sliced mushrooms in this easy stir-fry. If your family likes spicy foods, increase the curry powder as much as you'd like.

Chapter 5

Seafood

Serves 4

4 halibut fillets

3 tablespoons olive oil, divided

Salt and pepper to taste

2 cups chopped, seeded tomatoes

⅔ cup pesto sauce

½ cup grated Parmesan cheese

Halibut Bruschetta

Bruschetta is an Italian appetizer of toasted bread slices topped with a fragrant tomato salad. In this recipe, halibut replaces the bread for an easy and elegant main dish.

1. Preheat broiler. Place fillets on broiler pan and brush with half of the olive oil; sprinkle with salt and pepper. In small bowl, combine tomatoes, remaining olive oil, pesto, and Parmesan cheese; season with salt and pepper to taste.

2. Broil halibut fillets for 8 to 12 minutes or until fish flakes easily when tested with a fork. Top with tomato mixture and broil for 1 to 2 minutes longer. Serve immediately.

Other Fish Choices

You can use other mild fish fillets in this easy, nutritious, and beautiful recipe. Think about using orange roughy, tilapia, or cod. This topping would also be wonderful on salmon or swordfish fillets or steaks. Cook all of these fish just until the fish flakes when you insert a fork and twist it.

Shrimp Scampi Kabobs

Lemon and garlic are the main seasonings in Shrimp Scampi. This is an easy way to make scampi on your grill. Serve with hot cooked rice.

Serves 6

3 lemons
¼ cup olive oil
4 cloves garlic, minced
1 teaspoon dried thyme
    leaves
½ teaspoon salt
⅛ teaspoon white pepper
1½ pounds large raw shrimp,
    cleaned
18 large mushrooms
2 yellow squash, cut into
    1-inch pieces

1. Prepare and preheat grill. Using lemon zester, remove peel from 1 of the lemons. Place in medium bowl. Squeeze juice from the peeled lemon and add to peel in bowl. Cut remaining lemons into 6 wedges each and set aside. Add oil, garlic, thyme, salt, and pepper to lemon mixture in bowl and mix well. Add shrimp and let stand for 10 minutes.

2. Drain shrimp, reserving marinade. Place shrimp, mushrooms, squash pieces, and lemon wedges alternately on twelve 8"-long metal skewers. Brush skewers with marinade, then grill 4 to 6 inches from medium-hot coals for 8 to 14 minutes, turning once, until shrimp are curled and pink and vegetables are tender. Brush skewers often with marinade. Discard any remaining marinade.

Cleaning Shrimp
If the shrimp you buy still have the shell and tail on them, you must clean them before use. Cut a shallow slit along the back; remove the shell, tail, and legs; then rinse out the dark vein running along the shrimp, using your fingers to remove it if necessary.

Serves 6

2 6-ounce cans crabmeat,
  drained
1 cup frozen pepper and
  onion stir-fry mix
1 10-ounce container
  refrigerated four-cheese
  Alfredo sauce
1½ cups shredded Monterey
  Jack cheese
12 6-inch spinach-flavored
  flour tortillas

Crab Burritos

*You can make these excellent burritos with two pouches
of boneless skinless salmon, 12 ounces of cooked small or
medium shrimp, or 2 cups of flaked and cooked fish.*

1. Preheat oven to 350°F. Drain crabmeat well, pressing with paper towel to absorb excess moisture. Place in medium bowl. Thaw pepper and onion mix in microwave on 30 percent power for 2 to 3 minutes; drain well and add to crabmeat. Stir in half of the Alfredo sauce and ½ cup Monterey Jack cheese.

2. Fill tortillas with 2 tablespoons crabmeat mixture and roll up. Place in 13" × 9" glass baking dish. Top each filled burrito with some Alfredo sauce and sprinkle with remaining Monterey Jack cheese. Bake for 10 to 16 minutes until burritos are hot and cheese is melted. Serve immediately.

Broiled Cod Montauk

Mayonnaise helps keep the fish moist while it cooks. Serve this simple dish with a lettuce and vegetable salad and some soft breadsticks.

~~~~~~~~

Serves 6

½ cup mayonnaise
1 teaspoon Dijon mustard
1 tablespoon lemon juice
2 tablespoons grated
    Parmesan cheese
½ teaspoon dried tarragon
    leaves
6 6-ounce cod fillets

1. Preheat broiler. In small bowl, combine mayonnaise, mustard, lemon juice, cheese, and tarragon, and mix well.

2. Place cod on broiler rack. Broil 4 to 6 inches from heat source for about 4 minutes. Remove from oven, turn fillets, and spread mayonnaise mixture over each fillet. Return pan to oven and broil for 3 to 5 minutes longer, until fish flakes when tested with fork and mayonnaise mixture begins to bubble and brown. Serve immediately.

Mayo: Low-Fat or Regular?
You can find mayonnaise in low-fat, no-fat, and regular versions; they all taste pretty much the same. You can use any type in most cooking recipes, salad dressings, and sandwich spreads. In baking, however, you should use full-fat mayonnaise unless the recipe says otherwise.

Poached Salmon with Alfredo Sauce

You can find jarred Alfredo and other cheese sauces by the pasta sauces in the supermarket; they are a good substitute for the refrigerated sauces.

1. In shallow saucepan large enough to hold fillets in a single layer, place water and wine. Bring to a boil over medium heat and add salmon. Reduce heat to low, cover pan, and cook for 8 to 10 minutes or until fish is opaque and flakes easily when tested with fork.

2. Meanwhile, in heavy saucepan, heat olive oil over medium heat. Add onion and cook until tender, about 4 to 5 minutes. Add Alfredo sauce and basil; cook and stir over low heat until sauce bubbles.

3. Place salmon on serving plates; cover with sauce and sprinkle with Parmesan cheese. Serve immediately.

Poaching
Poaching is cooking meat or fruit in a liquid that is just below the boiling point. This method retains and concentrates the flavor of the food, and the results are juicy and tender. Fish is usually poached because the delicate flesh cooks gently with this method and does not dry out.

Shrimp and Rice

*Serve this spicy shrimp dish with Lemon Cucumber Salad (page 204),
Mini Popovers (page 43) and Oatmeal Cookie Parfaits (page 274).*

~

Serves 4

2 tablespoons olive oil
1 onion, finely chopped
1 cup Texmati rice
1½ cups chicken broth
1 14-ounce can diced
    tomatoes with green
    chilies, undrained
1½ pounds medium raw
    shrimp, cleaned
½ teaspoon dried oregano
    leaves
⅛ teaspoon cayenne pepper

1. In large saucepan, heat olive oil over medium heat. Add onion; cook and stir until crisp-tender, about 3 to 4 minutes. Add rice and stir to coat. Add chicken broth, bring to a boil, then cover, reduce heat, and simmer for 15 minutes.

2. Add tomatoes to rice mixture and bring to a simmer. Add shrimp, oregano, and pepper, and simmer for 4 to 6 minutes, until rice is tender and shrimp are pink and curled. Serve immediately.

Easy Jambalaya

*Jambalaya is a festive Southern dish that usually takes hours to make. Serve this easy
version with some melon wedges, croissants, and ice cream sundaes for dessert.*

~

Serves 4

1 8-ounce package yellow
    rice mix
2 tablespoons olive oil
1 onion, chopped
1 14-ounce can diced
    tomatoes with green
    chilies
1 8-ounce package frozen
    cooked shrimp, thawed
2 Grilled Polish Sausages
    (page 141), sliced

Prepare rice mix as directed on package. Meanwhile, in large saucepan, heat olive oil over medium heat. Add onion; cook and stir for 4 to 5 minutes, until tender. Add tomatoes, shrimp, and sliced sausages; bring to a simmer, and cook for 2 to 3 minutes. When rice is cooked, add to saucepan; cook and stir for 3 to 4 minutes, until blended. Serve immediately.

Frozen Shrimp

You can buy frozen shrimp that has been shelled, deveined, and cooked. To thaw it, place in a colander under cold running water for 4 to 5 minutes, tossing shrimp occasionally with hands, until thawed. Use the shrimp immediately after thawing.

Serves 6

3 cloves garlic, minced
½ teaspoon salt
½ cup butter, softened
1½ cups fine bread crumbs
¼ teaspoon dried marjoram
   leaves
¼ teaspoon dried tarragon
   leaves
⅛ teaspoon white pepper
2 pounds cooked, shelled
   shrimp, thawed if frozen
¼ cup lemon juice

Shrimps de Jonghe

*The bread-crumb mixture for this elegant dish can be prepared ahead of time.
Purchase cooked, shelled, and deveined shrimp from your butcher.*

1. Preheat oven to 425°F. In medium bowl, mash garlic with salt to form a paste. Add butter and beat until combined. Add bread crumbs, marjoram, tarragon, and white pepper and mix well.

2. Butter a 2-quart casserole dish. In large bowl, combine shrimp and lemon juice; toss to coat, then drain shrimp. Layer shrimp and bread crumb mixture in prepared casserole dish. Bake for 15 to 20 minutes, until hot and bread crumbs begin to brown.

Purchasing Shrimp

You can find cooked, shelled, and deveined shrimp in the meat aisle of the regular grocery store. This product is also stocked in the freezer section of the meat aisle; thaw according to package directions. Fresh cooked shrimp should be used within two days. It should smell sweet and slightly briny; if there is any off odor, do not buy it.

Salmon Steaks with Spinach Pesto

*This elegant dish is perfect for company. Serve it with
Pasta Pilaf (page 224), Melty Cheese Bread (page 54), and Roasted
Sugar Snap Peas (page 227), with a bakery cake for dessert.*

Serves 6

¼ cup lemon juice, divided
2 tablespoons oil
½ teaspoon dried basil leaves
6 salmon steaks
1 10-ounce container
　　refrigerated pesto
½ cup frozen chopped
　　spinach, thawed and
　　drained
¼ cup chopped salted
　　cashews

1. In glass baking dish, combine 2 tablespoons lemon juice, oil, and basil leaves. Add salmon steaks, turn to coat, and let stand for 10 minutes at room temperature.

2. While steaks marinate, combine pesto, spinach, and remaining 2 tablespoons lemon juice in a blender or food processor. Process or blend until mixture is smooth. Place in small bowl and stir in cashews.

3. Remove steaks from marinade and place on broiler pan. Broil 4 to 6 inches from heat source for 5 minutes, turn steaks, and broil for 5 to 8 minutes longer, until fish flakes when tested with fork. Top each with a spoonful of the pesto mixture and serve.

Spark Up Pesto

Adding spinach and lemon juice to prepared pesto makes the sauce a bright green color and perks up the flavor. And adding more nuts, whether pine nuts, cashews, or walnuts, makes the sauce a bit crunchy. Spinach also adds more nutrition and helps cut the fat, and it doesn't alter the flavor.

Serves 4

1 tablespoon olive oil
1 red bell pepper, chopped
1 pound shelled, deveined
    large raw shrimp, thawed
    if frozen
1 9-ounce package
    refrigerated cheese
    ravioli
1½ cups water
¾ cup pesto sauce
½ cup grated Parmesan
    cheese

Shrimp Pesto Ravioli

You can use fish fillets, cut into cubes, in place of the shrimp, or substitute bay scallops. Serve this easy dish with some breadsticks and a fruit salad.

1. In heavy skillet, heat oil over medium heat. Add red bell pepper and stir-fry for 3 to 4 minutes, until crisp-tender. Add shrimp; cook and stir for 4 to 6 minutes, until shrimp curl and turn pink. Remove shrimp and peppers from skillet.

2. Add ravioli and water to skillet and bring to a boil over high heat. Reduce heat to medium-high, cover, and simmer for 4 to 6 minutes, until ravioli are hot, stirring occasionally. Drain off excess liquid and return shrimp and pepper to skillet. Cook and stir over medium-high heat, stirring occasionally, until shrimp are cooked and mixture is hot. Stir in pesto, place in serving dish, sprinkle with cheese, and serve.

Honey Mustard Salmon

Honey and mustard make an irresistible flavor combination with rich and savory salmon fillets. You can multiply this recipe for a larger crowd; marinating and cooking times remain the same.

Serves 4

⅓ cup honey mustard salad dressing
2 tablespoons honey
½ teaspoon dill seed
2 tablespoons butter, melted
4 6-ounce salmon fillets

⁓

1. In shallow casserole dish, combine salad dressing, honey, dill seed, and butter and mix well. Add salmon fillets and turn to coat. Cover and let stand at room temperature for 10 minutes.

2. Prepare and preheat grill or broiler. Remove salmon from marinade and place, skin-side down, on grill or broiler pan. Cover and grill, or broil, 6 inches from heat for 8 to 12 minutes, until salmon is cooked and flakes when tested with a fork, brushing with remaining marinade halfway through cooking time. Discard remaining marinade. Serve immediately.

Menu Ideas
Any fish dish is delicious served with a salad made from baby spinach. Toss together spinach, sliced water chestnuts, sliced mushrooms, and red bell pepper, and drizzle with some creamy garlic salad dressing. Top it with croutons or Parmesan shavings. Add some ready-to-bake breadsticks and your meal is complete.

Serves 3–4

½ pound spaghetti pasta
4 pounds cleaned mussels
¼ cup olive oil
6 cloves garlic, minced
1 red bell pepper, cut into strips
½ teaspoon dried oregano leaves
1½ cups dry white wine
Salt and pepper to taste

Garlic Mussels

This is such a beautiful dish; the shiny black mussel shells contrast with the red pepper and the creamy beige flesh. Serve it with fresh fruit and crusty bread.

1. Bring a large pot of water to a boil; cook spaghetti pasta according to package directions. Meanwhile, place mussels in a colander; pick over them to remove any opened mussels; rinse well and set aside.

2. In large stockpot big enough to hold the mussels, heat olive oil over medium high heat. Add garlic; cook and stir until fragrant, 1 to 2 minutes. Add red bell pepper; cook and stir for 3 to 4 minutes, until crisp-tender. Sprinkle with oregano and pour wine into pot; bring to a boil. Add salt and pepper, then add mussels.

3. Cover pot and turn heat to medium-low. Cook, shaking pan frequently, for 4 to 7 minutes or until all mussels open. (Discard any mussels that do not open.) Remove mussels and bell peppers from pot and place in serving bowl. Strain liquid and pour half over mussels. Combine remaining liquid with cooked and drained spaghetti; serve immediately with the mussels.

About Mussels

Mussels used to be difficult to prepare because they needed to be cleaned, debearded, and scrubbed. Now you can buy them precleaned, with the beards off; just rinse and use. Be sure to discard open mussels and those with broken shells before cooking, and discard mussels that aren't open after cooking.

Fruity Tuna Steaks

Curry powder, orange juice, and apricot jam add great flavor to tender tuna steaks. Because the steaks are simmered in the sauce, they pick up more flavor.

Serves 4

2 tablespoons olive oil
1 onion, chopped
2 teaspoons curry powder
⅓ cup frozen orange juice concentrate
2 tablespoons water
¼ cup apricot jam
Salt and pepper to taste
4 6-ounce tuna steaks

1. In heavy skillet, heat olive oil over medium heat. Add onion; cook and stir for 2 minutes. Sprinkle curry powder over onions; cook and stir for 2 to 3 minutes longer, until onions are crisp-tender.

2. Add orange juice concentrate and water to skillet along with apricot jam and salt and pepper. Bring to a boil, then reduce heat to a simmer and add tuna. Cook for 8 to 10 minutes per inch of thickness, turning tuna once during cooking time, until fish flakes when tested with fork. You can serve tuna medium-rare if you'd like.

3. Place tuna on serving plate. If necessary, reduce sauce by turning heat to high and simmering until thickened, 3 to 4 minutes. Pour sauce over tuna and serve.

Serves 4–6

2 tablespoons olive oil
4 cloves garlic, minced
1 serrano pepper, minced
1 cup dry white wine
2 pounds sea scallops
1 teaspoon salt
⅛ teaspoon cayenne pepper
2 tablespoons butter

Steamed Spicy Scallops

*A peppery wine sauce finished with butter coats these
tender scallops that are steamed to perfection.*

1. In large saucepan, heat olive oil over medium heat. Add garlic and ser-
    rano pepper; cook and stir for 2 to 3 minutes, until fragrant. Add wine,
    reduce heat to low, and simmer while cooking scallops.

2. Meanwhile, place water in the bottom of a steamer and bring to a boil
    over high heat. Sprinkle scallops with salt and cayenne pepper and
    place in steamer top. Place over boiling water, cover, and steam scal-
    lops for 2 minutes. Gently stir scallops, cover again, and steam for 2 to
    5 minutes, until scallops are opaque.

3. Remove serrano pepper sauce from heat and swirl in butter until melted.
    Place scallops on serving plate and top with sauce. Serve immediately.

Scallops

*There are three kinds of scallops available. Sea scallops are the largest,
about 30 to the pound, and are white, sometimes with an orange tint.
Bay scallops are smaller, about 50 to the pound, are sweet and white
with a hint of pink. And calico scallops, the smallest of all, are darker in
color and not as tender.*

Scallop Tacos

These pretty tacos are sweet, spicy, and crunchy. Serve them with a pineapple and melon salad for a cooling contrast.

Serves 4

2 tablespoons olive oil
1 onion, chopped
1 pound scallops
½ teaspoon salt
2 teaspoons chili powder
½ teaspoon cumin
¼ teaspoon red pepper flakes
8 taco shells
1 cup mango salsa
2 cups finely shredded
      cabbage

1. Preheat oven to 375°F. In a heavy skillet, heat olive oil over medium-high heat. Add onion; cook and stir until tender, about 4 to 5 minutes. Meanwhile, sprinkle scallops with a mixture of salt, chili powder, cumin, and red pepper flakes. Add to skillet; cook for 2 minutes, then turn scallops and cook until opaque, about 2 to 4 minutes.

2. While scallops are cooking, put taco shells on a baking sheet and heat in the oven until crisp, about 5 to 7 minutes. Combine mango salsa and cabbage in medium bowl.

3. Make tacos with cabbage mixture, heated taco shells, and scallop mixture and serve immediately.

Salsa

There are so many types of salsa available today. You can find mango salsa, black bean salsa, vegetable salsa, and plain old tomato salsa in any supermarket. They range in spiciness from mild to extra hot. Be sure to read labels carefully to make sure you're buying the flavor and heat intensity you want.

Serves 3–4

3 tablespoons butter
1 red bell pepper, finely
    chopped
8 eggs
2 tablespoons water
½ teaspoon salt
⅛ teaspoon white pepper
1 pound cooked shrimp
1½ cups grated Havarti
    cheese

Shrimp Omelet

*This fluffy omelet filled with shrimp, bell pepper, and cheese is perfect
for a lazy Sunday brunch served with caramel rolls and a citrus salad.*

1. In large nonstick skillet, melt butter over medium heat. Add bell pepper; cook and stir for 3 to 4 minutes, until crisp-tender. Meanwhile, in large bowl, beat eggs with water, salt, and pepper.

2. Add egg mixture to pan. Cook for 2 minutes. Continue cooking, lifting egg mixture to allow uncooked portion to flow underneath. When eggs are almost set but still glossy after about 4 minutes longer, top with shrimp and cheese. Cover and cook for 2 more minutes, until cheese melts. Fold omelet and serve immediately.

Serves 6

½ cup chili sauce
1½ cups pasta sauce
2 cups medium cooked
    shrimp
2 tablespoons olive oil
6 4- to 6-ounce mild white
    fish fillets
½ teaspoon salt
⅛ teaspoon red pepper flakes
2 tablespoons lemon juice

Fish Creole

*You can use any mild white fish fillets in this flavorful recipe;
halibut, orange roughy, grouper, or cod would be good choices.*

1. Preheat oven to 450°F. In medium saucepan, combine chili sauce and pasta sauce; bring to a boil over medium-high heat. Reduce heat to medium and simmer for 5 minutes, stirring frequently. Stir in shrimp, cover, and remove from heat.

2. Meanwhile, place oil in glass baking dish. Arrange fish in dish and sprinkle with salt, pepper flakes, and lemon juice. Bake for 8 to 10 minutes or until fish flakes easily when tested with a fork. Place on serving dish and top with shrimp sauce. Serve immediately.

Salmon Florentine

Jarred four-cheese Alfredo sauce is a great timesaver. Find it near the pasta in the regular grocery store; stock up, because you can make many recipes with it.

Serves 4

4 6-ounce salmon fillets
1 teaspoon salt
⅛ teaspoon white pepper
½ teaspoon dried Italian
    seasoning
2 tablespoons olive oil
1 10-ounce jar four-cheese
    Alfredo sauce
1 cup frozen chopped spinach,
    thawed and well drained
½ cup grated Parmesan
    cheese

1. Preheat broiler. Sprinkle salmon with salt, pepper, and Italian seasoning and drizzle with olive oil. Place on broiler pan and let stand for 5 minutes.

2. In large skillet, heat Alfredo sauce over medium-low heat until bubbly. Place salmon fillets under broiler 4 to 6 inches from heat source for 5 minutes. Stir spinach into Alfredo sauce and let simmer over low heat. Turn salmon fillets and broil for 3 to 4 minutes longer, until salmon is almost done.

3. Place salmon on ovenproof serving platter and top with Alfredo-sauce mixture. Sprinkle with Parmesan cheese. Broil for 2 to 4 minutes, until cheese melts and begins to brown. Serve immediately.

4 6-ounce red snapper fillets
½ teaspoon salt
⅛ teaspoon white pepper
½ teaspoon dried thyme
    leaves
1 lemon
2 cups sliced mushrooms
2 cups sliced yellow summer
    squash
⅓ cup dry white wine

Red Snapper en Papillote

*Parchment paper not only holds in the steam to cook this delicate
fish to perfection, it makes for a beautiful presentation too.*

1. Preheat oven to 400°F. Cut four 12" × 18" rectangles from parchment paper and trim each into a large heart shape. Fold in half, then unfold and place one fillet in the center of each heart half. Sprinkle with salt, pepper, and thyme leaves. Thinly slice lemon and place on fillets.

2. Arrange vegetables around the fish and sprinkle everything with the wine. Fold the other half of the parchment paper over the food and crimp the edges together to seal. Place on cookie sheets and bake for 12 to 16 minutes or until fish flakes when tested with a fork. Place parchment packages on plates to serve.

Parchment or Foil?
You can use parchment paper or foil to cook food en papillote. *The parchment paper makes a prettier presentation at the table, but the foil is a better choice when the recipe cooks longer than 15 minutes, because the paper can burn. Let your guests open their packages at the table; warn them to be careful of the steam.*

Mussels in Spicy Broth

Serve the broth on the side after straining for another course;
top with some minced parsley, cilantro, or chopped green onions.

Serves 3–4
_____

4 pounds fresh mussels,
    cleaned
2 oranges
2 tablespoons olive oil
1 cup sliced mushrooms
1 jalapeño pepper, minced
2 cups fish stock
½ teaspoon salt
⅛ teaspoon red pepper flakes

1. Pick over mussels, discarding any that stay open when tapped and those with broken or cracked shells. Rinse and set aside. Remove 1 teaspoon orange zest from oranges and squeeze juice; set aside.

2. In a large stockpot, heat olive oil over medium heat and add mushrooms and jalapeño pepper. Cook and stir for 4 to 5 minutes, until mushrooms begin to brown. Remove mushrooms with slotted spoon and set aside. Add fish stock, orange juice and zest, salt, and red pepper flakes; bring to a boil.

3. Add mussels, cover pot, and cook until the mussels open, about 4 to 7 minutes, shaking pot frequently and rearranging mussels once during cooking time. Transfer mussels to serving bowl. Serve broth with mushrooms as a separate course.

Fish Stock

If you can't find fish stock in cans or boxes, you can make your own. In a large pot, combine 1 pound fish trimmings (not salmon) with 1½ quarts water; a bay leaf; a quartered onion; 3 garlic cloves; 2 stalks celery, chopped, including leaves; and 1 teaspoon salt. Simmer for 20 to 30 minutes, strain broth, and freeze.

Serves 4

1 cup jasmine rice
2 cups chicken broth
2 lemons
½ cup butter
1½ pounds medium raw
    shrimp, cleaned
¼ teaspoon garlic powder
⅛ teaspoon garlic pepper
½ teaspoon garlic salt

Microwave Shrimp Scampi

*This dish can be multiplied to serve more people.
You must proportionally increase the microwave cooking
time: if you double the shrimp, double the cooking time.*

1. Combine rice and chicken broth in medium saucepan and bring to a boil over high heat. Cover pan, lower heat to medium low, and simmer for 15 minutes.

2. Meanwhile, grate lemon zest from lemons and squeeze juice. Combine the zest, juice, and butter in microwave-safe dish. Microwave on high for 2 minutes. Sprinkle shrimp with garlic powder, garlic pepper, and garlic salt and add to butter mixture; toss to coat shrimp. Cover and microwave on high for 2 minutes. Uncover dish, stir shrimp, cover, and microwave on high for 1 to 3 minutes longer, until shrimp curl and turn pink.

3. Let shrimp stand, covered, for 2 to 3 minutes. Fluff rice with a fork. Serve shrimp and sauce over rice.

Quick-Cooking Rice

You don't have to use instant rice when you want some in a hurry. Read labels at the grocery store. There are some kinds of rice, including Texmati and jasmine, that cook in only 15 minutes. As a bonus, those rice varieties are fragrant and full of flavor.

Chapter 6

Chicken and Turkey

1 pound boneless, skinless
   chicken breasts
Salt and pepper to taste
2 tablespoons olive oil
2 cloves garlic, minced
2 cups frozen bell pepper and
   onion stir-fry
2 tablespoons lemon juice
½ cup crumbled feta cheese

Greek Chicken Stir-Fry

*Stir-fry with a twist! These ingredients add spark and great
flavor to a typical chicken stir-fry. Serve over steamed rice,
prepared instant couscous, or hot cooked noodles.*

1. Cut chicken breasts into 1-inch pieces and sprinkle with salt and pepper. Heat olive oil in a wok or large skillet over medium-high heat. Add chicken and garlic and stir-fry until chicken is cooked, about 4 to 5 minutes. Remove chicken and garlic to plate with slotted spoon and set aside.

2. Add frozen vegetables to skillet and stir-fry for 5 to 7 minutes until hot and crisp-tender. Add chicken to skillet and sprinkle with lemon juice. Stir-fry for 1 minute longer. Sprinkle with feta cheese, remove pan from heat, cover, and let stand for 2 to 3 minutes longer to melt cheese. Serve immediately.

Greek Food
Seasonings and ingredients that add a Greek flavor include feta cheese, oregano, olives, spinach, filo dough, pita bread, rice, fresh seafood, grape leaves, lamb, and yogurt. The food is fairly spicy, with some unusual food combinations that include spinach and raisins, and beef and olives.

Herbed Chicken Breasts

Serve these well-flavored, tender chicken breasts with a rice pilaf, a spinach salad, and some oatmeal cookies for dessert.

Serves 8

2 tablespoons olive oil
2 tablespoons butter
2 cloves garlic, cut in half
¼ cup lemon juice
2 tablespoons chopped flat-
    leaf parsley
½ teaspoon dried thyme
    leaves
½ teaspoon salt
⅛ teaspoon white pepper
8 chicken breasts

1. In a small saucepan, combine olive oil, butter, and garlic over medium heat. Cook and stir until garlic sizzles; then remove garlic and discard. Add lemon juice, herbs, and salt and pepper to oil and butter in pan; stir; and remove from heat. Let cool for 5 to 10 minutes. Loosen chicken skin from the flesh and pour a tablespoon of the lemon herb mixture between the skin and flesh. Smooth skin back over flesh.

2. Place chicken pieces, skin-side down, on broiler pan. Brush with lemon mixture. Broil chicken, 4 to 6 inches from heat source, for 7 to 8 minutes, brushing often with the lemon mixture. Turn chicken and broil 6 to 9 minutes longer, brushing frequently with lemon mixture, until chicken is thoroughly cooked. Discard any remaining lemon mixture.

Chicken Breasts: Boned or Not?
Chicken breasts are sold boneless and skinless, and with bone in and skin on. The one you choose depends on what you're cooking. The skin and bone do add more flavor, so in simple broiled recipes, bone-in chicken is a good choice. When you want cubed chicken for stir-fries and sandwiches, boneless, skinless breasts are better.

Serves 4

¼ cup flour
½ teaspoon salt
⅛ teaspoon pepper
½ teaspoon dried marjoram
   leaves
4 boneless, skinless chicken
   breasts
¼ cup butter
1 cup chicken stock
½ cup white grape juice
1 cup red grapes, cut in half

Chicken Veronique

*Sweet and tart grapes complement juicy and tender chicken
in this wonderful recipe perfect for entertaining. Make sure to
serve it over hot cooked rice to soak up the delicious sauce.*

1. On a shallow plate, combine flour, salt, pepper, and marjoram. Coat chicken breasts in this mixture. In a heavy skillet over medium heat, melt butter. Add chicken breasts and cook for 4 minutes. Turn chicken over and cook 3 to 6 minutes longer, until chicken is just done. Remove chicken from pan and cover with foil to keep warm.

2. Add stock and grape juice to pan and bring to a boil, scraping up pan drippings. Boil over high heat for 6 to 8 minutes, until sauce is reduced and thickened. Return chicken to pan along with red grapes, and cook over low heat for 2 to 3 minutes, until grapes are hot and chicken is tender.

Serves 6

6 boneless, skinless chicken
   breasts
¼ cup lemon juice
1 teaspoon salt
⅛ teaspoon pepper
½ teaspoon dried thyme
   leaves
¼ cup unsalted butter
½ cup grated Parmesan
   cheese

Parmesan Chicken

*This simple recipe demands the highest quality ingredients. Serve it
with some hot cooked couscous, bakery rolls, and melon wedges.*

1. Cut chicken breasts into 1-inch pieces. Sprinkle with lemon juice, salt, pepper, and thyme leaves. Let stand at room temperature for 10 minutes.

2. Melt butter in a heavy saucepan over medium heat. Sauté chicken until thoroughly cooked, about 5 to 6 minutes, stirring frequently. Sprinkle cheese over chicken, turn off heat, cover pan, and let stand for 2 to 3 minutes to melt cheese. Serve over hot cooked couscous.

Basil Spinach Risotto

This recipe does not contain chicken, but it does use chicken broth to add fabulous flavor. Be sure to save some to make Basil Spinach Risotto Cakes (page 104).

Serves 4

3 tablespoons olive oil
1 onion, finely chopped
1½ cups Arborio rice
½ teaspoon dried basil leaves
4 cups chicken broth
2 cups chopped fresh spinach
1 cup grated Parmesan
    cheese

1. In a heavy saucepan, heat olive oil over medium heat. Add onion; cook and stir for 4 to 5 minutes, until tender. Add rice; cook and stir until rice is opaque and coated. Sprinkle in basil leaves.

2. Meanwhile, in a medium saucepan, heat chicken broth over low heat. Add ½ cup of the chicken broth to the rice mixture; cook and stir until liquid is absorbed. Continue to add broth, ½ to 1 cup at a time, stirring frequently, until rice is tender and mixture is creamy.

3. Stir in spinach, cover pan, and let stand for 3 to 4 minutes, until spinach is wilted. Remove cover, stir in cheese, and serve.

About Risotto
Risotto is an Italian dish made from short-grain rice; Arborio is the most popular type. This rice has a lot of starch, which is released during the cooking and stirring process to thicken the broth. When finished, the rice should be tender but with a tiny bite still left in the middle, and the broth thick and smooth.

2 cups Basil Spinach Risotto
(page 103)
1½ cups soft bread crumbs,
divided
3 eggs, divided
½ cup shredded Gouda
cheese
3 tablespoons olive oil
½ cup basil pesto

Basil Spinach Risotto Cakes

These little cakes are full of flavor. Serve them with a mixed fruit salad and Braised Carrots (page 228), with Layered Brownies (page 252) for dessert.

1. In medium bowl, combine risotto, ½ cup bread crumbs, 1 egg, and Gouda cheese and mix well. Form into 8 small patties. In shallow bowl, beat remaining 2 eggs until combined. Place 1 cup bread crumbs on shallow plate. Dip each cake into the eggs, then into bread crumbs.

2. Heat olive oil in heavy skillet over medium-high heat. Sauté patties, 4 at a time, until golden brown on both sides and heated through, about 3 to 5 minutes per side. Place on serving platter and drizzle with the pesto. Serve immediately.

Pesto
You can find refrigerated pesto in the supermarket's dairy aisle, or make your own by combining 2 cups fresh basil leaves, 2 cloves garlic, ½ cup grated Parmesan cheese, and ½ cup olive oil in a blender; blend until puréed. Freeze in ice cube trays to store.

Herb-Crusted Chicken Breasts

Soaking chicken in buttermilk, even if just for a few minutes, makes it tender and juicy. You can use white or whole wheat bread in this easy and delicious recipe.

Serves 6

1 cup buttermilk
1 teaspoon salt
⅛ teaspoon cayenne pepper
6 boneless, skinless chicken
 breasts
3 slices bread
½ teaspoon dried thyme
 leaves
½ teaspoon dried basil leaves
½ teaspoon dried tarragon
½ cup grated Parmesan
 cheese
⅓ cup olive oil

1. Heat oven to 375°F. In large bowl, combine buttermilk with salt and cayenne pepper and mix well. Add chicken breasts, turn to coat, and set aside.

2. Place bread on cookie sheet and bake at 375°F until crisp, about 5 to 7 minutes. Remove from oven and break into pieces. Place in blender or food processor; blend or process until crumbs are fine. Pour crumbs onto large plate and add herbs and cheese; mix well.

3. Remove chicken from buttermilk mixture and roll in crumb mixture to coat. Set on wire rack. In a heavy skillet, heat olive oil over medium heat. Add chicken, two pieces at a time, and cook for 2 to 3 minutes on each side until browned. Remove to cookie sheet. Repeat to brown remaining chicken. Bake chicken at 375°F for 12 to 14 minutes or until thoroughly cooked. Serve immediately.

1½ pounds chicken tenders
1 teaspoon cayenne pepper
1 tablespoon hot pepper
    sauce
1 egg, beaten
½ teaspoon salt
1 cup dry bread crumbs
1 cup creamy blue cheese
    salad dressing
½ cup chopped celery
¼ cup olive oil

Spicy Chicken Tenders with Creamy Dip

This recipe is reminiscent of Buffalo Chicken Wings, a spicy appetizer that combines chicken with a creamy blue cheese dip.

1. Spread chicken tenders onto waxed paper. On shallow plate, combine cayenne pepper, hot pepper sauce, egg, and salt and mix well. Place bread crumbs on another plate. Dip chicken tenders, two at a time, into egg mixture then into bread crumbs to coat. Place on wire rack while coating remaining tenders.

2. In small bowl, combine salad dressing and celery; cover and chill until ready to serve. Heat olive oil in heavy skillet over medium heat. Fry chicken tenders, 4 or 5 at a time, for 6 to 9 minutes, turning once, until brown and crisp on the outside and fully cooked. Drain on paper towels as they are finished. Serve hot with the celery dip.

Chicken Tenders

Chicken tenderloin is part of the breast; it is a small thin muscle underneath, next to the bone. Chicken tenders can be made from the tenderloin or just cut from any part of the breast. They cook very quickly and are great for children, because their shape makes them easy to pick up, dunk, and eat.

Green Chili Chicken Burritos

Serve these easy burritos with salsa and guacamole. A mixed fruit salad would be a nice addition to the meal, with a bakery apple pie for dessert.

Serves 6

2 9-ounce packages grilled
    chicken strips
1 4-ounce can chopped green
    chilies, drained
1 cup sour cream
¼ teaspoon cayenne pepper
6 flour tortillas
1½ cups shredded Pepper
    Jack cheese, divided

1. Preheat oven to 400°F. In microwave-safe bowl, combine chicken strips and green chilies. Microwave on medium power for 2 to 3 minutes, stirring once during cooking time, until ingredients are hot. Stir in sour cream and cayenne pepper.

2. Divide mixture among the tortillas. Sprinkle with 1 cup of the cheese. Roll up to enclose filling. Place in 2-quart casserole dish and top with remaining cheese. Bake for 7 to 11 minutes, until cheese melts and burritos are hot.

Spice It Up

There are lots of ingredients you can use to add spice to your food. Canned chopped green chilies, jalapeño peppers, salsas, taco sauce, and chili powder are all good choices. You can also use cayenne pepper, Tabasco sauce, fresh chilies like habañeros and Anaheim peppers, and ground dried chilies.

1 pound boneless, skinless
  turkey thighs
3 tablespoons flour
1 teaspoon garlic salt
⅛ teaspoon white pepper
2 tablespoons olive oil
2 cups frozen green beans,
  thawed and drained
1 cup frozen soybeans,
  thawed and drained
1 cup chicken stock
2 tablespoons cornstarch

Turkey and Bean Stir-Fry

*Serve this quick and easy stir-fry over hot cooked rice,
along with a green salad and brownies for dessert.*

1. Cut turkey into 1-inch pieces. On shallow plate, combine flour, garlic salt, and pepper and mix well. Add turkey pieces and toss to coat.

2. In large skillet or wok, heat olive oil over medium-high heat. Add turkey; stir-fry for 4 to 5 minutes, until browned. Add beans and soybeans; stir-fry for 3 to 6 minutes longer, until hot. In small bowl, combine chicken stock with cornstarch and mix with wire whisk. Add stock mixture to turkey mixture; cook and stir over medium-high heat, until liquid bubbles and thickens. Serve immediately.

Thawing Frozen Vegetables
You can thaw frozen vegetables by placing them in a colander and running warm water over until thawed. Or you can use the defrost setting on your microwave oven. You can also let the vegetables stand at room temperature for 1 to 2 hours, until thawed. Be sure to drain well after thawing so you don't add too much liquid to the recipe.

Lemon Chicken en Papillote

*Lemon and chicken are perfect partners. The tart lemon tenderizes
the chicken and adds great flavor. Serve these "packages"
at the table and let your guests open them.*

~

1. Preheat oven to 425°F. Cut four 12" × 18" pieces of cooking parchment paper. Fold in half, cut into a half-heart shape, then unfold. Place chicken breasts on one side of the fold and sprinkle with salt and lemon pepper. Top with lemon slices.

2. Arrange summer squash and zucchini around chicken and sprinkle pine nuts over all. Fold hearts in half and seal the edges by tightly folding them together twice. Place on cookie sheets and bake for 10 to 15 minutes, until chicken registers 170°F on a meat thermometer. Serve immediately.

Serves 4

4 boneless, skinless chicken
   breasts
½ teaspoon salt
⅛ teaspoon lemon pepper
1 lemon, cut into thin slices,
   seeds removed
1 yellow summer squash,
   thinly sliced
1 zucchini, thinly sliced
¼ cup pine nuts

Chicken Fried Rice

*If you don't have leftover cooked chicken and rice, you can get
some cooked chicken from your local deli and purchase
cooked rice from any Chinese take-out place.*

~

Remove cooked meat from chicken; discard skin and bones. Cut chicken into 1-inch pieces. Heat olive oil in wok or heavy skillet. Add chicken and rice; stir-fry for 4 to 5 minutes, until heated, stirring gently to separate rice grains. Add peas, jam, soy sauce, and water and stir-fry for 4 to 5 minutes longer, until peas are hot and flavors are blended. Serve immediately.

Serves 4

2 cooked Herbed Chicken
   Breasts (page 101)
2 tablespoons olive oil
2 cups cooked rice (from
   Grilled Ham Steak, page
   130, or Creamy Chicken
   over Rice, page 115)
1 cup frozen sugar snap peas,
   thawed and drained
⅓ cup apricot jam
2 tablespoons soy sauce
¼ cup water

1 12- or 14-inch Boboli pizza
  crust
1 cup pizza sauce
4 cooked turkey cutlets (from
  Turkey Cutlets with
  Pineapple Glaze, page
  113)
1 8-ounce can pineapple
  tidbits, drained
1½ cups shredded Swiss
  cheese

Turkey Pizza

*Pizza is fun to make at home. Use your family's favorite
foods and flavors to create your own specialty. This one
is a variation of the classic ham and pineapple pizza.*

1. Preheat oven to 400°F. Place pizza crust on a large cookie sheet and
   spread with pizza sauce. Cut turkey cutlets into thin strips and arrange
   on pizza sauce along with well-drained pineapple tidbits. Sprinkle with
   cheese.

2. Bake pizza for 15 to 20 minutes or until pizza is hot and cheese is
   melted and beginning to brown. Let stand for 5 minutes, then serve.

Pizza Crusts

*There are lots of places to buy pizza crust. The deli department at your
local grocery store has Boboli pizza crusts, focaccia, thin prebaked
pizza crusts, and refrigerated pizza dough. You can even buy pizza
dough from your local pizza parlor; roll it out, bake for a few minutes
at 400°F, then freeze for later use.*

Spicy Chicken Paillards

Paillards (pronounced pie-YARDS) are thinly pounded pieces of meat, usually chicken or veal, which are coated in flour and spices and quickly sautéed.

⌒

Serves 4

4 boneless, skinless chicken
   breasts
½ teaspoon salt
Dash white pepper
1 egg, beaten
½ teaspoon Tabasco sauce
2 tablespoons water
⅓ cup flour
1 tablespoon chili powder
⅛ teaspoon cayenne pepper
2 tablespoons cornmeal
3 tablespoons butter

1. Place chicken breasts between two sheets of plastic wrap. Pound gently, starting at the middle and working out, until the breasts are about ⅓-inch thick. Sprinkle with salt and pepper.

2. In shallow bowl, combine egg, Tabasco sauce, and water and mix well to blend. On shallow plate, combine flour, chili powder, cayenne pepper, and cornmeal. Dip paillards, one at a time, into egg mixture, then into flour mixture to coat.

3. Heat a large skillet over medium-high heat. Add butter and heat until sizzling. Add chicken pieces, two at a time, and cook for 2 minutes. Turn and cook for 2 to 4 minutes longer, until chicken is just done: 165°F on an instant-read thermometer. Remove to serving platter and cover with foil to keep warm while you cook the other two paillards. Serve immediately.

1 pound turkey tenderloin
½ cup orange juice
2 tablespoons Dijon mustard
¼ cup honey
2 garlic cloves, minced
½ teaspoon salt
⅛ teaspoon pepper

Grilled Turkey Tenderloin

The marinade for this simple recipe is a nice blend of sweet and spicy. Serve the tenderloin with a mixed fruit salad and some toasted garlic bread.

1. Prepare and preheat grill. Butterfly the tenderloin by cutting it in half lengthwise, being careful not to cut all the way through. Stop about one inch from the other side. Spread the tenderloin open, cover it with plastic wrap, and pound gently with a meat mallet or rolling pin to flatten.

2. For marinade, combine remaining ingredients in a large resealable plastic bag. Add the turkey, close the bag, and knead the bag, pressing the marinade into the turkey. Let stand at room temperature for 10 minutes.

3. Cook turkey about 6 inches above medium-hot coals for 5 minutes; brush with any leftover marinade. Turn turkey and cook for 4 to 6 minutes on second side, until thoroughly cooked. Discard any remaining marinade.

The Tenderloin

Whether you are cooking beef tenderloin, pork tenderloin, or turkey tenderloin, remember that this popular cut is low in fat and should be cooked quickly. This cut comes from a part of the animal that isn't used much, so it is tender, with little connective tissue.

Turkey Amandine

This recipe is a great way to use up leftover Thanksgiving turkey;
and if you have gravy left after the feast, use that!
Serve over hot cooked couscous, mashed potatoes, or rice.

Serves 4

2 tablespoons olive oil
1 cup sliced carrots
2 cups chopped Grilled Turkey
    Tenderloin (page 112)
1 14-ounce jar turkey gravy
½ cup whipping cream
½ cup toasted sliced almonds

In heavy saucepan, heat olive oil over medium heat. Add carrots; cook and stir until crisp-tender, about 4 to 5 minutes. Add chopped turkey and stir. Add gravy and whipping cream and bring to a simmer. Cook for 3 to 5 minutes, until turkey and carrots are hot and tender. Sprinkle with almonds and serve.

Turkey Cutlets with Pineapple Glaze

Turkey cutlets cook very quickly and are a great choice for a fast meal.
Cook them just until done so they stay tender and juicy.

Serves 4

5 tablespoons olive oil,
    divided
1 onion, minced
1 8-ounce can crushed
    pineapple, drained
⅓ cup pineapple preserves
1 tablespoon finely minced
    gingerroot
8 turkey cutlets
¼ cup flour
1 teaspoon salt
⅛ teaspoon white pepper

1. In small saucepan, heat 2 tablespoons olive oil over medium-high heat. Add onion; cook and stir for 5 to 6 minutes, until onion begins to brown around the edges. Stir in pineapple, pineapple preserves, and gingerroot; bring to a boil. Lower heat to medium-low and simmer while preparing turkey.

2. Meanwhile, combine flour, salt, and pepper on shallow plate. Dip cutlets, one at a time, into flour mixture. Heat 3 tablespoons olive oil in large skillet over medium-high heat. Sauté cutlets, three or four at a time, for 2 to 3 minutes on each side, until browned and thoroughly cooked. Place on serving platter and top with pineapple mixture; serve immediately.

Serves 4
_____

1½ cups chicken broth
2 tablespoons chili powder
½ teaspoon salt
⅛ teaspoon cayenne pepper
4 boneless, skinless chicken
   breasts
1 cup chunky salsa
2 tablespoons tomato paste
2 tomatoes, chopped

Microwave Salsa Chicken

*Serve this delicious dish over couscous, topped with some
sour cream, chopped tomatoes, and diced avocado.*

1. Place chicken broth into a microwave-safe dish. Microwave on high for 3 to 5 minutes, until boiling. Meanwhile, sprinkle chili powder, salt, and cayenne pepper on the chicken and rub into both sides. Pierce chicken on the smooth side with a fork. Carefully place, smooth side down, in hot liquid in dish.

2. Microwave the chicken on high power for 8 minutes, then remove dish from oven and carefully drain off chicken broth. Meanwhile, in small bowl, combine salsa, tomato paste, and tomatoes and mix well. Turn chicken over, rearrange chicken in dish, and pour salsa mixture over. Return to microwave and cook for 2 to 6 minutes, checking every 2 minutes, until chicken is thoroughly cooked. Let stand for 5 minutes and serve.

Tomato Paste
Tomato paste is a concentrate of fresh tomatoes, sometimes made with seasonings like basil, garlic, and oregano. You can find it in cans or in tubes. Purchase it in tubes and you can add a small amount to particular dishes without having to store leftover paste.

Creamy Chicken over Rice

Serve this easy dish with some steamed asparagus,
a spinach salad, and ice cream sundaes for dessert.

Serves 4–6

1½ cups Jasmati rice
2½ cups water
4 boneless, skinless chicken
  breasts
1 teaspoon salt
⅛ teaspoon pepper
3 tablespoons olive oil
1 onion, finely chopped
1 10-ounce container
  refrigerated four-cheese
  Alfredo sauce
1 3-ounce package cream
  cheese, softened

1. In heavy saucepan, combine rice and water; bring to a boil over high heat. Cover, reduce heat to low, and simmer for 15 to 20 minutes, until rice is tender. Meanwhile, cut chicken into 1-inch pieces and sprinkle with salt and pepper. Heat olive oil in a large saucepan over medium heat. Add onion; cook and stir until crisp-tender, about 3 to 4 minutes. Add chicken; cook and stir until chicken is thoroughly cooked, about 5 to 6 minutes.

2. Add Alfredo sauce and cream cheese to chicken mixture; cook and stir over low heat until sauce bubbles. When rice is tender, fluff with fork. Serve chicken over rice.

Aromatic Rice Varieties

There are lots of different rice varieties available in the supermarket. Jasmati rice is the American version of jasmine rice, a fragrant long-grain rice that cooks quickly and is always fluffy. You can find basmati, Texmati, Wehani, Louisiana pecan, Della, and jasmine. These rices smell like nuts or popcorn while they cook.

4 boneless, skinless chicken
   breasts
½ teaspoon salt
⅛ teaspoon pepper
2 cups sliced mushrooms
3 garlic cloves, minced
1 cup pasta sauce
1½ cups shredded Gouda
   cheese

Grilled Chicken Packets

*This one-dish meal is so simple to make. You can make the packets ahead
of time and keep them in the fridge until it's time to grill and eat.*

1. Prepare and heat grill. Tear off four 18" × 12" sheets of heavy-duty aluminum foil. Place chicken breasts in center of each sheet and sprinkle with salt and pepper. Divide mushrooms and minced garlic among foil sheets and top each with pasta sauce. Sprinkle with cheese.

2. Fold foil over ingredients and seal the edges of the foil packets, making double folds on all of the seams. Place over medium coals and cover grill. Cook for 20 to 25 minutes, rearranging once during cooking time, until chicken is thoroughly cooked. Serve immediately.

Sautéed Chicken Patties

Caramelized onions add great flavor to these tender chicken patties. Serve them over mashed potatoes to soak up all the sauce.

Serves 4–6

4 tablespoons olive oil, divided
1 onion, finely chopped
1 teaspoon sugar
1 egg
2 cups panko, divided
½ teaspoon salt
⅛ teaspoon white pepper
1½ pounds ground chicken
1½ cups chicken broth
½ teaspoon dried marjoram leaves

1. Heat 2 tablespoons olive oil in heavy pan over medium heat. Add onion; cook and stir for 3 minutes, then sprinkle with sugar; cook, stirring occasionally, until onion begins to turn light brown, 8 to 10 minutes.

2. Meanwhile, in large bowl, combine egg, ½ cup panko, salt, and pepper and mix well. Add caramelized onions; do not rinse pan. Add ground chicken to egg mixture and mix gently but thoroughly. Form into 6 patties and coat in remaining panko.

3. Add remaining olive oil to pan used to cook onions; heat over medium heat. Add chicken patties, 3 at a time, and sauté for 4 minutes. Carefully turn patties and sauté for 3 to 6 minutes longer, until thoroughly cooked. Repeat with remaining chicken patties. Remove all chicken patties to serving platter. Add chicken broth and marjoram to saucepan and bring to boil over high heat. Boil for 2 to 3 minutes to reduce liquid; pour over chicken patties and serve.

Panko

Panko, or Japanese bread crumbs, are very light crumbs that make a coating exceptionally crisp and crunchy. You can substitute regular dry bread crumbs if you can't find them, but the coating won't be as crisp. Don't substitute soft, or fresh, bread crumbs, as the texture will be entirely different.

1½ cups chicken broth
½ teaspoon salt
⅛ teaspoon pepper
½ teaspoon dried thyme
    leaves
4 boneless, skinless chicken
    breasts
1 10-ounce package frozen
    broccoli, thawed
1 10-ounce container
    refrigerated four-cheese
    Alfredo sauce
1 cup crushed round buttery
    crackers

Microwave Chicken Divan

*This method of cooking chicken breasts in the microwave yields tender,
moist chicken. Serve with a spinach salad and some fresh fruit.*

1. Place chicken broth into a microwave-safe dish. Microwave on high for 3 to 5 minutes, until boiling. Meanwhile, sprinkle salt, pepper, and thyme on the chicken and rub into both sides. Pierce chicken on the smooth side with a fork. Carefully place, smooth side down, in hot liquid in dish.

2. Microwave the chicken on high power for 8 minutes, then remove dish from oven and carefully drain off chicken broth. Meanwhile, drain thawed broccoli and combine in medium bowl with Alfredo sauce. Rearrange chicken in dish, turn over, and pour broccoli mixture over; sprinkle with cracker crumbs. Return to microwave and cook for 3 to 6 minutes, checking every 2 minutes, until chicken is thoroughly cooked. Let stand for 5 minutes and serve.

Quick Chicken Cordon Bleu

Pancetta is Italian bacon that is cured with spices, but not smoked.
The deli department in your supermarket sells it thinly sliced.

Serves 4

1 cup grated Parmesan
   cheese, divided
4 boneless, skinless chicken
   breasts
8 slices pancetta
1 14-ounce jar Alfredo sauce
4 slices baby Swiss cheese

1. Preheat oven to 400°F. Place ½ cup Parmesan cheese on a plate and dip chicken breasts into cheese to coat. Wrap pancetta around chicken breasts and place in a 2-quart casserole dish. Bake for 10 minutes. In medium bowl, combine Alfredo sauce with remaining ½ cup Parmesan cheese.

2. Remove casserole from oven and pour Alfredo sauce mixture over chicken. Return to oven and bake for 10 minutes longer. Top each chicken breast with a slice of cheese and return to the oven. Bake for 5 minutes longer or until chicken is thoroughly cooked and cheese is melted.

Deconstructing Recipes
One way to make recipes simpler to make is to deconstruct them. Chicken cordon bleu is typically made by stuffing ham and cheese into chicken breasts and then baking. Wrapping the chicken in pancetta and topping with cheese results in the same taste but is much quicker to make.

4 chicken breasts
½ teaspoon salt
⅛ teaspoon white pepper
¼ cup Dijon mustard, divided
2 tablespoons honey
2 tablespoons mayonnaise
½ teaspoon dried thyme
    leaves
4 slices Muenster cheese

Mustard-Glazed Chicken Breasts

When broiling, be sure that you place the food the specified distance from the heat source. This recipe is excellent served with Braised Carrots (page 228) and a lettuce salad.

⟜⟶

1. Preheat broiler. Sprinkle chicken with salt and pepper and brush with 2 tablespoons Dijon mustard. Place on broiler pan, skin-side down, and broil 6 inches from heat source for 4 minutes.

2. Meanwhile, combine honey, mayonnaise, thyme leaves, and remaining 2 tablespoons Dijon mustard in small bowl. Turn chicken skin-side up and spoon on half of honey mixture. Return to oven and broil 6 inches from heat source for 4 minutes. Top with remaining honey mixture and place cheese slices on chicken. Return to oven and broil for 2 to 4 minutes, until chicken is thoroughly cooked and cheese is melted and begins to brown. Serve immediately.

Chicken Doneness
Chicken has to be cooked well done. Using a meat thermometer inserted in the thigh, not touching bone, whole chickens should be cooked to 180°F, chicken breasts to 165°F, ground chicken to 165°F, and chicken thighs to 170°F. Another test is to slice into the chicken; the juice should run clear with no tinge of pink.

Corn-Bread-Crusted Chicken Breasts

Serve this wonderful entrée with Herbed Couscous (page 222) and Honey-Orange Carrots (page 217). For dessert, serve Lemon Angel Cake (page 290).

Serves 6

2 3-inch squares Corn Bread
  (page 39)
½ teaspoon dried oregano
2 eggs, beaten
½ teaspoon salt
⅛ teaspoon cayenne pepper
6 boneless, skinless chicken
  breasts
2 tablespoons butter
2 tablespoons olive oil
1½ cups chunky salsa

1. Crumble Corn Bread finely and place in shallow bowl along with oregano; mix well. In another shallow bowl, beat eggs with salt and cayenne pepper. Dip chicken breasts into egg mixture, then place in Corn Bread crumbs to coat, pressing crumbs firmly onto chicken.

2. In heavy saucepan, heat butter and olive oil over medium heat until foamy. Add chicken and cook for 4 minutes, then carefully turn and cook for 4 to 8 minutes longer, until chicken is thoroughly cooked. Top chicken with salsa and serve.

Pesto Turkey Cutlets

The sauce for these cutlets is so delicious you must serve this over hot cooked rice or couscous, with steamed broccoli or green beans on the side.

Serves 6

12 turkey cutlets
⅓ cup flour
1 teaspoon salt
1 teaspoon dried basil leaves
⅛ teaspoon white pepper
¾ cup grated Parmesan
  cheese, divided
2 eggs, beaten
3 tablespoons olive oil
1 16-ounce jar four-cheese
  Alfredo sauce
1 10-ounce container
  refrigerated pesto

1. In small bowl, combine flour, salt, basil, pepper, and ¼ cup Parmesan cheese and mix well. Break eggs into shallow bowl and beat well. Dip cutlets into egg, then into flour mixture to coat. Place on wire rack.

2. Heat olive oil in heavy skillet over medium heat. Sauté cutlets, 4 at a time, for 3 minutes, then turn and cook for 2 to 3 minutes on other side. As cutlets are cooked, remove to a platter. When all cutlets are cooked, add Alfredo sauce to skillet; bring to a simmer.

3. Add pesto to skillet and stir to mix. Return cutlets to the pan with the sauce and heat for 1 to 2 minutes. Sprinkle with remaining ½ cup Parmesan cheese and serve immediately.

Serves 4

½ pound linguine pasta
2 cooked Herbed Chicken
    Breasts (page 101)
1½ cups heavy cream
1 10-ounce container
    refrigerated pesto
1 cup grated Parmesan
    cheese

Chicken Pesto Linguine

*This simple recipe is divine. Serve it with Lemon Pesto Pilaf (page 215)
and Roasted Sugar Snap Peas (page 227). For dessert,
Flaky Peach Tarts (page 289) are sublime.*

1. Bring a large pot of water to a boil and add linguine; cook according to package directions. Meanwhile, remove meat from chicken and coarsely chop. Bring cream to a boil in a heavy saucepan over high heat and add chicken. Reduce heat to medium; cook and stir until chicken is hot, about 3 to 4 minutes. Add pesto and remove from heat.

2. Drain linguine when cooked al dente and add to chicken mixture. Return to medium heat and toss using tongs until linguine is coated. Sprinkle with Parmesan cheese and serve immediately.

Boiling Cream
Whenever you are instructed to bring milk or cream to a boil, watch it carefully and don't leave the stove. Because of the proteins and fat in dairy products, they boil over very easily. When the milk or cream just begins to bubble, reduce the heat and stir or, if necessary, remove it from the heat until the foam subsides.

Chapter 7

Pork and Ham

Serves 4

4 boneless pork loin chops

4 garlic cloves, finely chopped

2 teaspoons cumin seed

½ teaspoon dried oregano
  leaves

½ teaspoon salt

⅛ teaspoon cayenne pepper

2 tablespoons olive oil

¼ cup orange juice

2 tablespoons lime juice

Cuban Pork Chops

*Evoke a taste of the tropics with this simple, well-flavored recipe. Serve it with
a rice pilaf, spinach salad and some cantaloupe slices drizzled with honey.*

1. Trim excess fat from pork chops. In small bowl, combine garlic, cumin, oregano, salt, and cayenne pepper and mix well. Sprinkle this mixture on both sides of chops and rub into meat. Let stand at room temperature for 10 minutes.

2. Heat olive oil in heavy saucepan over medium heat. Add pork chops and cook for 5 minutes. Carefully turn and cook for 5 minutes on second side. Add orange juice and lime juice and bring to a simmer.

3. Cover pan and simmer chops for 5 to 10 minutes or until pork chops are tender and just slightly pink in the center, and sauce is reduced. Serve immediately.

Ham Asparagus Wraps

The asparagus has to be cooked in this recipe because it doesn't bake long enough to soften. Use any flavor of cream cheese and bottled Alfredo sauce you'd like.

⸺

Serves 4

4 ¼-inch-thick slices deli ham
½ cup soft cream cheese with garlic
12 spears Grilled Asparagus (page 223)
1 10-ounce jar garlic Alfredo sauce
½ cup grated Parmesan cheese

Preheat oven to 375°F. Place ham on work surface and spread each piece with some of the cream cheese. Top each with three spears of asparagus and roll up. Place in 12" × 8" glass baking dish and pour Alfredo sauce over all. Sprinkle with Parmesan cheese. Bake at 375°F for 15 to 20 minutes, until ham rolls are hot and sauce is bubbling. Serve immediately.

Ham Slices

For recipes that require you to enclose other ingredients in ham slices, do not use the thin slices of boiled ham meant for making sandwiches. You can use slices from spiral sliced hams or go to the deli and ask for ham to be sliced from the whole ham.

Serves 4

½ cup golden raisins
1¼ cups orange juice, divided
¼ cup olive oil, divided
1 red onion, chopped
1 teaspoon sugar
4 center cut boneless pork
    chops
1 teaspoon salt
⅛ teaspoon pepper
1 teaspoon dried thyme

Pork Chops with Onion Conserve

You'll have three pans cooking on the stove while making this recipe, but it still takes only 30 minutes!

1. In small heavy saucepan, combine raisins and 1 cup orange juice; bring to a simmer over medium heat. Meanwhile, in another heavy saucepan, heat 2 tablespoons olive oil over medium heat. Add red onion; cook over medium heat for 10 minutes, stirring frequently, until onion begins to turn brown. Add sugar to onion; cook for 2 minutes. Add raisin mixture; bring to a boil over high heat, then reduce heat to low and simmer while cooking pork chops.

2. Meanwhile, sprinkle pork chops with salt, pepper, and thyme. Heat remaining 2 tablespoons olive oil in large skillet and add pork chops. Cook over medium heat, turning once, until pork is done, about 10 minutes. Remove pork from pan; cover to keep warm.

3. Add ¼ cup orange juice to drippings remaining in pan; turn heat to high and bring to a boil; reduce heat and simmer for 2 to 3 minutes, until juice is reduced. Return pork chops to pan along with onion/raisin mixture. Cover and cook for 2 minutes, then serve.

About Raisins

Raisins are dried grapes, but the way they are dried determines the color. Both golden and dark raisins are made from Thompson variety grapes, but the dark raisins are dried in the sun, while golden raisins are oven-dried. The sunlight causes the raisins to darken. Golden raisins may also be treated with sulfur dioxide; read labels carefully!

Ham and Asparagus Casserole

Ham and asparagus are natural partners; the sweet saltiness of the ham compliments the slight bitterness of the asparagus.

Serves 4

1 pound asparagus
1½ cups cubed fully cooked ham
1 10-ounce container refrigerated Alfredo sauce
1 cup shredded Gruyère cheese
½ teaspoon dried thyme leaves
1 cup bread crumbs
2 tablespoons olive oil

1. Snap tough ends off asparagus and discard. Place in saucepan and cover with water. Bring to a boil; boil for 3 to 4 minutes, until asparagus is just tender. Drain thoroughly. Place in 2-quart baking dish.

2. In medium saucepan, place ham cubes and Alfredo sauce; cook and stir over medium heat until sauce bubbles, about 4 to 6 minutes. Remove from heat and stir in cheese and thyme until cheese melts and mixture is smooth. Pour over asparagus in casserole.

3. Preheat broiler. In small bowl, combine bread crumbs and olive oil and toss to mix. Sprinkle over sauce mixture in casserole. Broil casserole 6 inches from heat for 4 to 6 minutes, until sauce is bubbly and bread crumbs are toasted. Serve immediately.

Menu Suggestions
Serve this rich and hearty casserole with Apple and Greens Salad (page 197) and Toasted Garlic Bread (page 53), with Chocolate Peanut Butter Pie (page 286) for dessert. Or choose Simple Spinach Salad (page 207) and Parmesan Crescents (page 43), with Raspberry Continental (page 276) for dessert.

Stovetop Lasagna

Serves 4–6

1 pound bulk sweet Italian sausage

1 onion, chopped

1 24-ounce package frozen ravioli

1 28-ounce jar pasta sauce

1 teaspoon dried Italian seasoning

1½ cups shredded Italian blend cheese

Serve this super-easy version of lasagna with a crisp green salad and some Cheese Breadsticks (page 50), with Fudgesicle Pie (page 292) for dessert.

1. Bring large pot of water to a boil. Meanwhile, in heavy skillet over medium heat, cook sausage and onion, stirring to break up sausage, until meat is browned. Drain sausage thoroughly, and wipe out skillet.

2. Add ravioli to boiling water; cook until almost tender, about 1 to 2 minutes. Drain well. In cleaned skillet, spread about 1 cup pasta sauce, then top with layers of sausage mixture, ravioli, and more pasta sauce. Sprinkle each layer with a bit of the dried Italian seasoning. Sprinkle with cheese. Cover and cook over medium heat, shaking pan occasionally, until sauce bubbles, cheese melts, and mixture is hot, about 5 to 8 minutes. Serve immediately.

Ham and Sweet Potatoes

Serves 6

1 tablespoon olive oil

1 onion, finely chopped

1½ pound cooked ham steak

½ cup orange marmalade

2 tablespoons reserved sweet potato liquid

¼ teaspoon nutmeg

1 15-ounce can sweet potatoes, drained, reserving 2 tablespoons liquid

1 15-ounce can mandarin oranges, drained

Sweet potatoes and oranges turn a ham steak into a real feast. This recipe is a good choice for smaller families for Thanksgiving or other holiday dinners.

1. In large skillet, heat olive oil over medium heat. Add onion; cook and stir until crisp-tender, about 3 to 4 minutes. Add steak to skillet along with marmalade, 2 tablespoons sweet potato liquid, and nutmeg. Cover and simmer for 10 minutes over medium-low heat.

2. Turn ham steak, then add sweet potatoes to skillet; cover and simmer for 5 minutes. Stir in mandarin oranges; cover and cook for 2 to 4 minutes longer, until hot. Serve immediately.

Pork and Apricot Skewers

This recipe is elegant enough for company. Serve with hot cooked rice and Toasted Garlic Bread (page 53), with a spinach salad on the side.

Serves 6

1½ pounds boneless pork
   tenderloin
1 cup apricot preserves
½ cup apricot nectar
12 dried whole apricots
2 onions
½ teaspoon dried thyme
   leaves

1. Prepare and heat grill. Cut pork into 1-inch cubes and place in medium bowl. Top with apricot preserves; let stand while preparing remaining ingredients. In small saucepan, combine apricot nectar and dried apricots; bring to a boil over high heat. Reduce heat and simmer for 3 minutes; remove apricots and set on wire rack to cool; pour hot nectar over pork cubes. Cut onions into 6 wedges each.

2. Drain pork, reserving marinade, and thread pork cubes, onion wedges, and apricots onto 6 metal skewers. Combine the reserved marinade with the thyme leaves in a small pan and bring to a boil over medium-high heat; reduce heat to low and simmer while skewers cook.

3. Grill skewers, covered, over medium coals for 5 minutes. Turn and brush with some of the simmering marinade. Cover and grill for 5 to 8 minutes longer, until pork is slightly pink in center and onions are crisp-tender; keep marinade simmering. Serve with the marinade on the side.

Kabobs

When you're making skewers or kabobs, there are different materials to choose from. Bamboo skewers must be soaked in water for at least 30 minutes before grilling so they won't burn while the food is cooking. Metal skewers are more durable, but use caution because they get very hot when on the grill.

Serves 4

1 cup Texmati rice

2 cups water

¾ cup orange marmalade

2 tablespoons frozen orange
    juice concentrate

2 tablespoons balsamic
    vinegar

2 tablespoons water

½ teaspoon dried marjoram
    leaves

½ teaspoon salt

⅛ teaspoon white pepper

1 1½-pound ham steak

Grilled Ham Steak

*Ham steak is a fully cooked slice of ham that may or may not contain a bone.
All you have to do is season it if you'd like and heat it.*

1. Prepare and heat grill. In large saucepan, combine rice and 2 cups water; bring to a boil over high heat. Reduce heat, cover, and simmer for 15 to 20 minutes. Meanwhile, in medium saucepan, combine all remaining ingredients except ham and bring to a boil. Reduce heat to low and simmer for about 4 minutes.

2. Place ham steak on grill and brush with some of the glaze. Cover and grill for 4 minutes; turn ham steak and brush with more of the glaze. Cover and grill for 3 to 5 minutes, until ham steak is thoroughly heated. Keep cooking marinade while ham is grilling. Serve with remaining marinade over rice.

Ham and Cheese Penne

This simple one-dish dinner recipe can be made with any frozen vegetable combo. You can even eliminate the pasta if you use a vegetable combo that includes pasta!

Serves 4

2 cups penne pasta
2 tablespoons olive oil
1½ cups frozen broccoli and
    cauliflower mixture
2 tablespoons water
2 cups cubed ham
1 10-ounce container
    refrigerated four-cheese
    Alfredo sauce
½ cup grated Parmesan
    cheese

1. Bring a large pot of water to boil; cook penne according to package directions. Meanwhile, heat olive oil in large saucepan over medium heat. Add frozen vegetables; sprinkle with 2 tablespoons water. Cover and cook over medium heat for 4 to 5 minutes until vegetables are almost hot, stirring once during cooking time. Add ham and Alfredo sauce; bring to a simmer.

2. Drain pasta when cooked and add to saucepan with ham mixture. Stir gently, then simmer for 2 to 3 minutes longer until vegetables and ham are hot. Sprinkle with Parmesan cheese and serve.

Al Dente

When cooking pasta, al dente *is a term used to indicate doneness. It means "to the tooth." Always test pasta by biting into it. When it's tender but still has a firmness to the center, it's done. Look at the pasta: you'll be able to see a small opaque line in the center after you bite it.*

2 pounds pork tenderloins
1 teaspoon salt
⅛ teaspoon pepper
⅓ cup frozen orange juice
concentrate, thawed
¼ cup honey
¼ cup Dijon mustard
1 tablespoon lemon juice
½ teaspoon dried oregano
leaves

Grilled Orange Pork Tenderloin

You can serve this elegant dish to company, along with Roasted Corn Salad (page 196), Herbed Couscous (page 222), Melty Cheese Bread (page 54), and Chocolate Raspberry Pie (page 275).

1. Prepare and heat grill. Cut pork tenderloins in half crosswise. Then butterfly the pork; cut the tenderloins horizontally in half, being careful not to cut through to the other side. Spread tenderloins open and place in large casserole dish. Sprinkle both sides with salt and pepper. In medium bowl, combine remaining ingredients and mix well. Spread on all sides of tenderloins and let stand for 10 minutes.

2. Grill tenderloins 6 inches from medium coals, covered, turning once, for 14 to 17 minutes, until a meat thermometer registers 160°F. Brush with any remaining marinade after turning. Discard remaining marinade. Slice tenderloins across the grain to serve.

Butterflying Meats

Butterflying meat cuts the cooking time almost in half. You can butterfly just about any cut of meat. Use a sharp knife and cut slowly, being sure not to cut all the way through to the other side. Spread the cut meat out, and if desired, use a meat mallet to gently pound it to flatten to an even thickness.

Sausage Stir-Fry

Serve this fresh-tasting stir-fry over hot cooked rice with chopped cashews on the side, along with a gelatin fruit salad.

~

Serves 4

1 pound sweet Italian
    sausages
¼ cup water
2 tablespoons olive oil
1 onion, chopped
2 yellow summer squash,
    sliced
1 cup frozen broccoli florets,
    thawed
¾ cup sweet-and-sour sauce

1. In large skillet, cook Italian sausage and water over medium heat for 6 to 8 minutes, turning frequently during cooking time, until water evaporates and sausages begin to brown. Remove sausages to plate and cut into 1-inch pieces.

2. Drain fat from skillet but do not rinse. Return to medium-high heat, add olive oil, then add onion. Stir-fry until onion is crisp-tender, 3 to 4 minutes. Add squash and broccoli; stir-fry for 4 to 5 minutes longer, until broccoli is hot and squash is tender. Return sausage pieces to skillet along with sweet-and-sour sauce. Stir-fry for 4 to 6 minutes, until sausage pieces are thoroughly cooked and sauce bubbles. Serve immediately.

Cooking Rice
Rice expands to three times its bulk when cooked. Each serving is about ½ cup, so if you want to serve six people, cook 1 cup of rice to make 3 cups. Combine 1 cup long-grain rice with 2 cups water and a pinch of salt in a saucepan. Cover, bring to a boil, reduce heat to low, and simmer for 15 to 20 minutes, until tender.

Serves 4

3 tablespoons olive oil

1 red onion, chopped

4 smoked pork chops

3 cups shredded red cabbage

1 Granny Smith apple, peeled
and chopped

1 cup apple juice

½ teaspoon dried thyme
leaves

½ teaspoon salt

⅛ teaspoon pepper

Skillet Pork Chops with Cabbage

Serve this hearty German feast with Smashed Potatoes (page 221) and a molded gelatin salad. For dessert, make Chocolate Peanut Butter Pie (page 286).

1. Heat olive oil in large skillet over medium heat. Add red onion; cook and stir for 3 to 4 minutes, until crisp-tender. Add pork chops; brown on both sides for about 3 minutes. Add cabbage and apple to the skillet; cook and stir for 3 minutes.

2. Pour apple juice over all and sprinkle with thyme leaves, salt, and pepper. Bring to a boil, then reduce heat, cover, and simmer for 10 to 15 minutes, until cabbage is crisp-tender and pork chops are hot and tender. Serve immediately.

Serves 4–6

1 16-ounce package seasoned
pulled pork in BBQ sauce

2 tablespoons oil

2 cups frozen onion and bell
pepper mixture

½ cup taco sauce

1 tablespoon chili powder

1 16-ounce can seasoned
refried beans

8 crisp taco shells

Pork and Bean Tacos

Serve these easy tacos with lots of toppings: sour cream, guacamole, shredded cheese, chopped pickled jalapeño peppers, and chopped tomatoes

1. Preheat oven to 350°F. Heat pulled pork in BBQ sauce as directed on package. Meanwhile, heat oil in heavy saucepan over medium-high heat. Add frozen vegetables, pulled pork in BBQ sauce, taco sauce, chili powder, and refried beans. Bring to a simmer and cook for 6 to 8 minutes, until vegetables and meat are hot.

2. Meanwhile, place taco shells on cookie sheet and heat at 350°F for 4 to 6 minutes. Fill taco shells with pork mixture and serve.

Italian Crispy Pork Chops

Serve these delicious little pork chops with Lemon Pesto Pilaf (page 215), Toasted Garlic Bread (page 53), Greens with Basil Dressing (page 206), and Chocolate Velvet (page 293) for dessert.

Serves 6–8

8 thin-cut boneless pork
  chops
2 eggs, beaten
2 tablespoons water
½ cup grated Parmesan
  cheese
1 cup panko
1 teaspoon dried Italian
  seasoning
½ teaspoon dried basil leaves
2 tablespoons butter
3 tablespoons olive oil

1. Place pork chops between two pieces of plastic wrap and pound with a rolling pin or meat mallet until about ⅓ inch thick. In shallow bowl, combine eggs and water and beat until blended. On shallow plate, combine cheese, panko, Italian seasoning, and basil and mix well. Dip pork chops into egg mixture, then into cheese mixture, pressing the cheese mixture firmly onto the chops. Place on wire rack when coated. Let stand for 10 minutes.

2. Heat butter and olive oil in a large skillet over medium-high heat. Fry the pork chops, 2 to 4 minutes on each side, until brown and crisp and just slightly pink inside. Serve immediately.

Panko Bread Crumb Substitutions
Panko are Japanese bread crumbs that are very light, dry, and rough. If you can't find them, make your own soft bread crumbs from a fresh loaf of bread, spread crumbs on a baking sheet, and bake them in a 350°F oven for 5 to 8 minutes, until dry and crisp.

Serves 4

¾ pound bulk pork sausage
1 cup shredded carrots
1½ cups shredded Colby
   cheese
6 (12" × 18") sheets frozen filo
   dough, thawed
½ cup butter, melted

Sausage Filo Rolls

Serve these crisp little bundles for a brunch along with Scrambled Eggs with Pesto (page 58), Caramel Rolls (page 49), and fresh orange juice and hot coffee.

1. Preheat oven to 400°F. In heavy skillet over medium heat, cook sausage until partially done, stirring to break up sausage, about 3 to 4 minutes. Stir in carrots; continue cooking, stirring frequently, until sausage is done and carrots are crisp-tender, 2 to 3 minutes longer. Drain well if necessary. Remove from heat, sprinkle cheese over sausage mixture, and let stand while preparing filo dough.

2. Place 1 sheet filo dough on work surface and brush with some butter. Continue layering filo sheets with butter. Cut filo stack into four 6" × 9" rectangles. Stir sausage mixture and divide among rectangles, placing at one 9" edge. Roll up filo, enclosing filling and folding in ends. Brush with more butter.

3. Place on parchment paper–lined baking sheets. Bake at 400°F for 20 to 23 minutes, until golden brown.

Filo Dough

You can find filo, or phyllo, dough in the freezer section of your supermarket near the frozen pie shells. Follow the thawing instructions carefully, and cover the dough that you aren't using with a damp paper towel so it doesn't dry out.

Sausage Quesadillas

*These crisp little sandwiches are delicious served
with some fresh tomato salsa for dipping.*

~~~

Serves 4

1 pound bulk pork sausage
1 onion, chopped
1 red bell pepper, sliced
½ teaspoon paprika
½ teaspoon ground cumin
2 teaspoons chili powder
8 10-inch flour tortillas
2 cups shredded Co-Jack
   cheese
2 tablespoons olive oil

1. Preheat oven to 375°F. In heavy skillet, cook pork sausage with onion over medium heat, stirring to break up sausage, about 4 to 5 minutes. When browned, drain off most of the fat. Add red bell pepper; cook and stir for 2 to 3 minutes. Sprinkle with seasonings and remove from heat.

2. Lay four tortillas on work surface. Sprinkle each with ¼ cup cheese and top with one-fourth of the sausage mixture. Sprinkle with remaining cheese and top with remaining tortillas. Place on two cookie sheets and brush quesadillas with olive oil. Bake for 7 to 10 minutes, or until cheese is melted and tortillas are lightly browned. Cut into wedges and serve.

Tortillas

Tortillas are available in two types, corn and flour. Flour tortillas are usually larger, used for quesadillas and burritos. They can be flavored with spinach, red pepper, garlic, and tomato. Flavored corn tortillas are also available, as well as the traditional white, yellow, and blue corn varieties.

Serves 4–6

1 pound Polish sausage
1 green bell pepper, chopped
1 18-ounce jar pasta sauce
1 16-ounce package
*   refrigerated mashed*
*   potatoes*
½ cup grated Parmesan
*   cheese*

Knock Bockle

This casserole is so hearty and comforting. Serve it with some steamed green beans and a simple green salad, with a chocolate cake for dessert.

1. Preheat oven to 425°F. Cut sausages into 1-inch slices; place in heavy skillet over medium heat and cook for 6 to 9 minutes, turning several times, until sausage is browned. Add green bell pepper; cook and stir for 2 minutes longer. Drain excess fat if necessary. Add pasta sauce and bring to a simmer.

2. Meanwhile, in medium bowl, combine potatoes and Parmesan cheese and mix well. Place sausage mixture into a 2-quart casserole dish and top with spoonfuls of the potato mixture. Bake for 15 to 20 minutes or until potatoes begin to turn light golden brown and sauce bubbles.

Serves 6

3 tablespoons olive oil
6 ½-inch boneless pork chops
1 teaspoon salt
⅛ teaspoon cayenne pepper
1 tablespoon chili powder
1 chipotle chile in adobo
*   sauce, minced*
2 tablespoons adobo sauce
½ cup salsa
1 8-ounce can tomato sauce

Southwest Pork Chops

These spicy pork chops are coated with layers of Tex-Mex flavor. Serve them with hot mashed potatoes, a cooling fruit salad, and a lemon meringue pie for dessert.

1. Place olive oil in heavy skillet and heat over medium heat. Meanwhile, sprinkle pork chops with salt, cayenne pepper, and chili powder and rub into meat. Add pork chops to skillet and cook for 4 minutes.

2. Meanwhile, combine chipotle chili, adobo sauce, salsa, and tomato sauce in a small bowl. Turn pork chops and cook for 2 minutes. Then add tomato sauce mixture to skillet, bring to a simmer, and simmer for 4 to 6 minutes, until chops are cooked and tender.

Pressure-Cooker Sausage Risotto

Your pressure cooker makes the most delicious risotto in less than half the time of traditional stovetop methods.

Serves 4

3 tablespoons olive oil, divided
1 pound bulk sweet Italian sausage
1 onion, finely chopped
2 cups Arborio rice
4 cups chicken stock, warmed
½ teaspoon dried Italian seasoning
½ cup grated Parmesan cheese

1. Turn the pressure cooker to high and add 2 tablespoons of the oil. Cook the sausage until almost done, stirring to break up meat, then add the onion and cook until the sausage is done and the onion is crisp-tender. Add remaining olive oil and the rice; cook and stir for 2 to 4 minutes, until the rice is coated and opaque.

2. Add ½ cup of the stock and cook, stirring constantly, for 2 to 4 minutes, until the liquid is absorbed by the rice. Add the remaining stock and Italian seasoning and lock the lid into place. Pressure cook on medium for 8 minutes. Let the pressure release, open the lid, and check the rice. If the rice isn't cooked al dente, lock the lid again and cook for 2 to 3 minutes longer. Release the pressure, open the lid, and stir in the Parmesan cheese until melted. Serve immediately.

Pressure Cookers

There are two kinds of pressure cookers: those that cook on the stove and those that are self-contained. You can brown food in either type of cooker before adding all the ingredients, sealing the cooker, and bringing it up to pressure. Regulate the heat on the stovetop models by adjusting the stove burners.

Ham Curry

Serve this delicious, rich curry over hot cooked rice and pair it with Toasted Garlic Bread (page 53) and a crisp mixed-lettuce salad with a honey mustard salad dressing.

1. In large skillet, heat olive oil over medium heat. Add onion; cook and stir for 4 to 5 minutes, until onion is tender. Sprinkle curry powder over onions; cook and stir for 1 to 2 minutes, until fragrant. Stir in Alfredo sauce and bring to a simmer.

2. Add ham and frozen baby peas and stir gently. Continue to cook over medium heat, stirring frequently, until sauce bubbles and ham and peas are hot. Serve immediately.

Curry Powder
Curry powder combinations vary according to the cook, and in India, the spices included vary according to region. Some recipes call for simmering the curry in butter or oil before adding other ingredients. This technique really brings out the flavors and aromas of the complex mixture.

Ham and Cheese Fondue

You'll find packaged fondue in the deli section of your supermarket. Serve this excellent dish with sliced apples, breadsticks, vegetables, and crackers.

In a heavy saucepan, melt butter over medium heat. Add onion; cook and stir until tender, about 5 to 6 minutes. Add ham and stir. Add fondue and stir to break up. Cook and stir over medium-low heat for 15 minutes or until fondue is melted and smooth, stirring almost constantly. Pour into a fondue pot and place over burner. Serve with long forks to spear the bread cubes and dip them into the fondue.

Grilled Polish Sausages

Make extra Polish Sausages and save them for Easy Jambalaya (page 85). This easy recipe is perfect for a summer cookout; serve potato salad and melon wedges on the side.

Serves 6

6 Polish sausages
1 cup beer
3 cups coleslaw mix
¾ cup coleslaw dressing
6 whole wheat hot dog buns, split

1. Prepare and preheat grill. Prick sausages with fork and place in sauce-pan with beer. Bring to a boil over high heat, then reduce heat to low and simmer for 5 minutes, turning frequently. Drain sausages and place on grill over medium coals; grill until hot and crisp, turning occasionally, about 5 to 7 minutes.

2. Meanwhile, combine coleslaw mix and dressing in medium bowl and toss. Toast hot dog buns, cut-side down, on grill. Make sandwiches using sausages, coleslaw mix, and buns.

Sausages

Just about any sausage can be substituted for another. Just be sure to read the package to see if the sausages you choose are fully cooked or raw. The fully cooked sausages need only to be reheated, but the raw ones should be cooked until a meat thermometer registers 170°F.

Chapter 8

Vegetarian and Pasta Dishes

2 15-ounce cans spicy chili
    beans, undrained
1 14-ounce can diced
    tomatoes with green
    chilies, undrained
1 12-ounce jar tomato salsa
1 tablespoon chili powder
1 green bell pepper, chopped
1 cup water

Spicy Vegetarian Chili

You can use this chili in so many ways: from the topping for Taco Salad (page 64), to filled stuffed baked potatoes, and as the base for enchiladas and burritos.

In a heavy saucepan, combine all ingredients. Bring to a boil, then reduce heat and simmer for 15 to 20 minutes, stirring occasionally, until peppers are crisp-tender and mixture is heated and blended. Serve immediately, topped with sour cream, grated cheese, and chopped green onions, if desired.

Canned Tomatoes
There are several different types of flavored tomatoes in the market. Fire-roasted tomatoes are broiled or roasted until the skins blacken, then they are chopped or diced. Tomatoes can be packed with garlic, with green chilies; there are Mexican-seasoned tomatoes and Italian-seasoned tomatoes. Stock up on several kinds to add kick to your recipes.

Vegetarian Curry Stir-Fry

You can increase the amount of curry powder you use depending on your preferences. Serve this delicious curry over some hot cooked basmati rice.

Serves 4

2 tablespoons olive oil
1 onion, sliced
2 green bell peppers, sliced
2 teaspoons curry powder
3 tablespoons flour
½ teaspoon salt
¼ teaspoon red pepper flakes
1 pound firm tofu, cubed
1 14-ounce can coconut milk

⌒

1. In heavy saucepan over medium-high heat, add olive oil. Cook onion and green bell peppers for 4 to 5 minutes, stirring frequently, until crisp-tender.

2. In small bowl, combine curry powder, flour, salt, and red pepper flakes. Sprinkle over onion mixture. Cook and stir for 3 to 4 minutes, until bubbly. Add tofu and coconut milk to the saucepan. Cook, stirring occasionally, over medium heat for 5 to 8 minutes, until sauce is thickened and tofu is hot. Serve immediately.

About Tofu
There are two different types of tofu available in the supermarket: regular and silken. Regular tofu is firmer than silken tofu. Firm or extra-firm regular tofu can be sliced or cut into cubes; it's perfect for stir-fries and grilling. Silken tofu is usually used for dressings or puddings.

1 tablespoon olive oil

3 tablespoons butter

8 eggs

⅓ cup heavy cream

2 teaspoons chopped freeze-
dried chives

Salt and pepper to taste

1¼ cups shredded Fontina
cheese

¼ cup grated Parmesan
cheese

Cheese Omelet

*Add any of your favorite vegetables to this easy omelet recipe. Serve
it with a fresh fruit salad and some croissants from the bakery.*

1. Place olive oil and butter in a large nonstick skillet and heat over medium heat. Meanwhile, beat eggs, cream, chives, salt, and pepper in large bowl until foamy. Add eggs to skillet and cook over medium heat for 5 to 8 minutes, lifting edges of the omelet as it cooks to allow uncooked egg mixture to flow underneath.

2. When egg is cooked but still glossy, sprinkle cheeses on top. Cover and let stand for 2 to 3 minutes off the heat. Uncover pan and fold omelet out onto heated serving plate. Serve immediately.

Cream or Water?

Believe it or not, a battle is raging over whether to add cream, milk, or water to eggs when making an omelet or scrambled eggs. Cream makes the eggs soft and fluffy; water makes the eggs fluffy but doesn't add any fat, so the eggs are not as creamy. All three additions work well; it's your choice.

Vegetable Pancakes

You can make this recipe ahead of time and refrigerate. When ready to serve, microwave the crepes at 70 percent power for 4–7 minutes until hot.

1. Prepare crepes or defrost if frozen. In medium saucepan, heat olive oil over medium heat. Add potatoes and peas; cook and stir until vegetables are hot and potatoes begin to brown. Remove from heat and sprinkle with tarragon, salt, and pepper.

2. Add half of the sour cream and mix well. Fill crepes with this mixture; roll to enclose filling. Place in microwave-safe baking dish. Spread crepes with remaining sour cream and sprinkle with cheese.

3. Microwave, covered, for 3 to 6 minutes on 70 percent power, rotating once during cooking time, until cheese is melted and crepes are hot. Serve immediately.

Crepes

You can find prepared crepes in the supermarket's produce section. If not, they're easy to make. Combine 1 cup milk, 2 eggs, ½ cup flour, 3 tablespoons melted butter, and ½ teaspoon salt in a blender. Blend until smooth. Heat 8" pan over medium heat. Cook ¼ cup batter, rotating the pan so batter covers the bottom. Turn the crepes once, then cool on a kitchen towel.

8 crepes
2 tablespoons olive oil
1 cup refrigerated hash brown potatoes
1 cup frozen baby peas
½ teaspoon dried tarragon leaves
½ teaspoon salt
⅛ teaspoon pepper
1 cup sour cream, divided
1½ cups shredded Gruyère cheese

Serves 4

1 pound linguine
2 tomatoes, seeded and
    chopped
1 10-ounce container basil
    pesto
½ cup toasted pine nuts
½ cup grated Parmesan
    cheese

Pesto Pasta

This simple recipe is bursting with the flavors of summer. You must make it only when tomatoes are ripe, sweet, and tender.

1. Bring large pot of water to a boil and cook linguine according to package directions.

2. Meanwhile, in serving bowl, place tomatoes and pesto. When linguine is cooked al dente, drain well and add to serving bowl. Toss gently to coat pasta with sauce. Sprinkle with pine nuts and cheese and serve.

Serves 4

1 cup vegetable broth
½ teaspoon dried thyme
    leaves
1 16-ounce package frozen
    pierogies
2 cups frozen baby peas
3 tomatoes, cut into wedges

Tomatoes and Pierogi

You can use canned whole tomatoes in this recipe if the fresh ones are not in top condition. Drain well and cut the tomatoes in half; add when directed in recipe.

In heavy saucepan, combine vegetable broth and thyme. Bring to a boil over high heat. Add pierogies, bring to a simmer, lower heat to medium, and cover. Simmer for 5 to 7 minutes, until pierogies are almost hot. Add baby peas and tomatoes, cover, bring to a simmer, and cook for 3 to 5 minutes longer, or until pierogies are heated through and vegetables are hot. Serve immediately.

Pierogies

Pierogies are large pasta half rounds that are stuffed with mashed potatoes and seasonings, usually onion and cheese. They are a Polish or Hungarian specialty that is sold individually frozen. They cook in only a few minutes and can be dressed with any pasta sauce.

Broccoli Frittata

A frittata is an open-faced omelet that is usually finished under the broiler. Serve it with some orange juice, whole wheat toast, and grapefruit halves.

Serves 4

2 tablespoons olive oil
1 onion, finely chopped
1½ cups frozen broccoli florets, thawed
6 eggs, beaten
⅓ cup whole milk
½ teaspoon garlic salt
⅛ teaspoon white pepper
Dash red pepper flakes
1 cup shredded Gouda cheese

1. Preheat broiler. In large ovenproof skillet, heat olive oil over medium heat. Add onion; cook and stir for 3 to 4 minutes, until crisp-tender.

2. Meanwhile, drain broccoli thoroughly and press between paper towels to remove more liquid. Add broccoli to skillet; cook and stir for 2 to 3 minutes, until hot. In large bowl, beat eggs with milk, garlic salt, white pepper, and red pepper flakes to taste. Pour into skillet.

3. Cook over medium heat, covered, for 4 to 5 minutes. Remove cover and run spatula under eggs to loosen; cook until edges are puffed and center is almost set. Sprinkle with cheese. Place skillet under broiler and broil for 2 to 4 minutes, until eggs are set and cheese is melted.

Flavored Salt and Pepper
There are quite a few flavored salts and peppers that add great flavor with no extra work. Garlic salt, onion salt, seasoned salt, celery salt, and lemon-garlic salt are popular flavors. Lemon pepper, garlic pepper, and seasoned pepper are also good items to keep on hand in your pantry.

Serves 4

2 tablespoons olive oil
1 onion, chopped
½ teaspoon crushed red
  pepper flakes
2 cups frozen broccoli and
  cauliflower combo,
  thawed
1 15-ounce can black beans,
  rinsed and drained
1½ cups shredded Pepper
  Jack cheese
4 10-inch flour tortillas

Veggie Burritos

*Burritos are made from flour tortillas rolled around a spicy
seasoned filling. Serve plain, or place in a baking pan,
cover with enchilada sauce, and bake until bubbly.*

1. Heat large skillet over medium heat. Add olive oil and onion; cook and stir for 3 to 4 minutes, until crisp-tender. Sprinkle with red pepper flakes; cook and stir for a minute. Drain the vegetable combo well, then add to the skillet; cook and stir for 3 to 5 minutes, until hot. Stir in black beans, cover, and let simmer for 3 to 4 minutes.

2. Meanwhile, warm tortillas by layering in microwave-safe paper towels and microwaving on high for 1 to 2 minutes. Spread tortillas on work surface, divide vegetable mixture among them, sprinkle with cheese, and roll up, folding in sides. Serve immediately.

Frozen Vegetable Combos
Browse through your grocer's freezer aisle and you'll find almost endless combinations of frozen vegetables to add nutrition to your recipes in just one step. The combos range from broccoli, cauliflower, and carrots to baby corn, red peppers, and peas. They'll keep for a year in your freezer, so stock up!

Mushroom Risotto

Risotto is a creamy, rich dish of short grain rice and vegetables. Cooking constantly while stirring releases starch from the rice which makes the mixture thick.

Serves 4–6

*3 tablespoons olive oil
1½ cups assorted fresh
   mushrooms, sliced
½ teaspoon dried thyme
   leaves
1 cup Arborio rice
4 cups vegetable stock
1 cup grated Parmesan
   cheese
2 tablespoons butter*

1. Place olive oil in large saucepan over medium heat. When hot, add the mushrooms and thyme. Cook and stir until mushrooms give up their liquid and the liquid evaporates, about 6 to 8 minutes. Then stir in rice; cook and stir for 3 to 4 minutes, until rice is opaque.

2. Meanwhile, heat vegetable stock in another saucepan; keep over low heat while making risotto. Add the stock to the rice mixture about one cup at a time, stirring until the liquid is absorbed.

3. When all the stock is added and rice is tender, remove from the heat, stir in cheese and butter, cover, and let stand for 5 minutes. Stir and serve immediately.

Fresh Mushrooms

The variety of fresh mushrooms is staggering. In the regular grocery store, you can find portobello, cremini, button, chanterelle, shiitake, and porcini mushrooms. Use a combination for a rich, deep, earthy flavor in just about any recipe. Just brush them with a damp towel to clean, then slice and cook.

1 15-ounce package
    refrigerated hash brown
    potatoes
3 tablespoons olive oil
1 onion, chopped
3 cloves garlic, minced
1–2 tablespoons curry powder
1 teaspoon salt
⅛ teaspoon red pepper flakes
2 cups frozen baby peas
1 cup sour cream

Potato Curry

This rich dish uses refrigerated prepared potatoes to save time.
Serve it with a fruit salad and some whole wheat breadsticks.

1. Drain potatoes well, if necessary. Spread on paper towels to dry. Meanwhile, in large skillet, heat olive oil over medium heat. Add onion and garlic; cook and stir for 3 to 4 minutes, until crisp-tender. Sprinkle curry powder, salt, and red pepper flakes into skillet; cook and stir for 1 minute longer.

2. Add potatoes to skillet; cook and stir for 8 to 10 minutes, until potatoes are hot and tender and browning around the edges. Stir in peas and cook for 2 to 3 minutes longer.

3. Remove from heat and stir in sour cream. Cover and let stand for 3 minutes, then serve immediately.

Artichoke Stir-Fry

Be sure to purchase artichoke hearts that have been packed in water, not marinated. Serve this dish over hot cooked couscous with Roasted Sugar Snap Peas (page 227).

Serves 4

1 14-ounce can artichoke
    hearts
3 tablespoons olive oil
2 cups cremini mushrooms,
    sliced
3 cloves garlic, minced
½ teaspoon salt
⅛ teaspoon pepper
½ teaspoon dried thyme
    leaves
1 15-ounce can cannellini
    beans, rinsed and
    drained
¼ cup reserved artichoke
    liquid
¼ cup grated Romano cheese

1. Drain artichoke hearts, reserving ¼ cup liquid; cut artichoke hearts in thirds and set aside. In large skillet, heat olive oil over medium heat. Add mushrooms; cook and stir for 4 to 5 minutes, until tender. Sprinkle with garlic, salt, pepper, and thyme leaves; cook and stir for 1 minute longer.

2. Add drained artichoke hearts and cannellini beans along with reserved artichoke liquid. Cook and stir for 4 to 5 minutes, until ingredients are hot. Sprinkle with Romano cheese, cover pan, remove from heat, and let stand for 4 minutes. Stir and serve immediately.

Complete Proteins

When planning vegetarian menus, it's important to consider complete proteins. Your body needs complete proteins to heal injuries and keep your body healthy. Beans and grains are a common combination that provides these proteins. You don't need to fulfill all the requirements in one day; balancing over a two-day period is just fine.

1 16-ounce package
    fettuccine
3 tablespoons olive oil
1 onion, finely chopped
1 pound raw medium shrimp
½ teaspoon salt
¼ teaspoon lemon pepper
1½ cups heavy cream or low-
    fat evaporated milk
1 cup grated Parmesan
    cheese

Shrimp Fettuccine

*Low-fat evaporated milk is a good substitute for heavy cream
because it is as thick as cream but contains much less fat.*

1. Bring a large pot of water to a boil and cook fettuccine according to package directions.

2. Meanwhile, heat olive oil in a large saucepan and add onion. Cook and stir for 4 to 5 minutes, until tender. Sprinkle shrimp with salt and pepper and add to saucepan; cook over medium heat for 4 to 5 minutes, until shrimp curl and turn pink. Add cream and heat for 2 minutes.

3. When pasta is cooked al dente, drain well and stir into shrimp mixture, tossing gently to combine. Cook over medium heat for 3 to 4 minutes, until sauce is slightly thickened. Add cheese and stir gently to coat. Serve immediately.

Recipe Substitutions
You can substitute scallops, clams, oysters, or cubed fresh fish fillets for shrimp in just about any recipe. Scallops are cooked just until opaque, clams and oysters until they plump, and fish fillets until they turn opaque and flake when tested with a fork.

Pasta with Spinach Pesto

Adding spinach to prepared pesto turns the color a bright green and adds flavor and nutrition, in addition to lowering the fat content.

Serves 8

½ cup frozen cut spinach

¾ cup grated Parmesan cheese, divided

1 10-ounce container prepared basil pesto

2 tablespoons lemon juice

1 16-ounce package campanelle or farfalle pasta

1. Thaw spinach by running under hot water; drain well and squeeze with your hands to drain thoroughly. Combine in food processor or blender with ¼ cup Parmesan cheese, pesto, and lemon juice. Process or blend until mixture is smooth.

2. Meanwhile, cook pasta as directed on package until al dente. Drain well, reserving ½ cup pasta cooking water. Return pasta to pan and add pesto mixture and ¼ cup pasta cooking water. Toss gently to coat, adding more pasta cooking water if needed to make a smooth sauce. Serve with remaining ½ cup Parmesan cheese.

Pasta Shapes

There are hundreds of different pasta shapes on the market. Campanelle, which means "bellflowers," is a crimped and ruffled pasta that holds onto thick sauces. Farfalle, or butterfly-shaped pasta, is a good substitute, as is penne rigate or mostaccioli. Browse through the pasta aisle in your supermarket for more ideas.

Serves 4–6

5 large beefsteak tomatoes
⅓ cup olive oil
1 12-ounce box linguine pasta
½ teaspoon salt
¼ cup chopped fresh basil
1 6-ounce wedge Brie cheese

Linguine with Tomato Sauce

The combination of basil, tomatoes, and Brie cheese with hot pasta is simply sensational. This recipe can only be made when tomatoes are in season.

1. Cut tomatoes in half and squeeze out seeds. Coarsely chop tomatoes and combine in large bowl with olive oil.

2. Bring a large pot of water to a boil and cook linguine pasta as directed on package. Meanwhile, add salt and basil to tomatoes and toss gently. Cut Brie into small cubes and add to tomatoes.

3. Drain pasta and immediately add to tomato mixture. Toss, using tongs, until mixed. Serve immediately.

Soft Cheeses

Soft cheeses include Brie, Camembert, and Reblochon. These cheeses have a tangy flavor and very soft texture, making them difficult to work with. When you need to slice or grate these cheeses, place them in the freezer for about 15 minutes. The cheese will harden, making it easier to handle.

Creamy Tomato Sauce with Meatballs

This wonderful 20-minute recipe is great for a last-minute supper or to serve for unexpected company. Use freshly grated Parmesan cheese for the best flavor.

Serves 6–8

1 16-ounce package frozen meatballs
1 28-ounce jar pasta sauce
1 16-ounce package linguine pasta
1 cup whipping cream
1 cup grated Parmesan cheese

1. Bring a large pot of water to a boil. Bake meatballs as directed on package until hot and tender. Meanwhile, place pasta sauce in large saucepan; heat over medium heat until it comes to a simmer. Simmer for 4 to 5 minutes.

2. Cook pasta according to pasta directions until al dente; drain well. Meanwhile, remove meatballs from oven and add to pasta sauce in saucepan along with whipping cream. Bring back to a simmer and cook over medium heat for 4 to 6 minutes, stirring occasionally. Serve over cooked and drained pasta with Parmesan cheese on the side.

About Frozen Meatballs
There are several types of frozen meatballs in your grocer's freezer section. You can find plain meatballs, beef meatballs made with wild rice, chicken meatballs, and meatballs seasoned with Italian spices. Keep a selection in your freezer and you'll have the makings for dinner in minutes.

1 14-ounce package frozen
  cheese tortellini
2 tablespoons olive oil
3 cloves garlic, minced
½ cup white wine or
  vegetable broth
2 cups frozen baby peas
¼ teaspoon onion salt
¼ cup chopped flat-leaf
  parsley

Tortellini in Wine Sauce

*This elegant recipe is perfect for a spur of the moment dinner party.
You can keep all of these ingredients on hand and dinner
will be on the table in under 15 minutes.*

1. Bring a large pot of water to a boil and cook tortellini as directed on
    package. Meanwhile, in a large saucepan, heat olive oil over medium
    heat. Add garlic; cook and stir for 2 minutes, until garlic just begins to
    turn golden. Add wine, peas, and salt and bring to a simmer.

2. Drain tortellini and add to saucepan with wine. Cook over low heat for
    4 to 5 minutes, until mixture is hot and slightly thickened. Add parsley,
    stir, and serve.

Serves 4–6

3 cups uncooked mostaccioli
  pasta
1 pound ground beef
1 onion, chopped
1 28-ounce jar pasta sauce
½ cup grated Parmesan
  cheese

Meaty Mostaccioli

*There are many varieties of jarred pasta sauce; you can find it with lots of vege-
tables, with meat, or just plain. Pick your favorite for this easy recipe.*

1. Bring a large pot of water to boil and cook pasta according to pack-
    age directions. Meanwhile, in heavy saucepan, cook ground beef with
    onion until beef is browned, stirring frequently to break up meat. Drain
    well, if necessary.

2. Add pasta sauce to ground beef mixture and bring to a simmer. When
    pasta is cooked al dente, drain and place on serving plate. Cover with
    pasta sauce mixture, sprinkle with cheese, and serve.

Linguine with Peas

This recipe is so simple, yet packed full of flavor. You can make it with spaghetti or fettuccine as well; just make sure to serve it as soon as it's cooked.

~

Serves 4–6

1 pound linguine pasta
¼ cup olive oil
1 onion, chopped
3 cups frozen baby peas
½ cup toasted pine nuts
1 cup cubed Gouda cheese

1. Bring a large pot of salted water to a boil and cook pasta according to package directions.

2. Meanwhile, heat olive oil in a heavy saucepan over medium heat and add onion. Cook and stir for 5 to 7 minutes, until onions are tender. Add peas; cook and stir for 2 to 4 minutes longer, until peas are hot. Turn off heat and add pine nuts and Gouda cheese; cover and let stand while you drain pasta. Toss pasta with pea mixture and serve immediately.

Cooking Pasta
Pasta must be cooked in a large amount of salted, rapidly boiling water. The proportions are 1½ quarts of water for every 3 ounces of dried pasta. When finishing a dish by adding the pasta to a sauce, slightly undercook the pasta. Some of the residual heat from the sauce will continue to cook the pasta in the last few seconds.

Serves 4

1 pound spaghetti
3 tablespoons fermented
*   black beans*
1 15-ounce can black beans
¼ cup olive oil
5 cloves garlic, minced

Black-Bean Spaghetti

*A combination of salty fermented black beans and
canned black beans is a delicious topping for spaghetti.
Serve it with a simple green salad and a fresh fruit salad.*

1. Bring a large pot of water to a boil and add the spaghetti. Cook according to package directions until al dente.

2. Meanwhile, place fermented black beans in a strainer and rinse; drain on paper towels. Drain the black beans and rinse, then drain again. Heat olive oil in large skillet over medium heat. Add garlic; cook and stir for 3 to 4 minutes, until garlic is fragrant. Do not let it burn.

3. When pasta is cooked, drain thoroughly and add to skillet along with fermented black beans and plain black beans. Toss until heated and mixed and serve immediately.

About Fermented Black Beans
Fermented black beans are actually black soybeans that are marinated in a mixture of garlic, salt, and spices. They are very strongly flavored and add a nice spicy kick to Asian dishes. If using more than 1 tablespoon, rinse them briefly to cut down on the salt.

Pasta Frittata

Leftover pasta can be made into this simple main dish. Just reheat it in boiling water for about 30 seconds, drain well, then continue with the recipe.

———

Serves 4

1 handful linguine pasta
8 eggs, beaten
¼ cup heavy cream
½ teaspoon dried Italian
　seasoning
½ teaspoon garlic salt
⅛ teaspoon garlic pepper
2 tablespoons olive oil
1 cup chopped mushrooms
1 cup grated Cotija or
　Parmesan cheese

1. Heat a large stockpot filled with water until boiling. Break linguine in half and add to pot. Cook linguine until almost al dente, about 5 to 7 minutes; drain well. Meanwhile, in large bowl, beat eggs with cream, Italian seasoning, garlic salt, and garlic pepper.

2. Preheat broiler. Heat olive oil in heavy ovenproof skillet over medium heat. Add mushrooms; cook and stir for 3 to 4 minutes, until almost tender. Add egg mixture to skillet along with drained pasta; arrange in an even layer. Cook over medium heat for 4 to 7 minutes, until eggs are almost set, lifting egg mixture occasionally to let uncooked mixture flow to bottom.

3. Sprinkle frittata with cheese and place under broiler for 3 to 5 minutes, until eggs are cooked and cheese is melted and beginning to brown. Serve immediately.

Menu Ideas
A frittata is a wonderful dish for a late-night supper. Serve it with a spinach salad made with sliced red and yellow bell peppers, croutons, and a creamy Italian salad dressing, and some Toasted Garlic Bread (page 53). For dessert, try Peanut Cakes (page 291).

2 tablespoons olive oil
1 red bell pepper, chopped
1 28-ounce jar pasta sauce
½ cup water
1 24-ounce package frozen
    ravioli
1 15-ounce can black beans,
    rinsed and drained
1½ cups shredded pizza
    cheese

Black-Bean Unstructured Lasagna

Lasagna in under 15 minutes! Serve this wonderful dish with a fresh green salad drizzled with Italian dressing, some crisp breadsticks, and ice cream for dessert.

Preheat broiler. Heat olive oil in large ovenproof skillet over medium heat. Add bell pepper; cook and stir for 2 to 3 minutes, until crisp-tender. Add pasta sauce and water; bring to a boil. Add ravioli, stir, bring to a simmer, and cook for 4 to 8 minutes, until ravioli are hot. Add beans and stir. Sprinkle with cheese, place under the broiler, and broil until cheese is melted and begins to brown. Serve immediately.

Modifying Equipment

If you don't have ovenproof pans or skillets, use heavy-duty foil to protect the handles. Wrap two layers of the foil around the handles and you can use the pans under the broiler. Foil can also be used to make a large pan smaller; just use it to build walls for the size pan you want. Fill the empty space with dried beans.

Chapter 9
From the Deli

Serves 4

3 cups deli three-bean salad
1 cup cubed cooked ham
1 cup grape tomatoes
1 yellow bell pepper, seeded
   and chopped
1 cup mushrooms, sliced

Ham and Three-Bean Salad

Make sure that you taste (and like!) the three-bean salad from your deli before using it in this recipe. Most delis will offer you a taste if you ask.

Drain salad and reserve ½ cup of the dressing. Combine all ingredients in medium bowl and toss with enough reserved dressing to moisten. Serve immediately; refrigerate leftovers.

Serves 8

1 quart deli potato salad
1 tablespoon chili powder
2 red bell peppers, chopped
1 pint cherry or grape
   tomatoes
1 jalapeño pepper, minced
2 cups canned corn, drained

Southwest Potato Salad

If you like your food extra spicy, use more chili powder or add more jalapeño peppers. If you're really brave, try habañero peppers!

Place potato salad in serving bowl and sprinkle evenly with chili powder. Add remaining ingredients and gently stir to mix thoroughly. Serve immediately or cover and chill for 1 to 2 hours to blend flavors.

Dress Up Potato Salad

It's easy to dress up plain potato salad. To make a curried potato salad, mix curry powder with chutney and stir into potato salad along with sliced green onions and sliced celery. For an All-American potato salad, add grape tomatoes, some chopped dill pickles, and some yellow mustard.

Spicy Veggie Pizza

Boboli pizza crusts are available in any deli and you can usually find plain pizza crusts there too. This easy pizza is delicious served with some deli fruit salad and cold milk.

⌒

Serves 4

2 cups marinated deli
    vegetables
1 12- or 14-inch Boboli pizza
    crust
1 10-ounce container garlic
    and herb cream cheese
1 cup shredded provolone
    cheese
½ cup grated Parmesan
    cheese

1. Preheat oven to 400°F. Chop the marinated vegetables into smaller pieces and place in saucepan with the marinade. Bring to a simmer over medium heat; simmer for 3 to 4 minutes, until vegetables are tender. Drain thoroughly.

2. Place pizza crust on a cookie sheet and spread with the cream cheese. Arrange drained vegetables on top and sprinkle with provolone and Parmesan cheeses. Bake for 15 to 18 minutes, until crust is hot and crisp and cheese is melted and begins to brown.

Make Your Own Pizza Crust
Make your own crust by combining 2 cups flour, 1 cup cornmeal, 3 tablespoons oil, 1 package yeast, and 1⅓ cups water in a bowl. Knead thoroughly, let rise, punch down, divide in half, and roll out. Prebake the crust at 400°F for 8 to 10 minutes, then cool, wrap well, and freeze until ready to use.

2 sheets puff pastry, thawed
4 cups deli candy bar salad
1 cup milk chocolate chips
½ cup finely chopped walnuts

Snickers Salad Éclairs

In many delis, there is a fabulous sweet whipped cream salad made with chopped candy bars. It stretches the definition of "salad," but it makes a delicious dessert.

1. Preheat oven to 425°F. On lightly floured surface, roll out each puff pastry sheet to a 12" × 12" square. Cut each in half horizontally to make four 6" × 12" pieces. Cut each into four 6" × 3" pieces (for a total of 16) and place on baking sheet. Bake for 8 to 10 minutes, until puffed and golden brown. Remove to wire rack and let cool for 10 to 15 minutes.

2. Split each rectangle of pastry in half horizontally and put the halves together with some of the salad. Meanwhile, melt chocolate chips in microwave oven for 2 minutes on 50 percent power; stir until smooth. Drizzle chocolate over filled rectangles and sprinkle with walnuts. Cover and refrigerate, or serve immediately.

Re-creating Deli Salads

If you can't find certain deli salads, re-create them! Most salads use a combination of fruits with whipped cream or nondairy whipped topping. The Snickers-Bar Salad is made with vanilla pudding, chopped candy bars, chopped walnuts, nondairy whipped topping, and chopped apples.

Simple Fruit Parfaits

*Make these pretty parfaits ahead of time and keep them
in the refrigerator until you're ready to serve them.*

Serves 8

2 cups frozen nondairy
topping, thawed
1 cup deli vanilla pudding
½ teaspoon cinnamon
2 cups deli fruit salad
1 cup granola

In medium bowl, combine topping, pudding, and cinnamon and fold together gently. Make parfaits by layering the fruit salad, topping mixture, and granola into tall parfait glasses, ending with granola. Serve immediately or cover and refrigerate for up to 4 hours.

Deli Fruit Salads
There are usually several kinds of deli fruit salads. You'll find plain mixed fruit with no dressing or a simple clear dressing, gelatin fruit salads, and fruit salads made with whipped cream or whipping topping. For this recipe, look for the plain mixed fruit salad.

Barbecued Roast Beef Sandwiches

*This recipe is great for using up leftover roast beef. The sauce
can also be used to make Sloppy Joe sandwiches; use 1½
pounds of cooked and drained ground beef for the roast beef.*

Serves 12

2 tablespoons olive oil
1 onion, chopped
½ cup steak sauce
1 8-ounce can tomato sauce
1½ pounds thinly sliced
cooked deli roast beef
12 sandwich buns, split and
toasted

1. In heavy skillet, heat olive oil over medium heat. Add onion and cook, stirring frequently, for 5 to 6 minutes, until onion is tender. Add steak sauce and tomato sauce and bring to a simmer. Stir in roast beef; simmer for 5 to 6 minutes, stirring frequently, until sauce thickens slightly and roast beef is heated through.

2. Make sandwiches using roast beef mixture and split and toasted sandwich buns. Serve immediately.

Serves 4–6

1 loaf Italian bread, unsliced
⅓ cup honey mustard/mayo
   combo
½ pound sliced deli ham
½ pound sliced deli turkey
½ pound sliced Muenster
   cheese

Hot Submarine Sandwiches

Use any combination of meats and cheeses for this easy and hearty sandwich recipe. Serve it with a deli fruit salad and a bakery pie for dessert.

Preheat oven to 400°F. Slice bread in half horizontally and place, cut sides up, on work surface. Spread cut surfaces with the honey mustard/mayo combo. Arrange ham, turkey, and Muenster cheese on bottom half of the bread, then top with second half. Wrap entire sandwich in foil. Bake for 20 to 23 minutes or until sandwich is hot, cheese is melted, and bread is toasted, opening foil for last 5 minutes of baking time to crisp bread. Slice into four to six portions and serve.

Mustard Combinations

There are many types and varieties of mustard combinations in the grocery store these days. From honey mustard to grainy mustard to mustard and mayonnaise blends, there's a large selection to choose from. Keep a supply on hand for making sandwiches from just about any leftover meat.

Corned Beef Sandwiches

These hearty sandwiches are perfect for a St. Patrick's Day celebration. Serve them with a deli fruit salad and Grasshopper Cookies (page 265) for dessert.

—⁓—

Serves 4

¼ cup mustard/mayonnaise combo
8 slices deli pumpernickel rye swirl bread
½ pound thinly sliced deli corned beef
2 cups deli coleslaw
4 slices deli Swiss cheese

Spread mustard/mayonnaise combo on the bread slices and make sandwiches with the corned beef, coleslaw, and Swiss cheese. Cut in half and serve with some deli dill pickles.

Salads in Sandwiches
When you're using any kind of prepared salads in sandwich recipes, you may need to drain the salad by placing it in a colander and letting it stand for a few minutes, or by using a slotted spoon to scoop the salad out of the container. If you're making sandwiches ahead of time, leave the salad out and add it just before serving.

Chicken Tortellini Salad

Most delis have a selection of prepared salads. Serve this gorgeous salad on some baby spinach leaves along with iced tea and bakery breadsticks.

—⁓—

Serves 4–6

1 quart deli tortellini salad
2 cups chopped deli chicken
1 red bell pepper, chopped
1 cup cubed Havarti cheese
½ cup mayonnaise

In large bowl, combine all ingredients and toss gently to coat. Serve immediately or cover and refrigerate up to 24 hours.

Salad Inspirations
Take some time to browse through your supermarket to find ideas for salads. In the produce section you'll find salad kits and lots of refrigerated dressings to inspire you. Many companies make salad kits that are placed in the meat aisle and some are in the grocery aisle near the bottled salad dressings.

Serves 4

¼ pound thinly sliced deli
  ham
¼ pound thinly sliced deli
  turkey
¼ pound thinly sliced deli
  Colby cheese
8 slices whole grain bread
1 cup fish batter mix
⅓ cup oil

Monte Cristo Sandwiches

*Find fish batter mix near the fish in the supermarket's meat aisle.
It makes a wonderful crispy coating on these delicious sandwiches.*

1. Make sandwiches using ham, turkey, cheese, and bread. In shallow bowl, prepare batter mix as directed on package.

2. Pour oil into heavy saucepan and heat over medium heat until a drop of water sizzles and evaporates. Dip sandwiches into batter mixture and immediately place in oil in saucepan. Cook over medium heat, turning once, until bread is golden brown and cheese is melted, about 3 to 5 minutes per side. Cut sandwiches in half and serve immediately.

Monte Cristo Sandwich Dips

Serve these dips with Monte Cristo Sandwiches or any grilled sandwich. For a sweet dip, combine ½ cup sour cream with ¼ cup raspberry jam and mix well. For a spicy dip, combine ½ cup mayonnaise with 2 tablespoons honey Dijon mustard and a teaspoon of chili sauce and blend well.

Crispy Chicken Stir-Fry

*Hot cooked rice is a must for this simple stir-fry recipe. Serve with
chopsticks and some green tea for an authentic quick Asian meal.*

Serves 4

2 fried deli chicken breasts
2 cups mixed salad
    vegetables from deli
    salad bar
2 tablespoons olive oil
1 onion, chopped
⅔ cup sweet-and-sour
    simmer sauce

Cut chicken meat off the bone; be sure to include some crisp skin on each
piece. Set aside. If necessary, cut salad vegetables into uniform pieces. In
large saucepan or wok, heat olive oil over medium high heat. Add onion and
salad vegetables and stir-fry for 4 to 7 minutes, until crisp-tender. Add chicken
pieces; stir-fry for 2 to 3 minutes, until hot. Add simmer sauce and stir-fry for 3
to 5 minutes, until hot. Serve immediately.

Roasted Chicken Penne

*A tender baby spinach salad with a raspberry vinaigrette,
some raspberries, and toasted slivered almonds is all
you need to make this easy recipe a complete meal.*

Serves 4

2 cups penne pasta
2 roasted deli chicken breasts
1 10-ounce jar garlic Alfredo
    sauce
½ cup chicken gravy (from
    deli or jar)
2 cups frozen mixed
    vegetables, thawed and
    drained

1. Bring a large pot of water to a boil and cook penne pasta according to
   package directions. Meanwhile, remove meat from chicken and shred.
   Combine with Alfredo sauce, chicken gravy, and vegetables in a large
   saucepan over medium heat. Cook, stirring occasionally, until sauce
   bubbles and chicken and vegetables are hot, about 8 to 10 minutes.

2. When pasta is cooked al dente, drain thoroughly and add to chicken
   mixture, stirring and tossing gently. Cook for another 1 to 2 minutes to
   heat through and serve.

1 package refrigerated pie
   crusts
1 7-ounce can artichoke
   hearts, drained
2 cups chopped deli roast
   beef
1½ cups diced Swiss cheese
⅓ cup sour cream

Roast Beef Calzones

Calzones are a baked Italian sandwich, usually made with pizza dough.
This version, made with pie crusts, is more delicate and flaky.

1. Preheat oven to 400°F. Let pie crusts stand at room temperature while preparing filling. Drain artichoke hearts, place on paper towels to drain further, and cut into smaller pieces. In medium bowl, combine artichoke hearts, chopped beef, cheese, and sour cream, and mix gently.

2. Place pie crusts on cookie sheet, placing the edges in the center of the cookie sheet, about 1 inch apart, and letting excess hang beyond the cookie sheet. Divide filling between pie crusts, placing on one half of each crust, leaving a 1-inch border. Fold the unfilled half of the pie crust (the part hanging beyond the cookie sheet) over the filling to form a half-moon shape. Press edges with a fork to firmly seal. Cut decorative shapes in the top of each crust. Bake for 18 to 24 minutes, until crust is golden brown and crisp and filling is hot. Let stand for 5 minutes, then cut into wedges to serve.

Pesto Potato Salad

This excellent salad is perfect for a picnic or cookout. Be sure to pack it in an insulated cooler with some ice packs, and discard leftovers after the picnic.

Serves 6–8

1 10-ounce container
    refrigerated pesto
½ cup mayonnaise
6 cups deli potato salad
½ cup grated Parmesan
    cheese
2 cups cubed Havarti cheese

In large bowl, combine pesto and mayonnaise; stir in potato salad until coated. Stir in cheeses and mix well. Serve immediately or cover and chill for up to 8 hours before serving.

Menu Ideas

Serve this potato salad along with Spicy Grilled Flank Steak (page 74), lots of tortilla chips and potato chips, and Grilled Asparagus (page 223). For dessert, make S'mores by toasting marshmallows over the coals and making sandwiches with the marshmallows, graham crackers, and chocolate bars.

Spinach and Fruit Ham Salad

For this recipe, purchase the deli fruit salad with a clear dressing, not the salad with the whipped cream dressing.

Serves 6

1 10-ounce bag baby spinach
2 cups (8 ounces) cubed deli
    ham
2 cups deli fruit salad
½ cup peach pie filling
1 cup pecan halves

In large serving bowl, arrange spinach. In medium bowl, combine ham with deli fruit salad and fold in pie filling. Add pecan halves and spoon salad over baby spinach; serve immediately.

Menu Suggestions

On hot summer days, serve cold main-dish salads on your back porch under a ceiling fan with some chewy bakery breadsticks on the side, some iced tea or Lemonade (page 36), and Oatmeal Cookie Parfaits (page 274) or Ice Cream with Mix-Ins (page 279) for dessert.

Serves 4

1 10- to 12-inch focaccia
    bread
¾ cup garlic Alfredo sauce
    (from 10-ounce jar)
8 ounces cold smoked
    salmon
1 8-ounce jar plain artichoke
    hearts, drained
1½ cups shredded Gouda
    cheese

Smoked Salmon Pizza

*If your deli makes a marinated vegetable salad that you like, cook it for
a few minutes over medium heat until tender, then drain thoroughly;
substitute it for the artichoke hearts in this simple recipe.*

Preheat oven to 400°F. Place focaccia on baking sheet. Spread with Alfredo sauce. Arrange salmon and artichoke hearts on pizza, then sprinkle with Gouda cheese. Bake for 18 to 22 minutes, until pizza is thoroughly heated and cheese is melted and beginning to brown. Serve immediately.

Smoked Salmon
Salmon is available hot-smoked or cold-smoked. Hot-smoked salmon, also called kippered salmon, is usually hard and slightly chewy and is a deep red color. Cold-smoked salmon, or lox, is pink and tender and is sliced very thin. Either type of salmon will work in this easy pizza.

Seafood Enchiladas

Serve these easy enchiladas with Lemon Cucumber Salad (page 204) and Garlicky Green Beans (page 226), with Cereal Caramel Chews (page 262) for dessert.

Serves 6

½ pound deli Muenster cheese
3 cups deli seafood salad
1 cup salsa
12 6-inch corn tortillas
1 10-ounce jar enchilada sauce

Preheat oven to 400°F. Shred cheese into large bowl or ask the deli to shred it. In another large bowl, combine seafood salad and salsa; stir in 1½ cups shredded cheese. Divide among corn tortillas and roll up. Place ½ cup enchilada sauce in bottom of 2-quart baking dish and lay filled tortillas on top. Drizzle with rest of enchilada sauce and sprinkle with remaining cheese. Bake for 20 to 23 minutes, until casserole is hot and bubbly. Serve immediately.

Asian Beef Rolls

This cold entrée wraps tender roast beef around crunchy coleslaw mix seasoned with Asian ingredients. Yum.

Serves 6

3 tablespoons hoisin sauce
¼ cup plum sauce
1½ cups coleslaw mix
¼ cup chopped green onion
6 slices cooked deli roast beef

In medium bowl, combine hoisin sauce and plum sauce and mix well. Stir in coleslaw mix and green onion and mix gently. Place roast beef slices on work surface and divide coleslaw mixture among them. Roll up beef slices, enclosing filling. Serve immediately or cover and refrigerate up to 8 hours before serving.

Menu Suggestions

These spicy and crunchy rolls are delicious paired with Cold Pea Soup (page 245) and Pumpkin Bread (page 38) for lunch on the porch on a hot summer day. For dessert, serve Oatmeal Cookie Parfaits (page 274) topped with a dollop of nondairy frozen whipped topping.

½ cup tomato sauce
4 slices deli meatloaf
4 slices deli Cheddar cheese
8 slices deli pumpernickel
   bread
¼ cup butter, softened

Grilled Meatloaf Sandwiches

*These great sandwiches are also the perfect way to use up
leftover meatloaf. Serve with large dill pickles from the deli and some
deli coleslaw, along with root beer and ice cream for dessert.*

Preheat dual-contact indoor grill or large skillet over medium-high heat. Spread tomato sauce onto meatloaf slices. Make sandwiches with coated meatloaf, cheese, and pumpernickel bread. Spread outside of sandwiches with softened butter and cook on grill or skillet, turning once, until bread is hot and crisp and cheese begins to melt, about 4 to 6 minutes for dual contact grill, and 6 to 10 minutes for skillet. Serve immediately.

Dual-Contact Grills
These grills are an easy way to grill just about any food. Just cut the cooking time in half, because the food cooks on both sides at the same time. Be sure to press the grill closed gently but firmly, to make good contact with the food.

Chapter 10

Sandwiches and Pizza

Serves 4

4 pita breads, unsplit
4 slices Swiss cheese
1 avocado
1 6-ounce can tuna, drained
½ cup tartar sauce
¾ cup shredded Swiss cheese,
    divided
½ teaspoon dried dill weed

Tuna Melts

*Tartar sauce is made of mayonnaise, pickles, and seasonings.
It is delicious paired with mild canned tuna and Swiss
cheese in these quick and easy sandwiches.*

1. Preheat oven to 400°F. Toast pita breads in oven until crisp, about 5 minutes. Remove from oven and top each one with a slice of Swiss cheese.

2. Peel avocado and mash slightly, leaving some chunks. Spread this on top of the Swiss cheese. In small bowl, combine tuna and tartar sauce with ¼ cup shredded Swiss cheese. Spread on top of avocado.

3. Sprinkle sandwiches with remaining shredded Swiss cheese and the dill weed. Bake for 7 to 11 minutes, until cheese melts.

Sandwich Melts

Melts are open-faced sandwiches, or sandwiches without a "lid," that are usually grilled, baked, or broiled to heat the filling and melt the cheese. Serve them with a knife and fork, and with a simple fruit salad or green salad for a hearty, quick lunch or dinner.

Salmon Avocado Sandwiches

*Look for salmon packed in pouches in your supermarket.
The new varieties are boneless and skinless, eliminating the
step of discarding the bone and skins from canned salmon.*

Serves 4

1 7-ounce pouch pink salmon,
   drained
1 avocado, peeled and diced
½ cup mayonnaise
½ teaspoon dried basil leaves
½ cup chopped tomato
4 hamburger or hoagie buns,
   split, toasted if desired

In small bowl, combine all ingredients except hamburger or hoagie buns and
mix gently but thoroughly. Divide mixture evenly between the hamburger or
hoagie buns and serve.

Curried Chicken Sandwiches

*Keep this delicious sandwich spread in your refrigerator
and let hungry teenagers make their own sandwiches! You could
substitute pitted, halved cherries for the red grapes if you'd like.*

Serves 4–6

2 cups cubed, cooked chicken
½ cup plain yogurt
⅓ cup chutney
1 teaspoon curry powder
1 cup red grapes, cut in half
3 pita breads, cut in half

In medium bowl, combine all ingredients except pita breads and stir well to
combine. Fill pita breads with chicken mixture and serve.

Cooking Chicken
*To cook chicken breasts for use in any recipe, place boneless, skinless breasts
in a pot and cover with half water and half canned chicken broth. Bring to a
simmer, then reduce heat and poach chicken for 8 to 12 minutes, until chicken
is thoroughly cooked. Let chicken cool in refrigerator, then chop. Reserve the
broth for use in other recipes.*

2 3-ounce packages cream
    cheese, softened
¼ cup sour cream
½ teaspoon dried dill weed
3 6-ounce cans small shrimp,
    drained
1½ cups chopped celery
    hearts
1 10-inch focaccia bread

Shrimp Sandwiches

*You can add some butter lettuce or watercress leaves to the
bottom half of the focaccia bread before adding the shrimp filling.
This is a good salad for a picnic because it's easy to carry.*

1. In medium bowl, beat cream cheese with sour cream and dill weed until smooth and fluffy. Stir in shrimp and chopped celery hearts.

2. Using serrated knife, cut focaccia bread in half horizontally. Spread bottom layer with cream cheese mixture and top with top layer. Cut into 8 wedges and serve.

Canned Seafood
Canned seafood can have a salty taste. You can rinse it before use, but be sure to drain it very well, and don't soak it. Canned salmon, crabmeat, and tuna, as well as surimi, or frozen faux crab, can all be substituted for canned shrimp in just about any recipe.

Stuffed Panini

You can stuff a hollowed-out loaf of bread with just about any combination of meats, cheeses, and salad dressings. Experiment, and have a taste-test party!

~

Serves 4

1 1-pound loaf round unsliced
    Italian bread
¼ cup creamy Italian salad
    dressing
¼ pound thinly sliced smoked
    turkey
¼ pound thinly sliced salami
½ pound sliced provolone
    cheese

1. Preheat oven to 400°F. Slice the top off the bread round and remove the center of the loaf, leaving a 1-inch border on the edges and the bottom. (Freeze the bread crumbs for another use or toast and use in Bread-Crumb Frittata, page 55.)

2. Spread half of the salad dressing in bottom and up sides of bread. Layer turkey, salami, and provolone cheese in the bread and drizzle with remaining salad dressing. Cover with top of bread round and place on baking sheet. Place an ovenproof skillet on top of sandwich to press it down as it bakes.

3. Bake sandwich for 15 to 20 minutes, until bread is toasted, filling is hot, and cheese is melted. Cut into wedges and serve.

Serves 4

8 slices bacon
¾ cup grated Parmesan
    cheese, divided
½ teaspoon dried thyme
    leaves
¼ cup mayonnaise
4 hoagie buns, sliced
2 tomatoes, thickly sliced

Bacon Crisp Sandwiches

*This unusual way of cooking bacon makes these sandwiches
simply superb. Be sure the tomatoes are ripe and juicy for best results.
You could also add some fresh lettuce leaves or baby spinach.*

1. Dip bacon slices in ½ cup Parmesan cheese and press to coat. Place 4 slices of the coated bacon on microwave-safe paper towels in a 12"×8" microwave-safe baking dish. Cover with another sheet of microwave-safe paper towels. Microwave on high for 3 to 4 minutes or until bacon is light golden brown. Repeat with remaining bacon slices.

2. Meanwhile, in small bowl, combine thyme, mayonnaise, and remaining ¼ cup Parmesan cheese and spread on cut sides of hoagie buns. Toast in toaster oven or under broiler until cheese mixture bubbles. Make sandwiches with the cooked bacon, tomatoes, and toasted buns and serve immediately.

Yields 3 cups

8 slices bacon
1 8-ounce container cream
    cheese with herbs,
    softened
⅓ cup mayonnaise
1 7-ounce pouch pink salmon,
    drained
½ cup chopped green onions

Bacon Salmon Sandwich Spread

*This fabulous spread is perfect to keep in the fridge for lunch
on the run. Have English muffins, pita breads, and whole wheat
sandwich buns on hand and let your family make their own.*

1. Cook bacon until crisp; drain on paper towels until cool enough to handle. Crumble bacon into small pieces.

2. In medium bowl, beat cream cheese until fluffy. Stir in mayonnaise and beat until smooth. Add reserved bacon, salmon, and green onions, and gently fold together. Cover and store in refrigerator up to 3 days. Make sandwiches using the spread.

Muffuletta

Muffuletta sandwiches are layered sandwiches that use olivada, or olive paste, as a spread between layers of meats and cheeses. Make them ahead of time and refrigerate until it's time to eat.

Serves 6

1 12-inch focaccia flatbread
⅓ cup bottled olivada,
   drained
½ pound thinly sliced Fontina
   cheese
¼ pound thinly sliced smoked
   turkey
¼ pound thinly sliced salami

1. Cut focaccia in half horizontally to make two thin round pieces. Spread cut side of both pieces with some of the olivada. Layer half of the Fontina cheese, a thin layer of olivada, smoked turkey, olivada, salami, olivada, and the rest of the Fontina cheese. Replace top of focaccia and press sandwich together gently.

2. Cut into wedges and serve immediately, or wrap whole sandwich in plastic wrap and chill for up to 8 hours.

Make Your Own Olivada

Combine 1 cup mixed olives (Kalamata, green, black, cracked) with ¼ cup olive oil, a few cloves of garlic, some thyme or marjoram, and a bit of pepper in a blender or food processor. Blend or process until olives are chopped. Store, covered, in the refrigerator and use it for sandwich spreads or as an appetizer dip.

½ cup bread crumbs
1 egg, beaten
½ teaspoon salt
¼ teaspoon cayenne pepper
¼ teaspoon cumin
1 teaspoon chili powder
1¼ pounds ground turkey
4 slices Pepper Jack cheese
4 whole wheat hamburger
    buns

Spicy Turkey Cheeseburgers

*Lots of spices make these burgers very flavorful. You could make a
Tex-Mex sandwich spread to put on the hamburger buns by combining
mayonnaise with some chopped chipotle peppers and adobo sauce.*

1. Prepare and preheat grill or broiler. In large bowl, combine bread
   crumbs, egg, salt, and seasonings and mix well. Add turkey and mix
   gently but thoroughly until combined. Form into 4 patties.

2. Cook patties, covered, 4 to 6 inches from medium heat for about 10
   minutes, turning once, until thoroughly cooked. Top each with a slice
   of cheese, cover grill, and cook for 1 minute longer, until cheese melts.
   Meanwhile, toast the cut sides of hamburger buns on the grill; make
   sandwiches with turkey patties and buns.

Make Recipes Your Own

*Once you get the hang of making a recipe quickly, think about varying
the ingredients to make it your own. For instance, Spicy Turkey
Cheeseburgers could be made with chutney, curry powder, and Havarti
or provolone cheese. Or make them Greek burgers with feta cheese,
chopped olives, and some dried oregano leaves.*

English Muffin Pizzas

These little pizzas can be topped with just about anything. Use cooked ground beef, drained chopped green chilies, and Pepper Jack cheese for Mexican pizzas; or chopped ham, drained pineapple tidbits, and Co-jack cheese for Hawaiian pizzas.

Preheat oven to broil. Place English muffin halves on baking sheet and top each one with pizza sauce. Layer mushrooms and pepperoni over pizza sauce. Sprinkle cheese over pizzas. Broil pizzas, 4 to 6 inches from heat source, for 2 to 4 minutes or until pizzas are hot and cheese is melted, bubbly, and beginning to brown. Serve immediately.

Serves 6–8

8 English muffins, split and toasted
1½ cups pizza sauce
1 6-ounce jar sliced mushrooms, drained
1 cup pepperoni, sliced
2 cups shredded mozzarella cheese

Mexican Chicken Pizzas

These individual pizzas are full of Tex-Mex flavor. Serve them with a simple fruit salad and an ice cream pie for dessert.

1. Preheat oven to 400°F. Place tortillas on two cookie sheets and bake for 5 to 8 minutes until tortillas are crisp, reversing the cookie sheets halfway through cooking time and turning tortillas over once.

2. In small bowl combine beans, taco sauce, oregano, and chili powder and mix well. Spread evenly over baked tortillas. Top with chicken strips and cheese. Bake for 12 to 18 minutes or until pizzas are hot and cheese is melted and beginning to brown, reversing cookie sheets halfway through cooking time. Cut into wedges and serve.

Serves 8

8 flour tortillas
1 16-ounce can refried beans
½ cup taco sauce
½ teaspoon dried oregano
1 tablespoon chili powder
2 9-ounce packages refrigerated grilled cooked chicken strips
2 cups shredded Pepper Jack cheese

Serves 6–8

1 16-ounce package frozen
    meatballs, thawed
1 15-ounce jar pasta sauce
1 cup frozen onion and
    pepper stir-fry combo,
    thawed and drained
4 hoagie rolls, sliced and
    toasted
1 6-ounce package sliced
    provolone cheese

Open-Faced Hoagies

*Thaw the meatballs by leaving the package in the refrigerator overnight,
or follow instructions on the package to thaw in the microwave.*

1. Cut thawed meatballs in half and place in heavy saucepan with pasta
   sauce. Cook over medium heat, stirring occasionally, until sauce bubbles and meatballs are hot.

2. Stir in onion and pepper stir-fry; cook and stir for 3 to 5 minutes, until
   vegetables are hot and tender. Preheat broiler.

3. Top each hoagie roll half with meatball mixture and place on broiler
   rack. Top each with a slice of cheese. Broil 6 inches from heat source for
   3 to 6 minutes, until cheese is melted and bubbly. Serve immediately.

Provolone Cheese

*Provolone cheese is a mild cheese with a slightly smoky taste that's
made from cow's milk. It is usually aged for a few months so the texture
is slightly firm. You can buy provolone aged for up to a year. This aged
cheese has a more intense flavor and firm texture, similar to Parmesan
cheese.*

Smashed Avocado Sandwiches

Mashing avocados with salad dressing helps prevent the avocados from turning brown. These rich sandwiches must be made with juicy, ripe tomatoes and ripe avocados.

~

Serves 4–6

3 avocados
⅓ cup creamy Italian salad
   dressing
4 hoagie buns, sliced and
   toasted
4 plum tomatoes, sliced
8 slices Muenster cheese

1. Preheat broiler. Peel and seed avocados; place in small bowl along with salad dressing. Mash, using a fork, until almost blended but there are still some pieces of avocado visible.

2. Place bottom halves of buns on broiler pan and spread with half of avocado mixture. Top with tomato slices and cover with cheese slices. Broil 6 inches from heat source for 2 to 5 minutes or until cheese is melted and begins to bubble. Spread top halves of buns with remaining avocado mixture and place on top of cheese. Serve immediately.

Tomatoes

Most tomatoes are full of seeds and liquid. This juiciness, desirable in salads, is less so in sandwiches and pizzas. Choose plum tomatoes for these recipes because there is more flesh and fewer seeds. Or you can seed tomatoes before use by cutting in half and gently squeezing them over the sink to remove seeds, jelly, and excess liquid.

4 pita pocket breads

3 tablespoons olive oil,
    divided

2 tablespoons mustard

6 ounces sliced cooked ham

6 ounces sliced Muenster
    cheese

½ cup sliced roasted red
    peppers, drained

Pita Paninis

*Roasted red peppers are sold in jars in the condiment aisle of the supermarket.
Drain them on paper towels before layering them in this sandwich.*

1. Heat dual-contact indoor grill. Using a sharp knife, split the pocket breads into 2 round pieces. In small bowl, combine 1 tablespoon olive oil and mustard and mix well. Spread this mixture on inside halves of the pita breads.

2. Layer ham, Muenster cheese, roasted red peppers, and more Muenster cheese on one side of each pita bread. Top with remaining pita bread sides. Spread outside of sandwiches with remaining 2 tablespoons olive oil.

3. Place each sandwich on dual-contact indoor grill and close the cover. Grill for 2 to 4 minutes, until cheese is melted and bread is golden brown and toasted. Cut sandwiches in half and serve.

Indoor Grills

If you like to make a lot of grilled sandwiches, buying a dual-contact indoor grill or panini grill is a good investment. They come in many different sizes, are nonstick for easy cleanup, and they heat up quickly. You can find some grills that are equipped with different surfaces to make patterns on the bread as it cooks.

Spinach Cheese Pizzas

Nutmeg really helps to bring out spinach's rich flavor. This may seem like a strange addition to pizza, but try it—you'll like it!

~

1. Preheat broiler. Place bagels on a cookie sheet. In heavy saucepan, heat olive oil over medium heat and add onion; cook and stir for 4 to 6 minutes, until onion is tender. Add pizza sauce and nutmeg; bring to a simmer.

2. Meanwhile, drain the thawed spinach in a colander or strainer, then drain again by pressing between paper towels. Spread bagel halves with pizza sauce mixture and top evenly with the spinach. Sprinkle with cheese. Broil 6 inches from heat for 4 to 7 minutes, until cheese melts and sandwiches are hot.

Serves 6–8

6 bagels, split and toasted
2 tablespoons olive oil
1 onion, chopped
1 8-ounce can pizza sauce
Pinch ground nutmeg
1 cup frozen chopped spinach, thawed
1½ cups shredded mozzarella cheese

Smoked Salmon Pizza

Cold-cured smoked salmon is a better choice than hot-cured for this recipe because the salmon is softer and sliced much thinner. Ask your grocer or butcher if you aren't sure about the salmon you buy.

~

1. Heat oven to 400°F. Place pizza crust on cookie sheet. Spread with cream cheese and arrange smoked salmon and bell pepper slices on top. Sprinkle evenly with provolone cheese.

2. Bake for 18 to 22 minutes or until crust is hot and crisp and cheese is melted. Serve immediately.

Serves 4

1 10- or 12-inch Boboli pizza crust
1 8-ounce package garlic and herb soft cream cheese
½ pound thinly sliced smoked salmon
1 red or orange bell pepper, thinly sliced
1½ cups shredded provolone cheese

Serves 4

1 10- or 12-inch Boboli pizza
    crust
1 cup pizza sauce
½ teaspoon dried oregano
    leaves
1 cup crumbled feta cheese
    with garlic and herbs
½ cup sliced black olives
2 cups shredded mozzarella
    cheese

Greek Pizza

Feta cheese, tomatoes, garlic, and olives give this pizza a Greek flair.
Serve it with a simple spinach salad and Grape and Melon Salad (page 200).

1. Preheat oven to 400°F. Place pizza crust on a cookie sheet and spread evenly with pizza sauce. Sprinkle with oregano. Arrange feta cheese and olives over sauce and top with mozzarella cheese.

2. Bake for 10 to 16 minutes or until crust is hot and crisp and cheese is melted and beginning to brown. Serve immediately.

Feta Cheese
Feta cheese usually comes cut into small blocks and packed in a brine solution. You can find several different varieties of flavored cheese, including garlic and herbs, sun-dried tomato, plain, peppercorn, basil and tomato, and low fat. Don't drain the brine before you use the cheese, because it helps preserve the cheese.

Meatball Pizza

This simple pizza can be made with cooked and drained ground beef or sausage instead of the meatballs. Serve with a green salad and carrot sticks.

Serves 4

1 14-inch prepared pizza crust
1½ cups pizza sauce
½ teaspoon dried oregano
    leaves
½ teaspoon dry mustard
½ 16-ounce bag frozen
    meatballs, thawed
1 cup frozen onion and bell
    pepper stir-fry combo
2 cups shredded pizza cheese

1. Preheat oven to 400°F. Place pizza crust on a cookie sheet. In small bowl, combine pizza sauce with oregano and dry mustard and mix well. Spread over pizza crust.

2. Cut meatballs in half, and arrange, cut-side down, on pizza sauce. Sprinkle with onion and bell pepper stir-fry combo, then with pizza cheese. Bake at 400°F for 18 to 23 minutes or until crust is golden brown and cheese has melted and begins to brown. Serve immediately.

Pizza Cheese
Pizza cheese is usually a blend of Cheddar, mozzarella, and provolone or Monterey Jack cheeses, and sometimes Parmesan or Romano. It's available preshredded in the dairy section of your supermarket. You can substitute Co-Jack cheese for the pizza cheese blend—it is a blend of Colby and Monterey Jack cheeses.

1 10-ounce container
    refrigerated pizza dough
2 tablespoons olive oil
½ teaspoon dried oregano
    leaves
2 cups cubed cooked Grilled
    Turkey Tenderloin (page
    112)
½ cup sour cream
2 tablespoons orange juice
1 green bell pepper, chopped
¼ teaspoon salt
⅛ teaspoon pepper

Orange Turkey Focaccia Sandwiches

*The combination of warm, freshly baked focaccia and
cold turkey filling is really wonderful. Serve with some
carrots sticks and potato chips for a great lunch.*

1. Preheat oven to 350°F. To make focaccia, unroll pizza dough and place
   on cookie sheet. Gently stretch to a 10" × 12" rectangle. Cut into eight
   5" × 3" rectangles and separate slightly. Press fingers into dough to
   dimple. In small bowl combine olive oil and oregano leaves and drizzle
   over dough. Bake for 14 to 18 minutes or until the focaccia pieces are
   light golden brown. Remove to wire racks.

2. Meanwhile, in medium bowl, combine turkey with remaining ingredients and blend well. Store in refrigerator while dough is baking, if necessary. When dough is baked, make sandwiches with the turkey filling
   and two rectangles of the baked focaccia. Serve immediately.

Focaccia Substitutions
*You can substitute any type of bread for the focaccia in this easy recipe.
Split croissants; toast split English muffins; use whole grain bread slices,
toasted or not; or try crusty French bread slices. The sandwiches made
with bread slices can be grilled on a dual-contact indoor grill until crisp
and brown.*

Seafood Pizza

You could add some vegetables like sliced mushrooms and chopped red or orange bell peppers to this elegant pizza.

Serves 4

1 14-inch prepared pizza crust
1 cup bottled four-cheese
   Alfredo sauce
½ teaspoon dried dill weed
1 cup cooked shrimp
1 cup lump crabmeat
1½ cups shredded mozzarella
   cheese

1. Preheat oven to 400°F. Place pizza crust on cookie sheet. Spread with Alfredo sauce and sprinkle with dill weed. Arrange shrimp and crabmeat on sauce, and sprinkle with mozzarella cheese.

2. Bake for 18 to 23 minutes or until crust is golden brown and cheese is melted and begins to brown. Serve immediately.

Open-Faced Chicken Sandwiches

These easy sandwiches can be made with any leftover meat: roast beef, ham, cooked turkey, or even shrimp.

Serves 4

4 whole wheat English
   muffins, split
2 cooked Mustard-Glazed
   Chicken Breasts (page
   120)
¾ cup double Cheddar
   Alfredo sauce (from
   10-ounce jar)
½ cup shredded carrots
¾ cup grated Parmesan
   cheese, divided

Preheat broiler. Toast English muffins under broiler and set on cookie sheet. Chop chicken breasts. In medium bowl, combine chicken with Alfredo sauce, shredded carrots, and ½ cup Parmesan cheese. Divide among English muffins and sprinkle with remaining ¼ cup Parmesan cheese. Broil 6 inches from heat source for 4 to 7 minutes, until sandwiches are hot and sauce is bubbling and begins to brown. Serve immediately.

Serves 4

1 cooked Herbed Steak
    (page 75)
1 cup jarred roasted red
    peppers, drained
8 slices French bread
2 cups shredded Muenster
    cheese
¼ cup butter

Grilled Steak Sandwiches

*Not only does this recipe stretch one steak to feed four people,
the combinations of flavors and textures are simply superb!*

Cut steak into ¼-inch-thick pieces against the grain. Slice the red peppers into strips. Place four bread slices on work surface and top each with ¼ cup cheese. Arrange one-fourth of the steak strips and red peppers on top of each. Top each with another ¼ cup cheese, then top with remaining bread slices. Spread butter on the outsides of the sandwiches. Grill on a dual-contact grill for 2 to 4 minutes, until sandwiches are hot and cheese is melted, or cook on a preheated griddle or skillet, turning once, about 5 to 6 minutes.

Slicing Bread for Sandwiches

When you're slicing French or Italian bread for sandwiches, be sure to cut the bread on the diagonal. That way there's more surface area and you get larger pieces to hold more filling ingredients. Use a serrated bread knife and grasp the bread firmly with your nondominant hand.

Chapter 11

Salads

2 tablespoons oil

1 10-ounce package frozen
   corn

1 green bell pepper, chopped

1 red bell pepper, chopped

2 tomatoes, chopped

¾ cup creamy garlic salad
   dressing

½ teaspoon dried Italian
   seasoning

½ teaspoon salt

⅛ teaspoon pepper

Roasted Corn Salad

*Roasting corn helps concentrate the sweetness of this
vegetable, and makes the kernels slightly chewy. It's
delicious mixed with crisp peppers and ripe tomatoes.*

1. Preheat oven to 400°F. Brush baking sheet with oil and set aside. Thaw corn under running water and drain well; dry with paper towels and spread onto prepared baking sheet. Roast at 400°F for 10 to 15 minutes, stirring once during cooking, until corn browns slightly around edges. Remove to serving bowl.

2. Add bell peppers and tomatoes and toss to mix. In small bowl, combine salad dressing, Italian seasoning, salt, and pepper and mix well. Drizzle over corn mixture and toss to coat. Serve immediately or cover and chill up to 8 hours.

Apple and Greens Salad

You can make the dressing ahead of time, but be sure to prepare the apples just before serving, or they will darken.

Serves 4

⅓ cup oil
3 tablespoons apple cider
    vinegar
¼ cup sugar
½ teaspoon celery seed
¼ teaspoon salt
⅛ teaspoon pepper
2 apples, cored and sliced
4 cups butter lettuce, torn
    into bite-sized pieces
1 cup curly endive

In small bowl, combine oil, vinegar, sugar, celery seed, salt, and pepper and mix well with wire whisk to blend. Place apples, lettuce, and endive in serving bowl and pour dressing over salad; toss gently to coat. Serve immediately.

Apple Varieties

Choose apple varieties according to whether you want a sweet or tart taste. Granny Smith apples are generally tart, while Golden Delicious and Red Delicious apples are sweeter. Gala apples have a sweet and honeylike taste, while Jonathans, McIntosh apples, and Cortlands are more tart.

Serves 4–6

1 pound fresh broccoli
1 cup sliced fresh mushrooms
3 strips bacon, cooked and
    crumbled
½ cup honey mustard salad
    dressing
½ cup cubed Swiss cheese

Broccoli Swiss Cheese Salad

*This salad is similar to a popular deli salad; to
make it identical, add some golden raisins.*

1. Cut florets from broccoli, and cut stems into 2-inch pieces. Place in heavy saucepan, cover with water, and bring to a boil. Simmer for 6 to 8 minutes, until broccoli is crisp-tender. Drain well and place in serving bowl.

2. Add mushrooms and bacon; toss gently. Drizzle with salad dressing and toss again. Sprinkle with cheese and serve.

Salad Substitutions
Salad recipes are made for substituting! Just about any vegetable can be substituted for another. Crumble cauliflower florets into a salad in place of mushrooms, slice crisp jicama as a substitute for bell peppers, and use blanched asparagus in place of green or wax beans (and vice versa!).

Greek Lentil Salad

This salad is a great choice for a light lunch or brunch. It's a vegetarian salad that offers complete protein with the combination of cracked wheat and lentils. Top it with some crumbled feta cheese for even more flavor.

1. Place cracked wheat in medium bowl and cover with boiling water. Set aside. In heavy skillet, combine lentils and 2 cups water and bring to a boil. Cover and simmer for 20 minutes, until tender; drain if necessary. Drain cracked wheat, if necessary. In small bowl, combine salad dressing and oregano.

2. Meanwhile, cut tomatoes in half, gently squeeze out the seeds, and chop. Peel cucumber, cut in half, remove seeds, and slice.

3. In serving bowl, combine cracked wheat, lentils, vegetables, and salad dressing; toss gently to coat and serve immediately.

Serves 6

¾ cup cracked wheat
1½ cups boiling water
¾ cup lentils
2 cups water
½ cup red wine vinaigrette salad dressing
¼ teaspoon dried oregano leaves
2 tomatoes
1 cucumber

Bacon and Spinach Salad

Baby spinach is wonderfully tender, with a rich and mild taste. It's perfect in this salad, accented with crisp bacon and creamy Havarti cheese.

1. In medium saucepan, cook bacon until crisp. Drain on paper towels until cool enough to handle, then crumble. Combine cooked bacon, spinach, and cheese in serving bowl.

2. In small bowl, combine mayonnaise, buttermilk, salt, and pepper and mix well with wire whisk to blend. Drizzle half of dressing over spinach mixture and toss to coat. Serve with remaining dressing.

Serves 6–8

4 strips bacon
1 pound baby spinach leaves
1 cup cubed Havarti cheese
½ cup mayonnaise
½ cup buttermilk
½ teaspoon seasoned salt
⅛ teaspoon white pepper

Serves 8

1 cantaloupe
2 cups green grapes
¼ cup honey
2 tablespoons lime juice
¼ teaspoon salt

Grape and Melon Salad

*This simple salad is the perfect accompaniment to a grilled steak,
or serve it for breakfast along with frozen waffles and maple syrup.*

1. Cut cantaloupe in half and scoop out seeds. Using a melon baller, remove the flesh from the rind. Place cantaloupe balls in a serving dish along with the grapes.

2. In small bowl, combine honey, lime juice, and salt and stir well with a wire whisk until combined. Drizzle over fruit mixture and serve.

About Cantaloupe
Cantaloupe flesh does not turn brown when exposed to air, so you can make this salad ahead of time. Ripe cantaloupes smell ripe, and they give slightly when pressed with the fingers. They should be firm and heavy for their size, with an even webbing over a greenish-gold skin.

Paella Rice Salad

Paella is a Spanish dish that combines rice with shrimp, sausages, chicken, peas, and saffron. This salad is a simplified version of the classic recipe.

Serves 4

1 cup uncooked long-grain
    rice
2 cups water
¼ teaspoon saffron threads
    (or ½ teaspoon turmeric)
1 cup frozen baby peas
1 cup sliced celery
½ pound cooked, shelled
    shrimp
⅔ cup creamy Italian salad
    dressing

1. In medium saucepan over high heat, combine rice, water, and saffron. Cover and bring to a boil; lower heat and cook for 15 to 20 minutes, until rice is tender. Stir in baby peas during final 3 minutes of cooking time. Remove from heat and let stand for 5 minutes, then fluff rice mixture with fork.

2. Place rice mixture in serving bowl and add celery and shrimp; toss gently. Drizzle with salad dressing and toss again, then serve, or cover and refrigerate up to 8 hours.

Refrigerated Salad Dressings

Browse through your grocery store's produce aisle and you'll find many flavors of refrigerated salad dressings. These dressings are usually richer than shelf-stable bottled dressings, and are made with fresh ingredients. They must be stored in the refrigerator; keep a supply of your favorites on hand.

2 cups cubed cooked chicken breast
1½ cups blueberries
3 nectarines, sliced
¾ cup mayonnaise
¼ cup mango chutney
½ teaspoon curry powder

Chicken Salad with Nectarines

Use any combination of fresh fruit in this simple and elegant salad. You can also try different flavors of chutney to vary the taste.

In serving bowl, combine chicken, blueberries, and nectarines and toss gently. In small bowl, combine mayonnaise, chutney, and curry powder and mix well. Spoon over chicken mixture and toss gently to coat. Serve immediately.

Chutney
Chutney is a cooked sauce made of fruit juices, dried fruits, and spices. You can usually find pineapple chutney, mango chutney, or cranberry chutney in the condiment aisle of your grocery store. There are also many recipes for making your own chutney; blueberry is a homemade favorite.

Serves 6

2 nectarines
2 cups sliced strawberries
2 cups blueberries
1 cup cubed Havarti cheese
½ cup poppy seed salad dressing

Fruit and Cheese Salad

The fruits of summer—strawberries, raspberries, melons, peaches, and blackberries—can all be used in this refreshing and beautiful salad.

Slice nectarines and discard pits. Combine with remaining ingredients in a serving bowl and toss gently to coat. Serve immediately or cover and refrigerate up to 2 hours before serving.

Wilted Lettuce Salad

This warm salad can be a meal in itself. Serve it with some Melty Cheese Bread (page 54) and fresh fruit for a light lunch or late-night supper.

⁓

Serves 4–6

1 head romaine lettuce
1 head butter lettuce
1 cup sliced cremini
    mushrooms
5 slices bacon
3 tablespoons apple cider
    vinegar
1 teaspoon sugar
½ teaspoon dry mustard
¼ teaspoon salt
⅛ teaspoon pepper

1. Wash lettuces, dry, and tear into bite-size pieces; place in serving bowl along with mushrooms. Cook bacon in heavy skillet over medium heat, turning frequently, until crisp. Remove bacon to paper towels to drain; crumble when cool enough to handle.

2. Remove pan from heat; drain all but ¼ cup bacon drippings from pan. Carefully add remaining ingredients and stir with wire whisk; return to medium heat and bring to a boil. Immediately pour over lettuces and mushrooms in salad bowl; toss to wilt lettuce. Sprinkle with bacon and serve immediately.

Cremini Mushrooms

Cremini mushrooms can be found in most supermarkets in the produce section. They are actually small portobello mushrooms, those large, dark mushrooms that are so perfect for grilling or stuffing. Creminis have more flavor than button mushrooms do; wipe them with damp paper towels, cut off the stem, and slice.

CHAPTER 11: SALADS

203

Serves 6

3 cucumbers
1 teaspoon salt
2 tablespoons sugar
1 6-ounce container lemon-
    flavored yogurt
⅓ cup sour cream
2 tablespoons lemon juice
1 teaspoon sugar
½ teaspoon dried thyme
    leaves
⅛ teaspoon white pepper

Lemon Cucumber Salad

*The cucumbers are sprinkled with salt and sugar before
dressing to draw out any sour taste and to reduce their
high water content, so the salad dressing isn't diluted.*

1. Peel cucumbers and slice thinly. Place in colander and sprinkle with salt and 2 tablespoons sugar. Let stand for 15 minutes, then toss cucumbers and press to drain out excess liquid. Rinse cucumbers, drain again, and press between paper towels to dry.

2. Meanwhile, in large bowl, combine yogurt, sour cream, lemon juice, 1 teaspoon sugar, thyme, and pepper and mix well to blend. Gently stir in drained cucumbers, then serve.

Summer Squashes

Summer squashes, like zucchini and yellow squash, are thin skinned and excellent eaten raw. They can be substituted for cucumbers or mushrooms in most salads. Unless the skins are waxed, they don't need to be peeled, just cut into sticks, julienne, cubes, or slices.

Turkey Waldorf Salad

Waldorf Salad is traditionally made of chopped apples and walnuts in a creamy dressing. Adding turkey to this salad elevates it to a main dish delight.

———

Serves 6

3 Granny Smith apples
1 cup golden raisins
1 cup coarsely chopped
   toasted walnuts
2 cups chopped cooked
   turkey breast
1½ cups mayonnaise
⅛ teaspoon allspice
⅛ teaspoon white pepper

Core apples and coarsely chop. Combine in medium bowl with raisins, walnuts, and turkey. In small bowl, combine mayonnaise, allspice, and pepper and blend well. Spoon over turkey mixture and toss to coat. Cover and refrigerate for 10 to 15 minutes to blend flavors. Store leftovers in refrigerator.

Toasting Walnuts

Toasting walnuts concentrates and brings out the flavor. To toast them, spread on a shallow baking sheet and bake in a 350°F oven for 10 to 15 minutes, stirring twice during baking time. Or microwave the nuts: place in a single layer on microwave-safe plate and heat at 100 percent power for 2 to 4 minutes, until fragrant.

Serves 6

8 cups salad greens
½ cup yogurt
½ cup mayonnaise
¼ cup buttermilk
⅓ cup chopped fresh basil
    leaves
½ teaspoon dried basil leaves
½ teaspoon salt
⅛ teaspoon white pepper

Greens with Basil Dressing

The dressing can be served with any green or vegetable salad. It will keep, well covered, in the refrigerator for about 3 to 4 days.

Place salad greens in a serving bowl. In a food processor or blender container, combine remaining ingredients. Process or blend until the basil leaves are very finely chopped. Drizzle dressing over the salad, toss, and serve.

Fresh and Dried Herbs
Using fresh and dried herbs in the same recipe is an easy way to increase the depth of flavor. Many dried herbs taste different than their fresh counterparts. Dried basil, for instance, has a smokier flavor than fresh. And dried thyme has a more intense mint flavor, while the fresh tends to be more lemony.

Simple Spinach Salad

This beautiful salad can be served with some Corn Bread (page 39) or hot biscuits for a simple lunch, or as a side dish for a casserole, soup, or stew.

Serves 4

4 cups baby spinach leaves
½ cup toasted pine nuts
1 cup frozen baby peas
1 cup grape tomatoes
½ cup basil vinaigrette salad dressing

Toss together spinach and pine nuts in serving bowl. Place peas in a colander and run hot water over them for 1 to 2 minutes to thaw. Drain well and add to spinach mixture along with grape tomatoes. Drizzle with half of the salad dressing and toss gently. Serve immediately with remaining dressing on the side.

Tiny Tomatoes

There are some new small tomatoes on the market. Grape tomatoes are about the size of grapes; they are sweet, tender, and juicy. Cherry tomatoes are less popular since grape tomatoes burst onto the scene, but they are still available; they come in red and yellow varieties. And sweet currant tomatoes are about half the size of cherry tomatoes.

Yields 6 cups

2 cups frozen soybeans
1 15-ounce can green beans,
  drained
1 15-ounce can wax beans,
  drained
¾ cup red wine vinaigrette
  salad dressing
2 tablespoons red wine
  vinegar
⅓ cup sugar
¼ teaspoon dried tarragon
  leaves
Dash black pepper

Three-Bean Salad

*Three-Bean Salad is typically marinated in a sweet and sour salad dressing.
You can use any combination of beans you'd like, selecting from green beans,
wax beans, kidney beans, chick peas, black beans, red beans, and soybeans.*

1. Bring large pot of water to a boil and cook frozen soybeans for 2 to 3 minutes, until tender. Drain and rinse with cold water. Combine in serving bowl with green beans and wax beans.

2. In small saucepan combine salad dressing, vinegar, sugar, tarragon, and pepper; whisk over low heat until sugar is dissolved. Pour over bean mixture and stir gently. Let stand for 10 minutes, then serve. Store leftovers in refrigerator.

Serves 6

1 10-ounce container basil
  pesto
½ cup mayonnaise
1 cup cubed smoked Gouda
  cheese
2 red bell peppers, chopped
1 18-ounce package frozen
  cheese tortellini

Pasta and Cheese Salad

*Of course, you can add any number of fresh vegetables to
this simple salad. Sliced mushrooms, yellow summer squash,
cucumbers, and spring onions would all be nice additions.*

Bring large pot of salted water to a boil. Meanwhile, in large bowl, combine pesto and mayonnaise and blend well. Stir in cheese and chopped peppers. Add tortellini to pot of water and cook according to package directions until done. Drain well and stir into cheese mixture. Serve immediately or cover and chill for 2 to 3 hours.

Smoked Turkey Fruit Salad

This delicious dressing, made by puréeing ripe strawberries with yogurt and minty thyme leaves, makes this salad simply spectacular.

Serves 6–8

1 quart strawberries
½ cup vanilla yogurt
¼ teaspoon salt
¼ teaspoon dried thyme
    leaves
1 ripe cantaloupe
2 cups chopped smoked
    turkey
1 pint raspberries

1. Wash and hull the strawberries and cut in half. In food processor or blender, combine yogurt, salt, thyme, and ½ cup of the sliced strawberries. Process or blend until smooth.

2. Cut cantaloupe in half and remove seeds. Cut flesh into chunks.

3. In serving bowl, combine remaining strawberries, cantaloupe, and turkey. Drizzle dressing over and toss gently to coat. Top with raspberries and serve.

Raspberries
Raspberries are a very delicate fruit. They must be used within a day or two of purchase. Do not rinse raspberries before you are ready to use them because they develop mold very easily. Never toss them with a salad; use them as a garnish on top.

Serves 6

2 tablespoons olive oil

2 cups chopped ham, divided

2 cups frozen bell pepper and
onion stir-fry combo

1 head romaine lettuce

1 cup mayonnaise

1 tablespoon brown sugar

2 tablespoons grated
Parmesan cheese

Layered Ham Salad

*Layered salads were big in the 1970s and 1980s.
They are a great choice for a buffet. Be sure to use a clear
glass serving dish so all the beautiful layers are visible.*

1. In heavy skillet, heat olive oil over medium heat. Add ¼ cup of the chopped ham; cook and stir until ham pieces are crisp around the edges. Remove ham to paper towel to drain. Add bell pepper and onion combo; cook and stir for 3 to 5 minutes, until vegetables are hot and tender.

2. Clean and chop romaine lettuce. In large bowl, layer half of the lettuce followed by half the bell pepper mixture and half the remaining 1¾ cups ham. Repeat layers.

3. In small bowl combine mayonnaise with sugar and cheese. Spread over top of salad and sprinkle with the fried ham bits. Serve immediately or cover and refrigerate for 2 to 3 hours before serving.

Sugared Almond Green Salad

Sugared almonds add wonderful crunch and flavor to this simple salad made with tender salad greens and sweet mandarin oranges.

———

Serves 4–6

2 tablespoons butter
½ cup sliced almonds
3 tablespoons sugar
6 cups mixed salad greens
1 15-ounce can mandarin
    oranges, drained, juice
    reserved
2 tablespoons reserved juice
    from oranges
½ cup honey mustard salad
    dressing

1. In small heavy saucepan, melt butter over medium heat until foaming. Stir in almonds; cook and stir for 2 to 4 minutes, until almonds begin to show color. Sprinkle sugar over almonds; cook and stir for another minute. Remove to paper towel to drain and cool.

2. In serving bowl, combine salad greens and drained oranges and toss gently. In small bowl, combine 2 tablespoons reserved orange juice and the salad dressing and whisk to blend. Drizzle over salad and top with sugared almonds.

Sugared Almonds
Sugared almonds are easy to make, but you must make sure to watch them carefully as they cook, and never leave the stove. They burn easily! Make a large batch and store them in an airtight container in a cool place. You can sprinkle them over many salads; try them on Ambrosia (page 212). They'll keep up to 3 weeks.

Serves 6

1 8-ounce container frozen whipped topping, thawed

⅓ cup reserved pineapple juice

1 cup cottage cheese

2 14-ounce cans mandarin oranges, drained

1 15-ounce can crushed pineapple, drained, reserving juice

1 cup shredded coconut

Ambrosia

Ambrosia is an old-fashioned salad that is sweet and delicious. It always includes oranges and coconut along with a sweet whipped dressing; the rest is up to you!

In serving bowl, combine whipped topping, reserved pineapple juice, and cottage cheese; stir with wire whisk until blended. Fold in remaining ingredients. Cover and chill for 15 minutes before serving. Store leftovers in refrigerator.

Whipped Cream or Frozen Topping?

You can use heavy cream, whipped until stiff with a few spoonfuls of powdered sugar, for the frozen whipped topping in this simple salad. If you are watching fat and calories, look for low-fat nondairy frozen whipped toppings in your grocery store's frozen-food aisle. Any frozen topping must thaw in the refrigerator for 6 to 8 hours.

Chapter 12

Side Dishes

1 12-ounce package
    refrigerated mashed
    potatoes
1 egg, beaten
¼ cup grated Parmesan
    cheese
2 tablespoons sour cream
½ teaspoon dried basil leaves
2 tablespoons milk
2 tablespoons grated
    Parmesan cheese

Duchess Potatoes

*This recipe is a great way to use up leftover mashed or riced potatoes.
You may need to add some more milk if you use leftover
homemade potatoes, since they can dry out when refrigerated.*

1. Preheat oven to 375°F. In large bowl, combine all ingredients except milk and 2 tablespoons Parmesan cheese and beat well until combined. Spoon or pipe mixture into 16 mounds onto parchment paper–lined cookie sheets. Brush with milk and sprinkle with 2 tablespoons Parmesan cheese.

2. Bake potatoes for 15 to 20 minutes or until tops are beginning to brown and potatoes are hot. Serve immediately.

Prepared Potatoes
You can find prepared refrigerated mashed potatoes in your supermarket's dairy aisle, or perhaps in one of the refrigerated endcaps at the end of the aisles. There are many different types of refrigerated prepared potatoes; look for hash brown potatoes and scalloped potatoes, too.

Risi Bisi

This Italian version of rice with peas is simple and delicious, the perfect side dish for a grilled steak.

⌐

Serves 6

2 tablespoons olive oil
1 onion, finely chopped
1½ cups long-grain rice
2 10-ounce cans chicken broth
½ cup water
1 cup frozen baby green peas
½ cup grated Parmesan cheese

1. In heavy saucepan, heat olive oil over medium heat. Add onion; cook and stir until onion is translucent. Add rice; cook and stir for 2 minutes. Add chicken broth and water and bring to a boil. Cover pan, reduce heat, and simmer mixture for 15 to 20 minutes, until rice is almost tender.

2. Add peas, cover, and cook over medium-low heat until peas are hot and rice is tender, 3 to 5 minutes. Stir in cheese and serve.

Lemon Pesto Pilaf

This simple pilaf has so much flavor and the most beautiful color. You can find prepared pesto in the refrigerated section of your supermarket, near the cheeses and eggs.

⌐

Serves 4–6

1 tablespoon butter
1 cup long-grain white rice
2 cups chicken or vegetable broth, heated
2 tablespoons lemon juice
½ teaspoon lemon zest
¼ cup prepared pesto

In heavy saucepan, melt butter over medium heat. Add rice; cook and stir for 3 to 4 minutes, until rice is opaque. Add broth, stir well, cover, bring to a boil, reduce heat to low, and simmer for about 15 to 20 minutes, until rice is tender. Stir in lemon juice, zest, and pesto; remove from heat and cover; and let stand for 3 to 4 minutes. Fluff rice with fork and serve.

Lemon Zest
Lemon zest is the outer skin of the lemon; use just the yellow part, because the white pith can be bitter. Lemon zesters and microplane graters are the best tools to use since they only remove the yellow part of the skin.

Serves 6

2 tablespoons olive oil
1 onion, finely chopped
3 cups frozen green beans
1 red bell pepper, cut into
    strips
1 tablespoon lemon juice
½ teaspoon salt
½ teaspoon dried thyme
    leaves

Green Beans with Red Peppers

*You can buy frozen julienned green beans or frozen cut green beans.
For this recipe, frozen cut green beans work best. The color combination
of the deep green beans and the bright red pepper is very festive.*

1. In heavy saucepan, heat olive oil over medium heat. Add onion; cook until onion is tender, stirring frequently.

2. Meanwhile, prepare green beans as directed on package and drain well. Add red bell pepper to saucepan with onions; cook and stir for 2 to 4 minutes, until tender. Add beans, lemon juice, salt, and thyme leaves; stir gently and cook until hot, about 2 to 3 minutes longer. Serve immediately.

How to Julienne Bell Peppers
To julienne bell peppers, hold them upright on a cutting board. Cut off the four sides of the pepper from the stem and core. Remove any extra seeds or ribs. Place each piece skin-side down on the cutting board and cut the peppers into thin strips. Discard stem and core.

Honey-Orange Carrots

These sweet-and-tart little carrots are perfect for a dinner party.
You can easily double or triple the recipe for a larger crowd.

Serves 4–6

1 16-ounce package baby
  carrots
2 cups water
2 tablespoons orange juice
  concentrate
2 tablespoons honey
2 tablespoons butter
¼ teaspoon dried thyme
  leaves

1. Rinse carrots and place in medium saucepan with water. Bring to a boil over high heat, then lower heat to medium and simmer carrots for 5 to 8 minutes, until just tender.

2. Drain carrots and return to pan. Stir in orange juice concentrate, honey, and butter; cook and stir over medium heat until sauce thickens and coats carrots, 2 to 4 minutes. Add thyme leaves and simmer for a minute, then serve.

Baby Carrots

Baby carrots are actually large carrots that have been carefully trimmed and shaped. They are sweeter than the carrots you remember from your childhood because they are a different variety that is bred to grow faster, longer, and with a higher sugar content.

*2 16-ounce cans sweet
   potatoes in syrup
½ cup brown sugar, divided
½ cup butter, divided
¼ cup reserved sweet potato
   liquid
½ cup chopped cashews
3 tablespoons flour
⅛ teaspoon nutmeg*

Praline Sweet Potatoes

*This recipe is excellent for an easy side dish for Thanksgiving. Since it takes
only about 20 minutes to make, you can prepare it just before serving.*

1. Drain sweet potatoes, reserving ¼ cup liquid. Place drained sweet
    potatoes in saucepan over medium heat along with ¼ cup brown sugar,
    ¼ cup butter, and ¼ cup reserved liquid. Mash potatoes as they heat,
    stirring frequently. Place in 1½-quart microwave-safe casserole.

2. In small bowl, combine cashews, remaining ¼ cup brown sugar, flour,
    and nutmeg and mix well. Melt remaining ¼ cup butter and add to
    cashew mixture; mix until crumbly and set aside.

3. Microwave potatoes on high power for 2 minutes, then stir well. Sprin-
    kle with cashew mixture and microwave on high 5 to 7 minutes longer
    or until potatoes are hot.

Sweet Potatoes

*Sweet potatoes are usually canned in a sweet syrup, but some are
canned in plain water; be sure to read the labels carefully. Sweet potatoes, whether canned or fresh, are a wonderful source of vitamins A and
C; in fact, one serving can provide more than 400 percent of the recom-
mended daily allowance of vitamin A.*

Glazed Squash

Acorn squash are green globes with scalloped sides. This dish is an excellent accompaniment to Cuban Pork Chops (page 124).

Serves 4

1 acorn squash
2 tablespoons water
2 tablespoons butter
2 tablespoons brown sugar
1 tablespoon honey
½ teaspoon dried tarragon leaves
½ teaspoon salt
⅛ teaspoon white pepper

1. Cut squash in half lengthwise and remove seeds and fibers from center. Place the squash halves cut side down on work surface and cut crosswise into 1-inch pieces. Place, skin-side down, in a microwave-safe 12" × 8" baking dish; sprinkle with 2 tablespoons water.

2. Cover with microwave-safe plastic wrap, vent one corner, and microwave on high power for 12 to 15 minutes, until flesh is almost tender when tested with fork. Uncover, drain if necessary, and let stand while assembling sauce.

3. In small microwave-safe bowl, combine remaining ingredients and microwave on high power for 2 minutes, then stir until sauce is smooth. Pour sauce over squash and microwave, uncovered, on high power for 3 to 4 minutes, until squash is tender, spooning sauce over squash twice during cooking time.

Winter Squash

Winter squash are hard-sided squashes that require cooking before they are edible. Acorn, butternut, delicata, buttercup, and pumpkin will all work in this easy microwave recipe. Any winter squash variety stores very well and will last up to 3 months if kept in a cool, dry place.

Serves 6–8

¼ cup olive oil
½ red onion, chopped
½ head red cabbage,
    chopped
2 tablespoons balsamic
    vinegar
½ teaspoon salt
⅛ teaspoon white pepper
2 Granny Smith apples, cored
    and sliced

Cabbage and Apples

*This dish is a perfect accompaniment to roasted pork
loin or smoked pork chops for a wonderful fall dinner.*

In heavy skillet, heat olive oil over medium heat. Add onion; cook and stir for
5 minutes, until crisp-tender. Add cabbage and vinegar; stir well. Cover and
cook over medium heat for 7 to 10 minutes, until cabbage is tender, stirring
once during cooking time. Sprinkle with salt and pepper and add apples.
Cover and cook for 3 to 4 minutes longer, until apples are hot and crisp tender. Serve immediately.

Preparing Cabbage
*To prepare cabbage, remove some of the tough or blemished outer leaves.
Using a large knife, cut cabbage in half through the center. Cut out the core
on both halves. Turn cabbage cut-side down and cut lengthwise. Cut crosswise, and cabbage will fall into bite-size pieces.*

Smashed Potatoes

When you cube potatoes they will cook in much less time.
This side dish is perfect to serve with a classic meatloaf.

Serves 6–8

6 russet potatoes
¼ cup butter
4 cloves garlic, minced
⅓ cup whole milk
½ teaspoon salt
1 tablespoon chopped fresh
    basil leaves

1. Peel potatoes and cut into 1-inch cubes; as you work, place the potatoes in a large saucepan filled with cold water. When all the potatoes are prepared, bring to a boil over high heat. Cover pan, lower heat, and simmer potatoes for 15 to 20 minutes, until potatoes are tender when pierced with fork.

2. Meanwhile, combine butter and garlic in small saucepan and cook over medium heat, stirring frequently, until garlic is fragrant and tender, about 2 minutes. Remove from heat. In another small saucepan, combine milk, salt, and basil and heat until steam forms.

3. When potatoes are tender, drain thoroughly, then return potatoes to hot pan and shake for 1 minute over medium heat. Add butter mixture and mash with a potato masher. Then add milk mixture and stir gently. Serve immediately.

The Fluffiest Mashed Potatoes

Adding butter to the potatoes before adding liquid helps ensure that the potatoes will be fluffy. The fat in the butter helps coat the starch granules in the potatoes so they don't absorb too much liquid and become sticky or gluey. Use this rule every time you make mashed or smashed potatoes for best results.

Serves 8

2 16-ounce packages frozen
    broccoli and cauliflower
    combo
1 16-ounce jar four-cheese
    Alfredo sauce
1 cup shredded Cheddar
    cheese
1½ cups soft bread crumbs
¼ cup butter, melted

Crispy Broccoli Casserole

This casserole is so good even your kids will like it!
Any vegetable is improved by being smothered in cheese
sauce and topped with crisp buttered bread crumbs.

Thaw vegetables according to package directions and drain thoroughly. Place in 13" × 9" glass baking dish. Top with the Alfredo sauce and sprinkle with the cheese. In medium bowl, combine bread crumbs and butter and toss to mix. Sprinkle over cheese. Bake casserole at 375°F for 20 to 23 minutes, until the sauce is bubbling, vegetables are hot, and bread crumbs begin to brown. Serve immediately.

Serves 6

2 tablespoons olive oil
1 onion, finely chopped
2 cups chicken or vegetable
    broth
½ teaspoon dried oregano
    leaves
½ teaspoon dried marjoram
    leaves
1 cup couscous

Herbed Couscous

Couscous actually isn't a grain; it is ground semolina pasta
that is usually precooked, so all you have to do is combine it
with boiling liquid and let stand until the liquid is absorbed.

In heavy skillet, heat olive oil over medium heat. Add onion; cook and stir until tender, about 5 minutes. Add chicken broth and herbs and bring to a rolling boil. Stir in couscous, then cover pan and remove from heat. Let stand for 5 to 10 minutes, or according to package directions, until liquid is absorbed. Fluff couscous mixture with fork and serve.

Grilled Asparagus

Grilling makes asparagus smoky and crisp tender. The combination of butter and olive oil adds extra richness.

——————————

1 pound asparagus
2 tablespoons butter
1 tablespoon garlic-flavored
    olive oil
1 teaspoon seasoned salt
⅛ teaspoon pepper

1. Hold asparagus spears between your hands and bend until they snap; discard the tough ends.

2. Prepare and preheat grill. In small saucepan, melt butter with oil, salt, and pepper. Brush asparagus with this mixture, then place on grill 6 inches from medium coals. Cover and grill asparagus, brushing frequently with butter mixture, for 5 to 9 minutes, until tender. Serve immediately.

Flavored Olive Oils
You can find flavored olive oils at gourmet and specialty shops, and in the regular supermarket. Garlic oil, lemon oil, and herb oils are a great way to add complex flavor with just one ingredient. Please do not make your own flavored oils; the risk of food poisoning is just too great because of the oil's anaerobic (oxygen-free) environment.

1 8-ounce package orzo
pasta
2 tablespoons butter
1 onion, finely chopped
3 cloves garlic, minced
½ teaspoon dried thyme
leaves
½ teaspoon salt
Dash pepper
½ cup grated Parmesan
cheese

Pasta Pilaf

*Orzo, or rosamarina pasta, is shaped like grains of rice. This recipe
is an excellent choice for people who have trouble cooking rice.*

1. Bring large pot of water to a boil and cook pasta according to package directions.

2. Meanwhile, melt butter in heavy saucepan and cook onion and garlic over medium heat for 4 to 5 minutes, until tender. Add thyme, salt, and pepper; cover; and remove from heat.

3. Drain the pasta thoroughly and add to onion mixture. Cook and stir over medium heat for 2 to 3 minutes, until hot and blended. Stir in Parmesan cheese and serve.

Orange Cauliflower

Tender cooked cauliflower florets are accented with orange juice that has been reduced to a syrupy sauce and flavored with marjoram. This is a great side dish to serve with roast chicken.

Serves 6

4 cups water
1 16-ounce package prepared
    cauliflower florets
2 tablespoons olive oil
1 onion, finely chopped
2 cloves garlic, minced
½ cup orange juice
½ teaspoon dried marjoram
    leaves
½ teaspoon salt
⅛ teaspoon white pepper

1. In large saucepan, place water and cauliflower florets. Bring to a boil over high heat, then cover, reduce heat to medium, and simmer for 6 to 7 minutes, until cauliflower is almost tender.

2. Meanwhile, in heavy skillet, heat olive oil over medium heat. Add onion and garlic and cook until tender. Add orange juice and seasonings and bring to a boil. Boil for a few minutes until slightly thickened.

3. When cauliflower is almost tender, drain well and add to orange juice mixture. Simmer for 2 to 4 minutes, spooning sauce over cauliflower, until sauce thickens and cauliflower is tender. Serve immediately.

About Cauliflower

Cauliflower is a cruciferous vegetable, related to broccoli. It is white because it grows wrapped in leaves that shield it from sunlight. The tender florets are creamy and mild when cooked, and crisp and tart when eaten raw. Look for cauliflower that is a creamy white color, with no discolored spots. It will keep in the refrigerator for 4 to 6 days.

Garlicky Green Beans

Serves 6

1 pound green beans
4 cups water
1 tablespoon olive oil
1 tablespoon butter
6 cloves garlic, peeled and
    chopped
1 shallot, peeled and chopped
½ teaspoon salt

*You can add more garlic to this simple and flavorful side
dish if you'd like. Just be sure to stir constantly while the garlic
and shallots are browning so they don't burn.*

1. Trim the ends off the green beans and cut each bean in half crosswise. Place in heavy saucepan and cover with water. Bring to a boil over high heat, then lower heat to medium and simmer for 5 to 8 minutes, until beans are crisp-tender.

2. Meanwhile, combine olive oil and butter in heavy saucepan and add garlic and shallot. Cook and stir over medium heat until the garlic is fragrant and turns light brown around the edges.

3. Drain beans and add to garlic mixture in pan along with salt. Cook and stir over medium heat for 2 to 3 minutes, until beans are coated. Serve immediately.

Types of Garlic
There are several forms of garlic that you can buy. Garlic powder is powdered dried garlic; ⅛ teaspoon is equal to one clove. Garlic salt is garlic powder combined with salt; ¼ teaspoon is equal to one clove. And garlic paste in a tube is puréed, concentrated garlic. One teaspoon is equal to one clove of garlic.

Roasted Sugar Snap Peas

You can sometimes find stringless sugar snap peas in the market. If you can't, to remove the string, cut off the very end of the pea, pull the string off and discard.

~~

Serves 6

3 cups sugar snap peas
2 tablespoons olive oil
½ teaspoon dried marjoram
   leaves
½ teaspoon garlic salt
⅛ teaspoon pepper

1. Preheat oven to 425°F. Remove strings from sugar snap peas, if desired. Place on baking sheet and sprinkle with remaining ingredients. Mix with your hands until the peas are coated.

2. Roast for 4 to 6 minutes, until peas just begin to brown in spots and are crisp-tender. Serve immediately.

About Sugar Snap Peas

Sugar snap peas are very sweet peas that are totally edible, including the pod. when purchasing, look for a bright green color with no dark or light spots and buy peas that are plump and crisp. Don't cook them too long; 2 to 3 minutes in boiling water is enough.

1 pound carrots
¾ cup water
¼ cup orange juice
1 tablespoon sugar
½ teaspoon salt
⅛ teaspoon white pepper
¼ teaspoon dried marjoram
*   leaves*
2 tablespoons butter

Braised Carrots

Braising means cooking food covered in a small amount of liquid until tender.
The liquid is then reduced to a syrup and poured over the food to serve.

1. Peel carrots and cut diagonally into 1½-inch chunks; set aside. In a heavy saucepan, combine remaining ingredients. Bring to a boil over medium heat.

2. Add carrots to the pan and cover. Reduce heat to low and simmer carrots, covered, for 5 to 8 minutes, until carrots are soft when pierced with a knife. Remove the carrots from the pan and place on serving plate. Increase heat to high and bring liquid to a boil. Boil for 3 to 5 minutes, until liquid is reduced and syrupy. Pour over carrots and serve.

Three-Bean Medley

This combination of beans is flavorful and delicious. And the sweet-and-sour salad dressing adds a nice punch of flavor. Serve it with a grilled steak and a mixed lettuce salad, with breadsticks on the side.

Serves 4–6

1 cup frozen green beans
1 cup frozen soybeans
1 cup frozen lima beans
½ cup sweet-and-sour salad dressing
¼ cup toasted pine nuts

1. Place the frozen green beans, soybeans, and lima beans in a heavy saucepan and cover with cold water. Bring to a boil, then reduce heat and simmer for 4 to 6 minutes, until all the beans are tender.

2. Drain beans thoroughly and return to saucepan. Add salad dressing and cook over medium heat until liquid comes to a boil and beans are glazed. Sprinkle with pine nuts and serve.

About Soybeans

Soybeans, also known as edamame, are grown in hairy pods; they are often served as a snack in the pod. The beans are high in complete protein and fiber and contain lots of isoflavones, which may help reduce the risk of cancer. And they taste great—nutty and sweet, with a buttery texture.

1 head broccoli, broken into
    florets
4 cups water
2 tablespoons olive oil
1 tablespoon butter
1 onion, chopped
3 cloves garlic, minced
2 tablespoons toasted
    sesame seeds

Broccoli Toss

*When broccoli is properly prepared, the florets are bright
green, tender, and mildly flavored. Serve this simple
side dish with a pasta casserole and a fresh fruit salad.*

1. Place broccoli florets in large saucepan and cover with water. Bring to a boil, then reduce heat and simmer, uncovered, for 5 to 7 minutes, until crisp-tender.

2. Meanwhile, place olive oil and butter in a skillet over medium heat. Add onion and garlic; cook and stir for 4 to 6 minutes, until crisp-tender.

3. Drain broccoli thoroughly and add to skillet with onion and garlic. Toss to coat broccoli with onion mixture. Sprinkle with sesame seeds, toss gently, and serve.

About Broccoli
The trick to cooking broccoli is to use a large amount of water and cook it, uncovered, very quickly. Use at least four cups of water for each head of broccoli. Follow these steps and your broccoli will be crisp-tender and mildly flavored.

Roasted Baby Beets

You can find baby beets in gourmet stores and farmer's markets. Look for candy cane beets, which are red and white striped, golden beets, or white beets.

Serves 4–6

1 pound baby beets
2 tablespoons olive oil
½ teaspoon salt
⅛ teaspoon pepper
3 tablespoons butter
1 tablespoon fresh oregano
    leaves

Preheat oven to 400°F. Cut off beet tops and root, if attached; scrub beets thoroughly. Cut beets in half. Place beets in large roasting pan and drizzle with olive oil; sprinkle with salt and pepper. Toss to coat. Roast for 20 to 25 minutes or until beets are tender when pierced with a fork. Place in serving bowl and toss with butter and oregano leaves until butter is melted. Serve warm.

Crunchy Puréed Squash

Frozen puréed squash is a fabulous convenience food that saves, literally, hours of work in the kitchen. This hearty side dish is perfect for Thanksgiving.

Serves 6

1 12-ounce package frozen
    puréed winter squash
¼ cup orange juice
2 tablespoons maple syrup
½ teaspoon salt
Dash white pepper
1 cup granola

In large saucepan, combine the frozen squash with orange juice and bring to a simmer. Cook for 6 to 8 minutes, until the squash begins to thaw. Stir in maple syrup, salt, and pepper; continue cooking for 3 to 4 minutes longer, until squash is hot and smooth. Place in 2-quart casserole dish and sprinkle with granola. Bake at 400°F for 12 to 15 minutes, until hot and granola browns slightly.

Serves 6

1 pound baby red-skinned
    potatoes
¼ cup butter
3 cloves garlic, minced
2 tablespoons fresh thyme
    leaves
2 tablespoons chopped fresh
    parsley
½ teaspoon salt
⅛ teaspoon white pepper

Herbed Baby Potatoes

*Baby potatoes cook quickly because they are so small. Removing a strip
of skin from the middle of the potatoes prevents splitting as they cook.*

1. Peel a strip of skin from the middle of each potato. Place in large pot
   and cover with cold water. Cover and bring to a boil over high heat.
   Uncover, lower heat, and cook potatoes until tender when pierced with
   a fork, about 12 to 14 minutes.

2. Meanwhile, combine butter and garlic in a small saucepan. Cook over
   medium heat for 2 to 3 minutes, until garlic is fragrant. Remove from
   heat.

3. When potatoes are done, drain thoroughly, then return potatoes to the
   hot pot. Let stand off the heat for 2 to 3 minutes, shaking occasionally.
   Place pot over medium heat and pour butter mixture over potatoes.
   Sprinkle with remaining ingredients, toss gently, then serve.

Preparing Fresh Herbs

*To prepare herbs with tiny leaves, like oregano, rosemary, marjoram,
and thyme, simply pull the leaves backward off the stem; chop if desired.
Herbs with larger leaves, like sage, mint, and basil, should be rolled into
a log and julienned.*

Chapter 13

Soup Recipes

Serves 6

1 tablespoon olive oil
1 onion, finely chopped
1 10-ounce container
   refrigerated Alfredo
   sauce
1½ cups chicken or vegetable
   broth
1½ cups whole milk
2 14-ounce cans diced
   tomatoes, undrained
½ teaspoon dried basil leaves
¼ teaspoon dried marjoram
   leaves

Tomato Bisque

A bisque is a rich soup that combines vegetables, stock, and milk or cream. Serve for lunch with some chewy breadsticks and a mixed fruit salad.

1. In heavy saucepan, heat olive oil over medium heat and add onion. Cook and stir until onion is tender, about 4 minutes. Add Alfredo sauce and chicken broth; cook and stir with wire whisk until mixture is smooth. Add milk and stir; cook over medium heat for 2 to 3 minutes.

2. Meanwhile, purée undrained tomatoes in food processor or blender until smooth. Add to saucepan along with seasonings and stir well. Heat soup over medium heat, stirring frequently, until mixture just comes to a simmer. Serve immediately.

Alfredo Sauce

Alfredo sauce is basically a white sauce, usually with some cheese added. You can find it in the refrigerated dairy section of your supermarket. It can also be found on the pasta aisle. In addition to Alfredo sauce, four-cheese sauce, cheddar pasta sauce, and roasted garlic Parmesan pasta sauce are available.

Super-Quick Beef Vegetable Stew

*There are so many types of fully prepared meat entrées in
your grocery store; browse the selection and stock up!*

Serves 6

3 tablespoons olive oil
1 onion, chopped
3 cloves garlic, minced
1 16-ounce package prepared
    roast beef in gravy
1 16-ounce package frozen
    mixed vegetables
1 10-ounce can cream of
    mushroom soup
2 cups water
½ teaspoon dried thyme
    leaves

1. In heavy large saucepan, heat olive oil over medium heat. Add onion and garlic; cook and stir until tender, 4 to 5 minutes. Meanwhile, cut the cooked roast beef into 1-inch chunks. Add to saucepan along with gravy, frozen mixed vegetables, soup, water, and thyme leaves.

2. Cook over medium-high heat until soup comes to a boil, about 7 to 9 minutes. Reduce heat to low and simmer for 6 to 7 minutes longer, until vegetables and beef are hot and tender. Serve immediately.

Soup or Stew?

The difference between soup and stew is the thickness of the liquid. Soups are generally thin, sometimes made with just broth or stock. Stews have ingredients that thicken the liquid, including potatoes, flour, cornstarch, or puréed vegetables. You can make any soup into a stew by adding some cornstarch dissolved in water.

Serves 6–8

1 pound sweet Italian bulk
  sausage
1 8-ounce package sliced
  mushrooms
4 cloves garlic, minced
3 14-ounce cans beef broth
1½ cups water
1 teaspoon dried Italian
  seasoning
⅛ teaspoon pepper
1 24-ounce package frozen
  cheese tortellini

Tortellini Soup

*This rich soup is full of flavor. Serve it with some water crackers,
a chopped vegetable salad, and melon slices.*

1. In large saucepan over medium heat, brown sausage with mushrooms
   and garlic, stirring to break up sausage. When sausage is cooked, drain
   thoroughly. Add broth, water, Italian seasoning, and pepper to saucepan and bring to a boil over high heat. Reduce heat to low and simmer
   for 8 to 10 minutes.

2. Stir in frozen tortellini and cook, stirring frequently, over medium-high
   heat for 6 to 8 minutes or until tortellini are hot and tender. Serve immediately.

Frozen or Refrigerated Tortellini?

*Refrigerated, or fresh, tortellini is found in the dairy aisle of the regular
grocery store. It is generally more expensive than the frozen, and
package sizes are smaller. Frozen tortellini and tortelloni take a bit
longer to cook. Choose your favorite and stock up.*

Cheesy Clam Chowder

This rich, thick, and super easy chowder can be made with any other seafood too. Think about using canned oysters, canned mussels, frozen cooked shrimp, or lump crabmeat.

Serves 6–8

2 10-ounce cans condensed broccoli cheese soup
2 cups half-and-half
2 cups milk
3 cups refrigerated hash brown potatoes
½ teaspoon dried marjoram
2 8-ounce cans clams, undrained
⅛ teaspoon pepper

Combine soup, half-and-half, and milk in large heavy saucepan. Bring to a boil, then add potatoes and marjoram. Bring to a boil again, reduce heat, and simmer for 15 minutes. Add clams and pepper and simmer for 5 to 10 minutes longer, until soup is hot and blended. Serve immediately.

Cheesy Shrimp Chowder

This rich chowder is very simple to make and has a wonderful rich flavor. Serve it with tiny oyster crackers, a baby spinach salad, and oatmeal cookies for dessert.

Serves 6

2 tablespoons olive oil
1 onion, finely chopped
2 cups frozen hash brown potatoes
1½ cups water
2 6-ounce cans medium shrimp, drained
1 16-ounce jar four-cheese Alfredo sauce
1 15-ounce can evaporated milk

1. In large saucepan, heat olive oil over medium-high heat. Add onion; cook and stir until tender, about 4 to 5 minutes. Add potatoes and water; bring to a boil, cover, lower heat, and simmer for 5 minutes, until potatoes are hot and tender.

2. Add shrimp, Alfredo sauce, and evaporated milk to saucepan. Stir well and heat over medium heat until the soup comes to a simmer; do not boil. Serve immediately.

Serves 6

1 26-ounce jar double
    cheddar pasta sauce
2 14-ounce cans chicken
    broth
2 15-ounce cans corn, drained
2 9-ounce packages frozen
    cooked Southwest-style
    chicken strips
½ teaspoon dried Italian
    seasoning
2 cups shredded sharp
    Cheddar cheese

Chicken Corn Chowder

Open four packages and grate some cheese, and you'll have a hearty, hot soup on the table in about 15 minutes. Serve with some crackers and fresh fruit.

In large saucepan, combine all ingredients except cheese and bring to a boil over medium-high heat. Reduce heat to low, cover, and simmer for 6 to 8 minutes, until chicken is hot. Stir in Cheddar cheese, remove from heat, and let stand, covered, for 3 to 4 minutes. Stir thoroughly and serve.

Frozen Precooked Chicken
There are lots of varieties of frozen precooked chicken in your supermarket's meat aisle. You can find cooked grilled chicken, chicken strips, and chopped chicken in flavors that range from Southwest to plain grilled. Some varieties come with a sauce; be sure to read the label to make sure you're getting what you want.

Savory Minestrone

Minestrone is a rich vegetable soup made with beans and pasta. It's really a meal in one bowl; serve with some toasted garlic bread and tall glasses of milk.

~

Serves 6

4 cups chicken broth
1 16-ounce package frozen mixed vegetables
1 15-ounce can cannellini beans, drained
½ teaspoon dried basil leaves
½ teaspoon dried oregano leaves
1 14-ounce can diced tomatoes with garlic, undrained
1½ cups elbow macaroni

In large saucepan, combine chicken broth and vegetables; bring to a boil over medium-high heat. When broth boils, add beans, basil, oregano, and tomatoes. Bring to a simmer, lower heat, and cook for 5 minutes. Add macaroni; stir and simmer for 8 to 9 minutes, until pasta is tender, then serve.

Canned Beans

Canned beans are a great convenience food to have on hand, but they do tend to be high in sodium. To reduce sodium, drain the beans, place them in a strainer or colander, and run cold water over them. Drain well again and use in the recipe.

Serves 6

2 tablespoons olive oil
1 onion, chopped
1 16-ounce package cooked
    ground beef in taco sauce
2 15-ounce cans chili beans,
    undrained
2 cups frozen corn
1 14-ounce can Mexican-
    flavored chopped
    tomatoes, undrained
2 cups water
1 tablespoon chili powder
½ teaspoon cumin
⅛ teaspoon cayenne pepper

Mexican Beef Stew

Serve this rich stew topped with a dollop of sour cream and some chopped avocados or guacamole for a cooling contrast.

In large saucepan, heat olive oil over medium heat. Add onion; cook and stir until crisp-tender, about 3 to 4 minutes. Add remaining ingredients and stir well. Bring to a simmer, reduce heat to medium-low, and cook for 10 to 15 minutes, until corn is hot and soup has thickened slightly. Serve immediately.

Spices
Spices have a shelf life of about a year; after that time, they lose flavor and intensity and should be replaced. To keep track, write the purchase date on the can or bottle, using a permanent marker. Periodically, go through your spice drawer or rack and discard older spices; be sure to write the ones you need on your grocery list.

French Onion Soup

Because the onions need to sauté for a fairly long time to develop caramelization, this recipe starts with frozen chopped onions. You can chop fresh onions, but the recipe will take longer than 30 minutes.

~

Serves 6

2 tablespoons olive oil
2 tablespoons butter
2 10-ounce packages frozen
    chopped onions
2 tablespoons flour
2 16-ounce boxes beef stock
6 slices French bread
¼ cup butter, softened
1½ cups shredded Gruyère
    cheese

1. In large saucepan, combine olive oil and 2 tablespoons butter over medium heat until butter is foamy. Add onions; cook over medium heat for 10 to 12 minutes, stirring frequently, until onions brown around edges. Sprinkle flour over onions; cook and stir for 2 to 3 minutes.

2. Stir in stock, bring to a simmer, and cook for 10 minutes. Meanwhile, spread French bread slices with ¼ cup butter. In toaster oven, toast the bread until browned and crisp. Sprinkle with cheese and toast for 2 to 4 minutes, until cheese melts. Divide soup among soup bowls and float the toasted cheese bread on top.

Boxed Stocks
If your grocery store carries boxed stocks, buy them. These stocks tend to be richer and less salty than canned stocks. If you don't use all of the stock, these boxes come with a flip-top lid so you can close the box and store them in the refrigerator for a couple of weeks.

Serves 6

1 16-ounce package frozen
   meatballs
2 cups 8-vegetable juice
2 cups frozen mixed
   vegetables
1 10-ounce can beef broth
3 cups water
½ teaspoon dried Italian
   seasoning
⅛ teaspoon pepper
1½ cups mini penne pasta

Vegetable Meatball Soup

*Frozen cooked meatballs are available in several flavors;
choose plain or Italian-style for this super-easy recipe.*

In large saucepan or stockpot, combine all ingredients except pasta and mix gently. Bring to a boil over high heat, then stir in pasta, reduce heat to medium-high, and cook for 9 to 11 minutes, until meatballs are hot, vegetables are hot, and pasta is tender. Serve immediately.

Substituting Pasta
You can substitute one shape of pasta for another as long as they are about the same size and thickness. Whichever pasta you choose, be sure to cook it al dente; this means cooked through, but with a firm bite in the center.

Pressure-Cooker Beef Stew

This stew tastes like it simmered for hours on your stove, but the pressure cooker makes quick work of the recipe. Serve with some crusty bread to soak up the wonderful sauce.

Cut steak into 1-inch cubes. Sprinkle meat with flour, garlic salt, and pepper and toss to coat. Heat oil in the pressure cooker and brown the coated beef, stirring frequently, about 5 to 7 minutes. Add remaining ingredients and lock the lid. Bring up to high pressure and cook for 20 minutes. Release pressure using quick-release method and stir stew. Serve immediately.

Serves 8

2 pounds bottom-round steak
3 tablespoons flour
½ teaspoon garlic salt
⅛ teaspoon pepper
3 tablespoons olive oil
3 russet potatoes, cubed
1 16-ounce package baby carrots
½ teaspoon dried thyme leaves
½ teaspoon dried oregano leaves
4 cups beef stock, heated
1 14-ounce can diced tomatoes with garlic, undrained

Tex-Mex Cheese Soup

As with all Tex-Mex foods, serve this hearty soup with salsa, sour cream, chopped avocado or guacamole, and crumbled crisp tortilla chips.

1. In heavy saucepan, heat olive oil over medium heat. Add onion; sauté until crisp-tender, about 3 to 4 minutes. Sprinkle taco seasoning mix over the onions and stir, then add corn, chicken broth, and water. Bring to a simmer and cook for 10 minutes, stirring occasionally.

2. Meanwhile, in medium bowl, toss cheese with flour. Add to soup and lower heat; cook and stir for 2 to 3 minutes, until cheese is melted and soup is thickened. Serve immediately.

Serves 4

2 tablespoons olive oil
1 onion, chopped
1 1.25-ounce envelope taco seasoning mix
1 15-ounce can creamed corn
2 10-ounce cans condensed chicken broth
1½ cups water
2 cups shredded Pepper Jack cheese
2 tablespoons flour

1 16-ounce package pork
roast au jus
1 4-ounce can chopped green
chilies, undrained
2 14-ounce cans chicken
broth
1 tablespoon chili powder
1 teaspoon ground cumin
½ teaspoon dried oregano
leaves
1 15-ounce can hominy,
drained
2 cups frozen corn
3 tablespoons flour
½ cup water

Quick Posole

*Posole is a Mexican stew made with hominy, green chilies,
and cubes of tender pork. Serve it with some blue corn tortilla
chips, guacamole, sour cream, and a green salad.*

1. Remove pork from package and cut into 1-inch cubes. Combine in large saucepan along with juice from pork, chilies, broth, chili powder, cumin, oregano, hominy, and frozen corn. Bring to a boil over high heat, then reduce heat to low, cover, and simmer for 12 to 15 minutes, until pork is hot and tender.

2. In small jar, combine flour and water and shake well to blend. Stir into stew and raise heat to medium. Cook and stir until stew thickens, about 5 to 8 minutes. Serve immediately.

Hominy

Hominy is made by removing the bran and germ from kernels of corn. It can be made by soaking the corn kernels in a weak solution of lye and water, or by physically crushing the corn. Yellow hominy is generally sweeter than the white. You can substitute barley for it in any recipe if you'd like.

Cold Pea Soup

This elegant soup is perfect for a hot summer evening. Serve it with some crisp croutons, a fruit gelatin salad, and some popovers fresh from the oven.

Serves 4

1 16-ounce package frozen
    baby peas
1 avocado, peeled and
    chopped
1 tablespoon lemon juice
2 cups chicken broth
½ teaspoon salt
⅛ teaspoon white pepper
¼ cup chopped mint

Place frozen peas in a colander and run cold water over them for 2 to 3 minutes to thaw, tossing occasionally. Place in blender container or food processor along with avocado and sprinkle with lemon juice. Add chicken broth, salt, and pepper and process until smooth. Pour into serving bowl and sprinkle with chopped mint.

Baby Peas

Try to find baby peas in the frozen aisle of your supermarket. They are much more tender than regular peas and have a sweet, fresh flavor. Do not cook them before adding to recipes; when adding to a pasta recipe, drain the pasta over the peas in a colander, or add them to a soup at the very end of the cooking time.

Serves 6

2 tablespoons olive oil

1 onion, chopped

3 cloves garlic, minced

2 15-ounce cans black beans, drained and rinsed

1 14-ounce can diced tomatoes with green chilies

2 14-ounce cans chicken broth

½ teaspoon cumin

⅛ teaspoon white pepper

Black Bean Soup

Serve this delicious soup with sour cream and chopped avocado for toppings, a spinach salad, and crisp breadsticks.

In heavy saucepan, heat olive oil over medium heat. Add onion and garlic; cook and stir for 3 to 4 minutes, until crisp-tender. Meanwhile, place black beans in a colander, rinse, and drain thoroughly. Using a potato masher, lightly mash some of the beans. Add all beans to saucepan along with remaining ingredients. Bring to a simmer; cook for 10 to 12 minutes, until blended.

Dried Beans

You can substitute dried beans for canned to reduce sodium. Rinse the beans and sort to remove any dirt or pebbles. Cover with cold water, bring to a boil, and boil for 1 minute. Cover and let stand for 1 hour. Drain the beans and cover with cold water. Simmer for about 2 hours, until beans are tender.

Potato Soup

*This creamy and rich soup uses two kinds of potatoes for
a nice depth of flavor. Serve with Green Beans with
Red Peppers (page 216) and Cheese Crackers (page 40).*

Serves 6

4 slices bacon
1 onion, chopped
1 5-ounce package cheese-
scalloped potato mix
3 cups water
1 15-ounce can evaporated
milk
2 cups frozen hash brown
potatoes
½ teaspoon dried dill weed
⅛ teaspoon white pepper

In heavy saucepan, cook bacon until crisp. Remove bacon, drain on paper towels, crumble, and set aside. Cook onion in bacon drippings until tender, about 5 minutes. Add potato mix and seasoning packet from potato mix along with remaining ingredients. Bring to a boil and simmer for 17 to 20 minutes, until potatoes are tender. If desired, purée using an immersion blender. Sprinkle with bacon and serve.

Precooked Bacon?

When recipes call for crumbled bacon, you can use the precooked version. But if the recipe calls for cooking the bacon and using the bacon fat to sauté other ingredients, you must used uncooked bacon. Or you can use the precooked bacon and use butter or olive oil as a substitute for the bacon fat.

2 tablespoons olive oil
1 onion, chopped
1 1.25-ounce package taco seasoning mix
1 15-ounce can kidney beans, drained
1 15-ounce can black beans, drained
2 14-ounce cans diced tomatoes with green chilies, undrained
1 cup water

Two-Bean Chili

This vegetarian chili can be varied so many ways. Add more beans, salsa, cooked ground beef or pork sausage, jalapeño peppers, or tomato sauce.

In heavy saucepan over medium heat, add olive oil and sauté onion until tender, about 4 to 5 minutes. Sprinkle taco seasoning mix over onions; cook and stir for 1 minute. Add drained but not rinsed beans, tomatoes, and water. Bring to a simmer; cook for 10 to 12 minutes, until thickened and blended.

Taco Seasoning Mix
You can make your own taco seasoning mix by combining 2 tablespoons chili powder, 2 teaspoons onion powder, 2 tablespoons cornstarch, 1 teaspoon dried oregano, 1 teaspoon dried red pepper flakes, 2 teaspoons salt, and ½ teaspoon cumin. Blend well and store in a cool dry place: 2 tablespoons equals one envelope mix.

Bean and Bacon Soup

This simple soup is great for kids' lunch boxes. Pack into an insulated thermos and provide some cheese crackers, baby carrots, and shredded Cheddar cheese for topping the soup.

~

Serves 4–6

1 8-ounce package bacon
1 onion, chopped
1 14-ounce can diced tomatoes, undrained
2 15-ounce cans pinto beans, drained
2 cups chicken broth

In large saucepan, cook bacon until crisp. Drain bacon on paper towels, crumble, and set aside. Drain off all but 2 tablespoons bacon drippings. Cook onion in drippings over medium heat for 3 to 4 minutes. Add remaining ingredients and bring to a simmer. Simmer for 10 to 12 minutes, then use a potato masher to mash some of the beans. Add reserved bacon, stir, and simmer for 5 minutes longer. Serve immediately or pour into warmed insulated thermoses and store up to 6 hours.

Sweet-and-Sour Pork Stew

Serve this delicious stew with a mixed lettuce salad, some crisp breadsticks, with a bakery layer cake for dessert.

~

Serves 4–6

2 tablespoons olive oil
1 onion, chopped
1 red bell pepper, chopped
1 8-ounce can pineapple tidbits, undrained
1 16-ounce package cooked sweet-and-sour pork
2½ cups water
½ cup long-grain rice
2 tablespoons cornstarch
⅓ cup water

1. In large saucepan, heat olive oil over medium heat. Add onion; cook and stir for 3 minutes until crisp-tender. Add red bell pepper; cook and stir for 2 to 3 minutes longer. Add undrained pineapple, pork with sauce, and 2½ cups water. Bring to a simmer, stir in rice, and cook for 10 minutes.

2. Meanwhile, in small bowl, combine cornstarch and ⅓ cup water and mix well. Stir into stew; cook and stir over medium heat for 5 to 8 minutes, until rice is tender and stew is thickened. Serve immediately.

5 cups chicken broth
1 cup shredded carrots
½ cup grated onion
2 eggs
1 egg yolk

Egg Drop Soup

*Because this soup is so simple it demands the best chicken stock.
Try to find the boxed chicken stock at your grocery store,
or order it online. You can also make your own stock.*

1. In heavy saucepan, combine chicken broth, carrots, and onion. Bring to a simmer; cook for 3 to 5 minutes, until vegetables are tender. Meanwhile, in small bowl, place eggs and egg yolk; carefully remove the chalazae (the white ropy strand that connects the egg white and the yolk). Beat eggs and egg yolk with a fork until smooth; do not overbeat.

2. Remove the saucepan from the heat. Using a fork, drizzle the egg mixture into the soup. When all the egg is added, stir the soup for 30 seconds, then serve immediately.

Make Your Own Chicken Stock

This recipe takes some time, but you can freeze it and it will add lots of flavor to your recipes. Cover one stewing chicken, some chopped onion, carrots, 1 bay leaf, some parsley, and celery with water and simmer for 3 to 4 hours. Strain broth, cool, pour into ice cube trays, and freeze, then package the cubes in freezer bags.

Chapter 14

Cookies and Candies

Serves 9

1 14-ounce package rich and
   fudgy brownie mix
⅓ cup sugar
1 egg
1 3-ounce package cream
   cheese, softened
1 cup semisweet chocolate
   chips

Layered Brownies

*Cream cheese and brownies are natural partners. This is a dual-use recipe;
you end up with layered brownies for tonight's dessert, and plain
brownies for this weekend's Brownie Parfait (page 281).*

1. Preheat oven to 375°F. Spray two 9" square pans with baking spray and
   set aside.

2. Prepare brownie mix as directed on package. Pour half of batter into
   one prepared pan and set aside. In small bowl, combine sugar, egg,
   and cream cheese and beat until smooth and blended.

3. Pour half of remaining brownie batter into second prepared pan. Top
   with cream cheese mixture, and pour last part of brownie batter over
   cream cheese mixture; marble with a knife.

4. Bake both pans of brownies for 19 to 22 minutes or until tops look dry
   and shiny. Remove from oven and immediately sprinkle cream cheese
   brownies with the chocolate chips; cover that pan with foil and let
   stand for a few minutes. Remove foil and spread chips evenly over
   brownies. Let cool completely. Cover and reserve plain brownies for
   the Brownie Parfait (page 281) or tuck into lunchboxes.

Low-Fat Products in Baking
*You can use low-fat cream cheese, low-fat milk, and low-fat sour cream
in baking, but do not use low-fat or whipped margarines or butter.
Those ingredients can contain a lot of water, which will ruin the struc-
ture of your baked products.*

No-Flour Peanut Butter Cookies

Believe it or not, these cookies turn out wonderfully with absolutely no flour of any kind! Do not use the refrigerated, or natural, type of peanut butter because the cookies will spread too much when they bake.

Yields 48 cookies

2 cups peanut butter
2 cups sugar
2 eggs
1 teaspoon vanilla
½ cup chopped peanuts
1 cup miniature semisweet chocolate chips

1. Preheat oven to 325°F. Line cookie sheets with parchment paper or Silpat silicon liners; set aside. In large bowl, combine peanut butter, sugar, eggs, and vanilla and mix well until blended. Stir in peanuts and chocolate chips.

2. Drop by teaspoonfuls onto prepared cookie sheets. Bake for 12 to 15 minutes, until cookies are just set. Cool for 5 minutes on cookie sheets, then carefully remove to wire racks to cool.

M&M's Cookies

You can use this basic formula to make an almost infinite variety of cookies. Use chocolate cake mix with walnuts, white cake mix with mini chocolate chips, or spice cake mix with raisins.

Yields 3 dozen cookies

1 18-ounce package yellow cake mix
1 cup quick-cooking oats
¼ cup butter, softened
2 eggs, beaten
1½ cups plain M&M's candies

Preheat oven to 350°F. In a large bowl, combine all ingredients except candies and beat until blended. Stir in candies, then drop mixture by tablespoons onto Silpat-lined cookie sheets. Bake for 12 to 15 minutes or until cookies are set. Let cool for 5 minutes on cookie sheets, then remove to wire racks to cool.

Yields 3 cups

1 cup brown sugar
½ cup sugar
⅓ cup orange juice
3 tablespoons butter, melted
1 teaspoon vanilla
3 cups mixed nuts

Candied Nuts

*Candied nuts are a wonderful snack to have on hand for the holiday season;
they also make great gifts packaged in decorative tins or glass jars.*

1. Preheat oven to 350°F. Grease a large cookie sheet with butter and set aside. Grease 2 large sheets of foil with butter and set aside.

2. In large bowl, combine brown sugar, sugar, orange juice, melted butter, and vanilla and mix well. Add nuts and toss to coat. Spread onto prepared cookie sheet. Bake for 10 to 15 minutes or until nuts are dark golden brown and sugar mixture bubbles. Stir nuts twice during cooking time. Immediately place nuts onto buttered foil, spreading thinly. Let cool, then break nuts apart before storing in airtight container.

Storing Nuts
Many nuts should be stored in the freezer before use, because the oils they contain can turn rancid quickly at room temperature. Pour the nuts into a freezer container such as a heavy-duty resealable freezer bag or a hard-sided plastic container, label, and freeze up to 6 months.

Marshmallow Treats

This is a twist on the traditional combination of Rice Krispie bars. Peanut butter and chocolate are added to toasted rice flakes cereal and it is formed around large marshmallows; the finished cookies look like popcorn balls.

———

Yields 12 cookies

4 cups miniature
    marshmallows
¼ cup peanut butter
2 tablespoons butter
4 cups toasted rice flakes
    cereal
1 cup miniature chocolate
    chips
12 large marshmallows

1. Combine miniature marshmallows, peanut butter, and butter in large microwave-safe bowl. Microwave on high for 1 to 3 minutes or until marshmallows are melted, stirring once during cooking time. Stir well to combine. Add rice cereal and miniature chocolate chips and mix well.

2. Form a scant ½ cup cereal mixture around each large marshmallow and form a ball, using greased hands. Refrigerate about 10 to 15 minutes, until firm. Wrap in cellophane and store at room temperature.

Substitutions
For a nice treat, you can substitute many things for the large marshmallows in these easy cookies. You can use chocolate Kisses, either milk chocolate or dark; miniature candy bars; dates; or dried apricots. Or you don't need a filling at all! The cereal mixture can also be pressed into a 13" × 9" pan and cut into bars.

Yields 16 bars

1 cup flour
½ cup quick-cooking oats
½ cup brown sugar
⅛ teaspoon allspice
⅓ cup butter, melted
1 cup chopped red grapes
2 tablespoons grape jelly

Streusel Grape Bars

*Grapes are a surprising and fresh filling for this rich oatmeal bar.
Serve them with a fork at the end of a company dinner,
or cut into small squares and tuck into lunchboxes.*

1. Preheat oven to 350°F. In large bowl, combine flour, oats, brown sugar, and allspice and mix well. Add melted butter; stir until mixture forms crumbs. Press half of crumbs into 9" square pan and set aside.

2. In small bowl, combine grapes with jelly and mix well. Spoon over crust in pan and spread evenly. Sprinkle grapes with remaining crumb mixture. Bake for 15 to 20 minutes or until bars are light golden brown. Cool and cut into bars.

Grapes

Almost all the grapes sold in produce departments today are seedless. They are called "table grapes" to distinguish them from grapes used to make wine. You can buy red, green, or blue-black grapes. Varieties include Flame, Thompson Seedless, Red Globe, Autumn Royal, and Christmas Rose.

Graham Fudge Squares

These no-bake bars have the most wonderful rich flavor and texture from the cinnamon graham cracker crumbs.

~~~~

Yields 36 squares

1 cup sugar
¾ cup flour
½ cup butter
1 15-ounce can sweetened
    condensed milk
2 cups semisweet chocolate
    chips, divided
1½ cups cinnamon graham
    cracker crumbs

1. Grease 9" square pan with butter and set aside. In heavy saucepan, mix sugar, flour, butter, and sweetened condensed milk. Bring to a boil over medium-high heat, stirring constantly. Let boil for 1 minute, stirring constantly. Remove from heat and add 1¼ cups of the chocolate chips. Stir until chocolate melts and mixture is smooth.

2. Add graham cracker crumbs and mix well. Spread in prepared pan and press down. In microwave-safe bowl, place remaining ¾ cup chocolate chips. Microwave on medium power (50 percent) for 1 minute. Remove and stir until smooth. Pour over bars and spread to cover. Chill in freezer for 10 to 15 minutes, then cut into bars to serve.

Yields 36 candies

1 12-ounce package
    semisweet chocolate
    chips
⅓ cup peanut butter
1 cup cashews
1 cup mini marshmallows
1 cup crisp rice cereal

Choco-Peanut Crunchers

These little chocolate and peanut butter candies are very easy to make and fun to eat. Make them with your kids at holiday time.

1. Line cookie sheets with parchment paper or waxed paper and set aside. In microwave-safe bowl, place chocolate chips and peanut butter. Melt at 50 percent power for 2 minutes, remove from microwave, and stir until chips melt and mixture is smooth. It may be necessary to microwave the mixture for 1 to 2 minutes longer, until the chips melt.

2. Stir in remaining ingredients until coated. Drop mixture by spoonfuls onto prepared cookie sheets and refrigerate until set. Store in airtight container at room temperature.

About Semisweet Chocolate

Semisweet chocolate is made of cocoa butter (made from roasted, ground cocoa bean nibs), sugar, and vanilla. Semisweet chocolate chips are generally a bit sweeter than bar chocolate. You can substitute one for the other. Chop semisweet chocolate bars into small pieces to use in place of the chips.

Graham Cracker Crisps

These crisp and crunchy little bar cookies are very fun to make. They taste like English toffee, but they aren't quite as hard or crunchy.

Yields 24 cookies

24 graham cracker squares
1 cup butter
1 cup brown sugar
1 cup chopped cashews
1½ cups milk chocolate chips

1. Preheat oven to 350°F. Place graham crackers in an ungreased 15" × 10" jelly-roll pan and set aside.

2. In medium saucepan, combine butter and brown sugar. Bring to a boil, stirring frequently, and boil for 1 minute or until sauce comes together and blends. Slowly pour this mixture over the graham crackers and sprinkle with cashews.

3. Bake for 8 to 12 minutes or until entire surface bubbles. Remove from heat and sprinkle with milk chocolate chips. Let stand for 10 minutes, then swirl through chips with knife to marble. Let cool and cut into squares along the cracker lines.

Chopping Nuts
You can chop nuts by placing them on a work surface and using a chef's knife to rock back and forth over the nuts. There are specialty hand-turned nut choppers that do a good job. You can also place the nuts in a heavy-duty resealable plastic bag and roll over the bag with a rolling pin.

Serves 8–10

1 12-ounce package
    semisweet chocolate
    chips
½ cup milk chocolate chips
1 15-ounce can sweetened
    condensed milk
1 cup chopped cashews
1 cup miniature
    marshmallows

Easy Fudge

*Use just about anything as the additions in this easy candy—
candy-coated chocolate pieces, gumdrops, peanuts, chopped candy
bars, macadamia nuts, or toffee bits would all be wonderful.*

1. Grease an 8" square pan with butter and set aside. In medium microwave-safe bowl, combine semisweet chocolate chips, milk chocolate chips, and sweetened condensed milk. Microwave on 50 percent power for 2 to 4 minutes, stirring once during cooking time, until chocolate is almost melted. Remove from oven and stir until chocolate melts.

2. Stir in cashews until mixed, then stir in marshmallows. Spread into prepared pan and let stand until cool.

Sweetened Condensed Milk

Sweetened condensed milk was invented in the 1800s to prevent food poisoning in infants and children that was caused by lack of pasteurization and refrigeration. It's a combination of milk and sugar with 50 percent of the water removed. Keep a can or two on hand because it's a great ingredient for making fudge and candies.

Chocolate Cream Peppermints

These rich little peppermints are so fun to make. They make a wonderful gift at Christmas or Hanukah packaged into a red, green, or blue box tied with a bow.

~

Yields 24 candies

2 tablespoons light cream
1 tablespoon butter
1½ cups powdered sugar
¼ teaspoon peppermint
    extract
1½ cups milk chocolate chips

1. Place cream in microwave-safe bowl and heat at 50 percent power for 30 seconds. Stir in butter until melted, then blend in powdered sugar and peppermint extract. Work with hands until creamy. Shape into ¾-inch balls, place on parchment paper–lined cookie sheets, and flatten to ⅛-inch thickness.

2. Place 1¼ cups of the chocolate chips in a 2-cup glass measuring cup and microwave at 50 percent power for 2 minutes. Remove from oven and stir in remaining chips until mixture is melted and smooth.

3. Dip each peppermint center into the chocolate, shake off excess, and place back onto cookie sheets. Place in freezer for 10 minutes, until chocolate is hardened. Store in airtight container.

Yields 16 bars

½ cup corn syrup
½ cup brown sugar
1 cup crunchy peanut butter
3 cups cornflakes
1 cup milk chocolate chips

Cereal Caramel Chews

These easy bars are crunchy and full of flavor, perfect for after-school munching or for a great treat in a lunch box. You could top them with butterscotch chips or semisweet chocolate chips instead.

1. Grease a 9" pan with butter and set aside. In heavy saucepan, combine corn syrup and brown sugar. Cook over medium heat until mixture boils, stirring frequently. Let boil for 2 minutes, stirring constantly.

2. Remove from heat and add peanut butter; stir until melted. Add cornflakes and stir gently, then spread into prepared pan. Press down with back of a greased spoon to form an even surface.

3. Place milk chocolate chips in small microwave-safe bowl. Microwave at 50 percent power for 1 to 1½ minutes, remove from oven, and stir until chips are melted. Pour over cereal mixture and spread; let cool. Cut into bars.

Storing Brown Sugar
Brown sugar can dry out and develop hard lumps if not stored properly. Decant the sugar from its plastic bag into a hard-sided container with a tightly sealing lid. You can put some foil on the sugar and place a bit of damp paper towel on the foil to keep the sugar moist. Change the paper towel when it dries out.

Crunchy Peanut Butter Sandwich Cookies

This rich chocolate peanut butter filling can be used as a frosting for brownies or cupcakes, or to fill any kind of cookie sandwich.

———

Place chocolate chips in medium microwave-safe bowl. Microwave on medium power for 1 minute, then remove and stir until chocolate is melted and smooth. Stir in peanut butter until smooth. Refrigerate for 10 minutes, stirring once. Make sandwiches using chocolate mixture and peanut butter cookies. Roll edges of cookie sandwiches in peanuts. Refrigerate for 10 to 15 minutes, until set. Store at room temperature.

Yields 12 cookies

1 cup semisweet chocolate chips
¼ cup milk chocolate chips
¼ cup peanut butter
24 No-Flour Peanut Butter Cookies (page 253)
1 cup chopped salted peanuts

Brown Sugar Bars

Be sure not to overbake these bars; watch them carefully while they are in the oven. They should be soft and chewy when cool.

———

Yields 9 bars

¾ cup brown sugar
¼ cup butter
1 teaspoon vanilla
1 egg
1 cup flour
1 teaspoon baking powder
½ cup candy-coated chocolate pieces
1 cup semisweet chocolate chips

1. Preheat oven to 350°F. Grease a 9" square pan and set aside. In saucepan, combine brown sugar and butter; cook and stir over medium heat until butter melts and mixture is smooth.

2. Remove from heat and add vanilla and egg; beat well. Stir in flour and baking powder. Then stir in candy-coated chocolate pieces. Spread into prepared pan. Bake for 12 to 16 minutes or until bars are very light golden brown and just set. Be careful not to overbake.

3. Immediately sprinkle bars with chocolate chips. Cover pan with foil and let stand for 1 to 2 minutes, until chips soften. Spread chips to cover bars, then cool on wire rack.

Yields 24 candies

3 cups milk chocolate chips, divided
½ cup cream of coconut
1 teaspoon vanilla
3 tablespoons butter, melted
1¾ cups powdered sugar
2 cups flaked coconut

Coconut Drops

These little candies taste just like the popular chocolate-covered coconut candy bar. You can use semisweet or dark chocolate instead of the milk chocolate if you'd like.

1. Set aside 2½ cups chocolate chips. Finely chop remaining ½ cup chocolate chips. Combine cream of coconut, vanilla, and butter in a large bowl and mix thoroughly. Add powdered sugar and mix well. Work in coconut and chopped chocolate with hands. Form mixture into 1-inch balls and place on waxed paper.

2. Place 2 cups milk chocolate chips in a microwave-safe glass measuring cup and heat at 50 percent power for 2 minutes. Stir chips until almost melted, then return to microwave. Heat at 50 percent power for 30 seconds. Remove from microwave and add remaining ½ cup chips. Stir until chocolate is melted and mixture is smooth.

3. Drop coconut balls, one at a time, into chocolate mixture and remove with a fork. Tap fork on side of glass measuring cup to shake off excess chocolate, then place coated candy on waxed paper. Refrigerate until set, then store at room temperature.

Cream of Coconut
Cream of coconut is not the same as coconut milk. Cream of coconut is smooth and quite thick, similar to sweetened condensed milk. It is made from fresh coconuts. Coconut milk is made by puréeing chopped coconut with water, and is often used in Thai and Asian main dishes.

Grasshopper Cookies

These easy cookies are based on the plain chocolate wafer cookies that are used to make the old-fashioned chocolate dessert of cookies layered with cream.

Yields 30 cookies

1 7-ounce jar marshmallow crème
½ teaspoon peppermint extract
3–5 drops green food color
1½ cups powdered sugar
1 12-ounce package semisweet chocolate chips, divided
1 10-ounce package chocolate wafer cookies

1. Place marshmallow crème in medium bowl and mix in peppermint extract and green food color. Stir in powdered sugar until blended, then stir in ¾ cup chocolate chips.

2. Place cookies on a wire rack and top each with a spoonful of the marshmallow crème mixture; spread to edges. Place in freezer for 10 minutes.

3. Meanwhile, place remaining 1¼ cups chocolate chips in glass measuring cup. Heat at 50 percent power in microwave oven until chips are almost melted, about 1½ minutes. Stir until chips are melted and mixture is smooth. Remove cookies from freezer. Spoon some of the chocolate mixture over each cookie to coat. Return to freezer for a few minutes to harden chocolate. Store in airtight container at room temperature.

Marshmallow Crème

Marshmallow crème, also known as marshmallow fluff, is a fat-free product usually made of corn syrup, sugar, egg whites, and vanilla. It will keep, unopened, in a cool place for about a year. To measure it, first oil the measuring cup and the crème will slip right out.

½ cup butter
1½ cups sugar
½ cup brown sugar
1 cup grated peeled Granny
    Smith apple
½ teaspoon cinnamon
3 cups quick-cooking
    oatmeal
1 cup chopped walnuts
½ cup powdered sugar

No-Bake Apple Cookies

*The pectin in the apple helps thicken the cookie mixture without baking.
Store these cookies in an airtight container at room temperature.*

1. In heavy saucepan, melt butter with sugars over medium heat, then stir in apple. Bring to a boil, then stir and boil for 1 minute. Remove from heat and add cinnamon, oatmeal, and walnuts; stir to combine. Let stand for 5 minutes.

2. Place powdered sugar on shallow pan. Drop apple mixture by teaspoons into powdered sugar and roll into balls. Place on waxed paper and let stand until the cookies are firm.

Yields 36 bars

2 cups crunchy peanut butter
2 cups sifted powdered sugar
½ cup butter, softened
2 cups crisp rice cereal
1 11.5-ounce package milk
    chocolate chips

Peanut Butter Bars

*Make sure you sift the powdered sugar for this recipe,
or there will be little bits of unmixed sugar in the bars.*

1. Butter bottom of 13" × 9" pan and set aside. In large bowl, combine peanut butter and sifted powdered sugar with butter; mix until well combined. Stir in rice cereal. Press in bottom of prepared pan.

2. In microwave-safe bowl, heat chips on 50 percent power for 2 minutes, then remove and stir until melted. Pour over peanut butter mixture in pan and spread to coat. Refrigerate until chocolate hardens.

Chocolate Date Balls

Dates and chocolate are a wonderful combination. These easy cookies are the perfect addition to a holiday cookie tray.

½ cup butter
¾ cup sugar
¼ cup brown sugar
1 cup chopped dates
1 egg
1 cup semisweet chocolate chips
½ teaspoon vanilla
1½ cups crisp rice cereal
1 cup powdered sugar

1. In heavy saucepan, melt butter, sugar, and brown sugar together over medium heat. Stir in dates and bring to a boil. Cook mixture, stirring constantly, for 3 to 4 minutes, until dates begin to melt. Add egg to mixture, beat well, and cook for 1 minute longer, stirring constantly. Add chocolate chips, remove pan from heat, cover, and let stand for 4 to 5 minutes. Add vanilla and stir until chocolate melts and mixture is blended.

2. Add rice cereal to date mixture. Spread powdered sugar onto shallow plate. Drop date mixture by tablespoons into powdered sugar and form into balls. Place on cookie sheet; let stand until cool and firm.

About Dates
You can buy dates in the baking aisle of the supermarket, and sometimes in the produce department. When choosing dates for baking and cooking, do not use the dates that are precut and rolled in sugar. They are often too dry and do not blend well in cookie dough.

2 cups buttery round cracker
crumbs
¾ cup butter, melted
1½ cups chopped macadamia
nuts
1 14-ounce can sweetened
condensed milk
1½ cups coconut

Macadamia Coconut Bars

*The saltiness of the buttery round cracker crumbs helps temper the
sweetness of the remaining ingredients in these easy bar cookies.*

1. Preheat oven to 350°F. In medium bowl, combine cracker crumbs with
   melted butter. Press into 13" × 9" pan. Sprinkle nuts over the crust, then
   evenly drizzle with sweetened condensed milk. Sprinkle coconut over
   milk.

2. Bake for 22 to 26 minutes or until edges are golden brown and bars are
   almost set. Let cool, then cut into bars.

Don't Use Evaporated Milk!
*Many cooks, especially beginning cooks, tend to confused sweetened
condensed milk with evaporated milk. Doing so will ruin your recipes!
Sweetened condensed milk is very thick and sweetened, while evaporated milk is simply milk with some water removed. Read labels!*

Macaroonies

Ground almonds and chocolate chips add interest to these simple cookies that are great for Passover because they contain no flour.

Yields 3 dozen cookies

¾ cup slivered almonds
1⅓ cups sugar, divided
2 cups coconut
3 egg whites
1 teaspoon vanilla
2 cups miniature chocolate
    chips

1. Preheat oven to 350°F. Line cookie sheets with Silpat liners and set aside. In food processor or blender, combine almonds with ⅓ cup sugar and process or blend until particles are fine. Stir in coconut and mix well.

2. In large bowl, beat egg whites until foamy. Gradually add remaining 1 cup sugar, beating until stiff peaks form. Fold in vanilla, coconut mixture, and chocolate chips.

3. Drop by tablespoons onto prepared cookie sheets. Bake for 8 to 12 minutes, until cookies are light golden brown around edges and are set. Cool on cookie sheets for 5 minutes, then remove to wire racks to cool.

Chapter 15

Desserts

Serves 8

½ cup sugar
1 teaspoon cinnamon
3 apples, peeled and chopped
½ cup butter
4 cups vanilla ice cream
8 shortbread cookies,
    crumbled
½ cup chopped toasted
    pecans

Caramel Apple Parfaits

*Choose crisp and tart apples for this simple fall dessert.
Granny Smith apples would be a good choice because
they hold their shape well even when cooked.*

1. In medium bowl, combine sugar, cinnamon, and apples and toss to coat. Melt butter in a heavy saucepan and add apple mixture. Cook over low heat for 10 to 12 minutes or until apples are tender and sauce is lightly caramelized. Remove from heat, pour mixture into a heat-proof bowl, and let stand for 10 minutes, stirring occasionally.

2. Make parfaits with apple mixture, ice cream, crumbled shortbread cookies, and pecans. Serve immediately.

Cooking Apples
There are apples that are best for eating out of hand, and those best for cooking. Cooking apples include McIntosh, Cortland, Rome Beauty, Jonathan, Haralson, and Granny Smith. The best apples for eating out of hand include Honeycrisp, Gala, Red Delicious, and new varieties including Sweet Sixteen and Honeygold.

Berry Cheese Cakes

*Use a combination of raspberries and blueberries, or raspberries
and sliced strawberries, or strawberries and blackberries
in this simple and elegant little dessert.*

~

Serves 8

1 8-ounce container soft
  cream cheese with
  pineapple
1½ cups powdered sugar
4 tablespoons pineapple
  preserves, divided
8 purchased individual
  sponge cake cups
2 cups mixed berries

1. In medium bowl, beat cream cheese until fluffy. Add powdered sugar and 2 tablespoons of the preserves and beat well until combined.

2. Carefully frost tops and sides of each sponge cake cup with the cream cheese mixture. In small saucepan over low heat, melt remaining preserves until thin. In small bowl combine the berries with the melted preserves and mix gently. Top each frosted sponge cake with some of the berry mixture and serve. You can prepare the cups ahead of time, refrigerate them, and top them with the berry mixture just before serving.

Recipe Substitution
You can use bakery or homemade cupcakes instead of the individual sponge cake cups if you'd like. Use a knife to cut a cone-shaped piece out of the top of the cupcakes, then frost as directed and spoon the berry mixture over the cupcakes before serving. Freeze the cupcake tops to use later in Raspberry Trifle (page 280).

Serves 4

1 3-ounce package instant
 chocolate pudding mix
1 cup chocolate milk
1 cup whipping cream
5 oatmeal cookies, broken
 into pieces
¼ cup toffee candy bits

Oatmeal Cookie Parfaits

*You can vary this dessert any way you'd like! Use any type of cookie, like choco-
late chip or peanut butter, vary the flavor of pudding mix, and use everything
from M&M's candies to chocolate chips to toasted nuts for a garnish.*

1. In medium bowl, combine pudding mix and chocolate milk and mix
   well with wire whisk until smooth and thickened. In small bowl beat
   cream until stiff peaks form; fold into pudding mixture.

2. Layer pudding mixture, cookies, and candy bits in parfait glasses.
   Serve immediately or cover and store in refrigerator up to 4 hours.

Desserts in an Instant
*Keep the ingredients for several of these easy desserts on hand in the
refrigerator and freezer and you can make dessert in an instant. For
instance, keep nondairy whipped topping and cookies in the freezer,
pudding mix and several types of candy in the pantry, and refrigerated
prepared pudding in the fridge.*

Mint Mousse

*This mousse must be served immediately for the best texture.
You can also pile it into a baked and cooled pie crust or
a chocolate cookie crumb pie crust and freeze it.*

Serves 8

*2 cups vanilla ice cream
2 cups mint chip ice cream
¼ teaspoon peppermint
    extract
¼ cup whipping cream
16 chocolate-mint-layered
    rectangular candies,
    coarsely chopped*

In blender or food processor, combine vanilla ice cream and mint chip ice cream, peppermint extract, and whipping cream; blend or process until smooth and creamy. Quickly spoon into parfait glasses or custard cups and top with chopped candies. Serve immediately.

Chocolate Raspberry Pie

*You can find prepared chocolate cookie pie crusts in the baking aisle of your
supermarket. Or make your own by combining 2 cups chocolate cookie
crumbs with ⅓ cup melted butter and pressing into a 9" pie pan.*

Serves 8

*1 cup semisweet chocolate
    chips
1 8-ounce package cream
    cheese, softened
1 9" chocolate cookie pie crust
¼ cup raspberry jelly
2 cups fresh raspberries*

1. Put chocolate chips in a small microwave-safe bowl. Microwave at 50 percent power for 1½ minutes; stir until chips are melted. Cut cream cheese into cubes and add to melted chips; beat well until smooth. Place mixture in refrigerator for 10 minutes.

2. Spread cooled chocolate mixture in bottom of pie crust. Put jelly in medium saucepan over low heat; cook and stir just until jelly is almost melted. Remove from heat and gently fold in raspberries just until coated. Place on top of the chocolate mixture. Serve immediately or cover and refrigerate until serving time.

Serves 9

1 9-inch round or square
    yellow cake layer
1½ cups powdered sugar
⅓ cup butter, softened
⅓ cup seedless raspberry jam
¾ cup whipping cream
3 tablespoons powdered
    sugar

Raspberry Continental

*Using premade and convenience foods means you can make this elegant
dessert in just minutes! This is an excellent cake for a birthday celebration.*

1. Using a serrated knife, carefully cut the cake horizontally through the
   middle to make two thin layers.

2. In small bowl, combine 1½ cups powdered sugar with butter, beating
   until light and fluffy. Stir in raspberry jam. Spread this mixture on the
   bottom cake layer and carefully top with the top layer.

3. In small bowl combine whipping cream and 3 tablespoons powdered
   sugar; beat until stiff peaks form. Frost top and sides of cake with
   cream mixture. Serve immediately or cover and chill in refrigerator for
   2 to 3 hours. Store leftovers in refrigerator.

Garnishes

*Garnishes make even purchased desserts look homemade. Use one of
the ingredients from the recipe to make a garnish. Grated chocolate
works well on any chocolate dessert, place fresh raspberries or strawberries on a dessert made with fruit, and mint sprigs look beautiful on
any dessert topped with whipped cream.*

Crunchy Ice Cream Cupcakes

Ice cream contains sugar, eggs, and milk and is the secret ingredient in these simple little cupcakes. If you'd like, you can frost them after they have cooled with any canned frosting.

Yields 24 cupcakes

2 cups vanilla ice cream
1 tablespoon butter
1 18-ounce package yellow
   cake mix
3 eggs
1½ cups granola, slightly
   crushed

1. Preheat oven to 350°F. Line 24 muffin tins with paper liners and set aside.

2. In microwave-safe bowl, place ice cream and butter. Microwave on 50 percent power for 1 to 3 minutes, until ice cream and butter melt. Remove from microwave and stir in cake mix and eggs; beat at medium speed for 2 minutes.

3. Fill lined muffin tins two-thirds full with batter and top each with a tablespoon of the crushed granola. Bake for 18 to 23 minutes or until cupcakes are rounded and top springs back when lightly touched with finger. Cool on wire racks.

Recipe Variations

Use chocolate ice cream and chocolate cake mix in this easy recipe, and top the cupcake batter with chocolate chips and nuts. Or use caramel ice cream and spice cake mix, topping the cupcakes with toffee bits. Use your imagination and invent your own special flavor!

Serves 10–12

1 9-inch round angel food
cake
4 1.4-ounce chocolate-
covered toffee bars
2 cups whipping cream
⅔ cup powdered sugar
⅓ cup chocolate syrup
1 teaspoon vanilla

Chocolate Toffee Torte

*This elegant torte is a wonderful finish for a company meal
because you can make it up to 8 hours ahead of time.
Use a serrated knife for slicing for best results.*

1. Using serrated knife, cut angel food cake horizontally into four equal layers. Place toffee bars in resealable plastic bag and crush with a rolling pin.

2. In large bowl, combine cream, powdered sugar, chocolate syrup, and vanilla. Beat until stiff peaks form. Frost layers of cake as you reassemble it, sprinkling crushed toffee bars on each layer. Frost top and sides of cake and sprinkle with remaining crushed toffee bars. Serve immediately or cover and chill for 2 to 4 hours. Store leftovers in refrigerator.

Ice Cream with Mix-Ins

This new trend in ice cream lets you decide what to add: one or all of the toppings! Work on a marble surface and let your guests pick the additions.

Serves 4

2–3 cups vanilla ice cream

1 cup Candied Nuts (page 254), chopped

4 squares plain Brownies from Layered Brownies (page 252)

4 Choco-Peanut Crunchers (page 258), chopped

4 Graham Cracker Crisps (page 259), chopped

Prepare all toppings. Let ice cream stand at room temperature for 10 minutes to soften slightly. Place ½ to ¾ cup ice cream on a cold marble or granite surface and sprinkle desired toppings over. Using two spatulas, chop the ice cream and the toppings together and fold until mixed. Scoop into a serving dish and continue with remaining ice cream and remaining toppings.

Marble Tiles
You can find inexpensive marble or granite tiles at discount stores and home improvement centers. It must be marble or granite to keep the ice cream cold while you work. Clean it thoroughly with soap and water and keep it in the freezer to make ice cream with mix-ins anytime.

Serves 6

8 vanilla cupcakes

3 tablespoons raspberry
  liqueur

½ cup raspberry jam

1 8-ounce dark chocolate bar,
  chopped

1 8-ounce container nondairy
  whipped topping,
  thawed

Raspberry Trifle

Ask at your bakery for cupcakes that are unfrosted. This easy dessert is delicious served immediately, but you can cover and refrigerate it for 24 hours if you'd like.

Unwrap the cupcakes and break into small pieces. In glass serving dish, place half of the cupcakes and sprinkle with half of the raspberry liqueur. Top with half of the raspberry jam, half of the chopped chocolate bar, and half of the whipped topping. Add remaining cupcakes, sprinkle with rest of the liqueur, top with remaining jam, and the remaining whipped topping. Sprinkle top with remaining chopped chocolate bar.

Liqueur Substitutions

When you're making recipes for children and the ingredient list calls for liqueur, substitute fruit juices or nectar like pear nectar or guava juice. Other substitutes include the liquid from maraschino cherries, thawed frozen fruit juice concentrates, or fruit syrups like black currant syrup.

Brownie Parfait

Use your favorite flavors of ice cream and toppings in this simple and indulgent dessert. You can use plain brownies from the Layered Brownies recipe (page 252) or purchase a pan of brownies from your supermarket or bakery.

Serves 8

5 plain brownies from Layered Brownies (page 252)
2 cups coffee ice cream
2 cups vanilla ice cream
1 cup chocolate fudge ice cream topping
½ cup English toffee bits

Cut brownies into 1-inch squares. Stir both flavors of ice cream until slightly softened. Layer brownies, ice cream, and fudge topping in 8 parfait glasses. Sprinkle with toffee bits. Serve immediately or freeze up to 8 hours; if frozen, let stand at room temperature for 10 to 15 minutes before serving.

Parfait Glasses
Parfait glasses and iced-tea spoons are the perfect utensils to use when making parfaits. The long and slender parfait glasses allow lots of beautiful layers to show through, and the iced-tea spoons are long enough to reach down to the bottom of the glasses.

Yields 24 tarts

24 frozen mini filo tart shells
½ cup apple jelly
½ teaspoon chopped fresh
   thyme leaves
½ cup blueberries
½ cup raspberries

Mini Fruit Tarts

*Your grocer's freezer section is a gold mine of prepared pie and tart shells.
Stock up on a few different types to make pies and tarts in minutes.*

1. Preheat oven to 375°F. Place tart shells on a cookie sheet and bake according to package directions. Remove to wire racks.

2. Meanwhile, heat apple jelly and thyme in a medium saucepan over low heat until jelly melts. Remove from heat and stir in berries. Put a couple of teaspoons of berry mixture into each tart shell and serve.

Herbs in Desserts

In the 1990s, using savory herbs in desserts became popular. Thyme, with its minty, lemony fragrance, is a natural partner with sweet and tart fruits. Rosemary is delicious with lemon desserts and in shortbreads, and lemon verbena is used in fruit jellies and cakes.

Blueberry Crisp

A crisp is a baked dessert that has a crumbly topping made of flour, sugar, butter, and usually oatmeal and nuts. Using canned pie filling streamlines this excellent recipe.

Serves 6

1 21-ounce can blueberry pie
    filling
½ cup flour
½ cup brown sugar
½ cup oatmeal
½ cup chopped walnuts
½ teaspoon cinnamon
¼ cup butter, melted

1. Preheat oven to 400°F. Pour blueberry pie filling into 9" square glass pan and set aside.

2. In medium bowl, combine flour, brown sugar, oatmeal, walnuts, and cinnamon and mix well. Pour butter into flour mixture and stir until mixture is crumbly. Sprinkle over blueberry pie filling. Bake for 20 to 25 minutes or until filling is bubbly and crust is light golden brown. Serve with ice cream or whipped cream.

Crisps, Crumbles, Grunts, and Cobblers
All of these old-fashioned, homey desserts are basically the same thing: fruits with some kind of topping. Crisps use oatmeal and nuts to form a crumbly topping; crumbles are the same thing. Grunts are more like a steamed pudding, sometimes cooked on top of the stove. Cobblers are similar to a deep-dish pie, with a thick biscuit-type crust.

1 14-ounce can sweetened
   condensed milk
1 8-ounce package cream
   cheese, softened
¼ cup lemon juice
1 9-inch graham cracker pie
   crust
1 18-ounce can cherry pie
   filling

Simple Cheesecake

Use any flavor of canned pie filling in this easy pie. You could even top it with some fresh berries mixed with a bit of jam or jelly.

1. In large bowl, combine condensed milk, cream cheese, and lemon juice; beat on low speed until smooth and combined. Pour into graham cracker crust. Place in freezer for 10 minutes.

2. Using a slotted spoon, remove the cherries from the pie filling, leaving a lot of the gel behind. Place cherries on cream cheese filling and serve, or cover and chill the pie up to 8 hours. Store leftovers in the refrigerator.

Cheesecake Toppings

There are many toppings that are delicious on cheesecake. Try mixing fresh berries with preserves or jelly, drizzle the dessert with chocolate and caramel ice cream toppings, beat whipping cream with chocolate syrup, or combine chopped nuts with chopped chocolate bars and marshmallows.

Strawberries with Sour Cream

There isn't an easier dessert on the planet, and this simple fruit recipe has the most wonderful sweet-and-tart flavor. You can make it with peaches, mangoes, grapes, or pears too; just use fruits that are acidic.

Serves 6

2 pints strawberries, stemmed and sliced
1 cup sour cream
½ cup brown sugar
¼ cup toasted pecans

In glass serving bowl, place one-third of the strawberries. Top with one-third of the sour cream, and sprinkle with one-third of the brown sugar. Repeat layers, ending with brown sugar. Top with toasted pecans and serve, or cover and refrigerate up to 8 hours.

Grilled Peaches

Grilling fruit makes the most wonderful dessert; the sugars caramelize and the fruits become very tender and sweet. Serve this after a cookout for a great finish.

Serves 4

4 peaches, cut in half
3 tablespoons brown sugar
3 tablespoons maple syrup
½ teaspoon cinnamon
½ cup heavy cream

Remove pits from peaches. Prepare and preheat grill. In small bowl, combine sugar, syrup, and cinnamon. Brush this mixture over both sides of peaches. Place peaches, cut-side down, 4 to 6 inches from medium coals. Grill, uncovered, for 2 to 3 minutes, then turn peaches and top with remaining brown sugar mixture. Grill for 1 to 2 minutes longer, then remove. Drizzle with cream and serve.

Serves 8–10

30 fudge-covered graham
    crackers
⅓ cup butter, melted
3 pints chocolate ice cream
¾ cup peanut butter
5 ounces peanut butter cups,
    chopped

Chocolate Peanut Butter Pie

*This is such an indulgent dessert, it's hard to believe that it uses
only five ingredients! Take it out of the freezer 15 minutes
before serving for the best flavor and texture.*

1. Crush graham crackers and combine with butter; press crumbs into 9"
   pie pan and set aside.

2. In blender container or food processor, combine ice cream and peanut
   butter; blend or process until combined. Fold in chopped candies and
   place in pie crust. Freeze until firm.

Graham Crackers
*There are many varieties of graham crackers on the market. You can find
chocolate-covered crackers, low-fat crackers, and cinnamon-flavored
and honey-flavored crackers. Choose any of them to make a wonderfully
easy and quick pie crust by crushing the crackers and mixing the crumbs
with some melted butter, then pressing into a pie pan.*

Sherbet Roll

You can use any flavor sherbet, sorbet, or ice cream in this easy and colorful recipe. Think about using other flavors of ice cream and topping for unlimited dessert variations!

Serves 6

1 quart vanilla ice cream
1 cup granola
1 quart lemon sherbet
½ cup caramel ice cream topping

1. Line a jelly-roll pan with parchment paper. Let ice cream stand at room temperature for 5 minutes, then spread evenly in prepared pan. Sprinkle granola over ice cream and return to freezer.

2. Let sherbet stand at room temperature for 5 minutes, then spoon and spread over granola. Return to freezer for 5 minutes.

3. Lift narrow end of parchment paper and use it to roll the ice cream and sherbet together, peeling the paper away from the ice cream as you roll. Place on serving plate and freeze until firm. To serve, slice roll and place slices cut-side down on a spoonful of caramel ice cream topping.

Ice Cream Desserts
Keep several flavors of ice cream, sorbet, and sherbet on hand in your freezer to make easy desserts in a flash. Also, when you're making an ice cream dessert, make one or two extra and keep them in the freezer, well covered and labeled, for unexpected company.

Serves 6

2 pints raspberries
1½ cups whipping cream
½ cup powdered sugar
½ teaspoon vanilla
½ cup chopped pecans,
    toasted
½ cup grated semisweet
    chocolate

Raspberry Fool

A fool is a soft parfait usually made with a puréed fruit and flavored whipping cream. Top it with more sweetened whipped cream and some mint sprigs.

1. Place raspberries in medium bowl and mash some of them, leaving some whole. In large bowl, combine cream, powdered sugar, and vanilla and beat until stiff peaks form.

2. Layer raspberries with whipped cream mixture, pecans, and grated chocolate in 6 parfait glasses. Serve immediately or cover and refrigerate up to 6 hours.

Whipping Cream

Heavy whipping cream must contain at least 36 percent butterfat. To whip cream, chill the bowl and the beaters in the freezer for 10 to 15 minutes. Begin whipping slowly, and gradually increase speed as the cream thickens. The cream is done when peaks droop slightly when the beaters are lifted.

Flaky Peach Tarts

*You should make these little mini tarts just before you
plan to serve them for best flavor and texture. Top them
with peach ice cream and some chopped cashews.*

Serves 6

*1 sheet frozen puff pastry,
   thawed*
2 peaches
⅓ cup peach jam
3 tablespoons brown sugar
⅛ teaspoon cinnamon

1. Preheat oven to 375°F. Roll pastry into a 9" × 12" rectangle. Cut pastry into twelve 3-inch squares and place on parchment paper–lined cookie sheets; set aside.

2. Peel peaches, remove pit, and cut into thin slices. Arrange peach slices on pastry and brush each with some of the peach jam. Sprinkle with brown sugar and cinnamon. Bake for 10 to 14 minutes or until pastry is puffed and golden and fruit is tender.

Topping Tarts
Tarts can be topped with sweetened whipped cream, ice cream, or hard sauce. To make hard sauce, beat ½ cup softened butter with 1 cup powdered sugar and 1 teaspoon vanilla. Serve on hot desserts; the mixture will melt into the dessert and form a sweet sauce.

Serves 10–12

1 9-inch round angel food
    cake
1¼ cups whipping cream
2 tablespoons powdered
    sugar
1 cup lemon curd
1½ cups chopped Candied
    Nuts (page 254)

Lemon Angel Cake

*Bakeries always have angel food cake available; also look for
them in the bakery department of your supermarket. Lemon curd is
available near the pie fillings and also in the gourmet foods aisle.*

1. Using a serrated knife, cut cake horizontally into 3 layers. In a large bowl, combine cream and powdered sugar; beat until stiff peaks form. Fold in lemon curd until blended.

2. Spread mixture between layers, sprinkling each layer with some of the Candied Nuts, and then frost top and sides with lemon mixture. Sprinkle top with remaining Candied Nuts. Serve immediately or cover and refrigerate up to 8 hours; store leftovers in refrigerator.

Recipe Variation

You can use just about any well-flavored, smooth, creamy filling, pudding, or custard in place of the lemon curd in this easy recipe. Try chocolate pudding, caramel pudding, or cream cheese frosting. You can also sprinkle the layers with toasted coconut, nuts, or chopped or crushed candy bars as you frost them.

Peanut Cakes

You can find plain cake layers at most bakeries; in some cases you will have to ask for them. These little cakes are kind of fussy to make, but so delicious.

Yields 9 cakes

1 9-inch square yellow cake
1 can vanilla frosting
¼ cup peanut butter
1–2 tablespoons milk
2 cups chopped salted
    peanuts

1. Cut cake into 9 squares and place on waxed paper–lined cookie sheets; set aside.

2. In medium bowl, combine frosting and peanut butter with enough milk to make a smooth spreading consistency. One at a time, frost all sides of the cake pieces with this frosting. When completely coated, drop cake pieces into the peanuts and roll to coat all sides. Serve immediately or cover and hold at room temperature for up to 8 hours.

Cake Layers
It's a good idea to keep some boxes of cake mix on hand, especially the single-layer-size mix. There are so many ways to use plain cake layers— frost them with canned frosting, layer them with pudding or ice cream for parfaits, and cut them into squares and frost individually.

Serves 6

1 21-ounce can apple pie
   filling
¾ cup brown sugar
1 teaspoon cinnamon
¼ teaspoon nutmeg
½ cup flour
½ cup oatmeal
⅓ cup butter, melted

Apple Crumble

*Use the crumbly topping with any flavor of canned pie filling;
peach would be very delicious. Top it with some vanilla
or caramel ice cream for extra decadence.*

1. Preheat oven to 400°F. Place pie filling into 1½-quart casserole. In medium bowl, combine sugar, cinnamon, nutmeg, flour, and oatmeal and mix well. Add melted butter and mix until crumbs form. Sprinkle crumbs over pie filling.

2. Bake for 15 to 20 minutes or until pie filling bubbles and crumb mixture is browned. Serve warm.

Serves 8

1 4-ounce package instant
   chocolate pudding mix
1 cup chocolate milk
2 cups vanilla ice cream
½ cup whipping cream
1 chocolate cookie crumb pie
   crust

Fudgesicle Pie

*This excellent recipe does taste just like a Fudgesicle in a pie crust. Garnish it
with chocolate-covered peanuts and some chocolate syrup.*

1. In large bowl, combine pudding mix with milk; mix with eggbeater or hand mixer for 1 minute until smooth and thickened. Using mixer on low speed, add vanilla ice cream and beat until combined.

2. In small bowl, beat cream until stiff peaks form. Add to ice cream mixture and beat just until combined. Pour into pie crust and freeze.

Chocolate Velvet

You can pile this mixture into a baked and cooled pie crust or a graham cracker crust and freeze to serve it as a pie; top wedges with some whipped cream and grated chocolate.

Serves 8

1 cup chocolate syrup
1 15-ounce can sweetened
  condensed milk
1 16-ounce container frozen
  whipped topping,
  thawed
½ teaspoon vanilla
⅓ cup sliced almonds, toasted

In large bowl, combine syrup and sweetened condensed milk and beat until smooth. Fold in whipped topping and vanilla. Sprinkle with almonds and serve immediately as a pudding, or place in 1-quart casserole dish, top with almonds, and freeze until solid.

Toasting Nuts

To toast nuts, place them on a shallow baking pan and bake at 350°F for 5 to 10 minutes, shaking pan frequently, until nuts are fragrant and just beginning to turn light golden brown. You can also microwave the nuts at 100 percent power for 3 to 5 minutes, until the nuts are fragrant. Let cool completely before chopping.

Appendix A

Shortcut Ingredients

Companies introduce thousands of new convenience products into the market every year. It's worth your time to stroll through your grocery store every month or so looking for new products and advances in food preparation.

Shelf-stable grocery products can be stored at room temperature without refrigeration. Keep a good selection of these products on hand in your pantry, organized by type.

- ✔ Cake mixes
- ✔ Cookie mixes
- ✔ Prepared frostings
- ✔ Bread mixes
- ✔ Dessert mixes
- ✔ Soup mixes and bases
- ✔ Self-rising flour
- ✔ Flavored rice mixes
- ✔ Dried fruit
- ✔ Fruit pie fillings
- ✔ Flavored oils
- ✔ Canned soups and stocks
- ✔ Breads and crackers
- ✔ Dry seasoning mixes

- ✔ Flavored pasta mixes
- ✔ Seasoned bread crumbs
- ✔ Prepared sauces
- ✔ Pasta sauces and tomato products
- ✔ Pasta
- ✔ Prepared salad dressings
- ✔ Pudding and pie filling mixes
- ✔ Canned and jarred fruit salads
- ✔ Stocks and broth in aseptic boxes
- ✔ Rice mixes
- ✔ Flavored vinegars
- ✔ Marinades

The number of prepared meat products has skyrocketed in recent years. From cooked deli meats to heat-and-eat entrées, these products not only make quick work of the main dish, but they can be used as an ingredient in recipes. For instance, Mexican Beef Stew (page 240) is made from cooked ground beef in a taco sauce. Excellent value-added meat products include:

- ✔ Preformed hamburger patties
- ✔ Precooked bacon
- ✔ Marinated meats
- ✔ Fully prepared entrées like pot roast in gravy, BBQ beef, and pulled pork
- ✔ Prestuffed and seasoned chicken and fish
- ✔ Chicken and turkey cutlets
- ✔ Chicken tenders
- ✔ Preseasoned turkey tenderloin
- ✔ Frozen precooked meatballs
- ✔ Fully cooked frozen shrimp
- ✔ Minute steaks and cubed stew meat
- ✔ Cooked ground beef in sauces
- ✔ Frozen stir-fry mixes
- ✔ Frozen seasoned burgers
- ✔ Fish fillets and steaks
- ✔ Smoked pork
- ✔ Cooked shredded chicken in sauces
- ✔ Marinated and smoked salmon
- ✔ Seafood dinner starters
- ✔ Breading and batter mixes
- ✔ Fajita kits
- ✔ Lunch kits
- ✔ Fully cooked sausages

The produce and dairy departments have perhaps changed the most over the past few years, with introductions of many value-added and prepared foods. Many of these items will keep after opening, under refrigeration, for several weeks. Be sure there is a "use by" date on them; if not, mark the date of purchase and discard after a few weeks. Produce and dairy products that will save you time include:

- ✔ Prewashed salad mixes
- ✔ Flavored tomato products
- ✔ Refrigerated hash brown potatoes, mashed potatoes, potato slices
- ✔ Vegetables from salad bar
- ✔ Sliced mushrooms
- ✔ Jarred minced garlic
- ✔ Preshredded cheeses
- ✔ Refrigerated pasta sauces
- ✔ Fresh pasta
- ✔ Pesto sauce
- ✔ Shredded coleslaw mix
- ✔ Shredded carrots
- ✔ Shredded cabbage
- ✔ Prepared polenta
- ✔ Fresh herbs
- ✔ Smoothie mixes
- ✔ Salad kits

In the frozen aisle of the supermarket, you'll find totally prepared meals as well as ingredients to make meals quickly. For instance, add some chopped chicken to any of the frozen vegetable combinations, especially those with sauce, and dinner is on the table in less than 15 minutes.

- ✔ Frozen chopped vegetables
- ✔ Frozen vegetable combinations
- ✔ Frozen chopped onions and pearl onions
- ✔ Ice cream combinations
- ✔ Frozen stuffed chicken entrées
- ✔ Prepared hash brown potatoes, mashed, French fries
- ✔ Pizzas
- ✔ Snack foods

- ✔ Prepared entrées
- ✔ Vegetables in sauce
- ✔ Meal starters
- ✔ Slow-cooker meal starters
- ✔ Frozen prepared garlic and cheese breads
- ✔ Breakfast pastries
- ✔ Frozen puff pastry and filo dough
- ✔ Frozen cakes and pies
- ✔ Frozen juices and beverages

And the deli department is bursting with wonderful precooked meats and vegetables, salads, cheeses, breads, and flavored oils and sauces. These ingredients do cost more than those you prepare yourself, but they are excellent time-savers. Not only can you serve them as is, but they are great components in many five-ingredient recipes (see From the Deli, page 163). Deli ingredients to look for include:

- ✔ Fully cooked rotisserie chicken
- ✔ Fried chicken
- ✔ Fully cooked roast beef
- ✔ Fully cooked ham
- ✔ Corned beef
- ✔ Unusual cheeses
- ✔ Sandwiches
- ✔ Fondue mix
- ✔ Pastrami and other sandwich meats
- ✔ Vegetable salads
- ✔ Potato salads
- ✔ Pizza

- ✔ Relishes
- ✔ Mashed potatoes
- ✔ Fruit salads
- ✔ Rolls
- ✔ Flavored oils
- ✔ Desserts
- ✔ Prepared breads
- ✔ Party trays
- ✔ Gelatin salads
- ✔ Cold cuts
- ✔ Soups
- ✔ Wraps and unusual breads

There are many products on the market that will help you organize your kitchen and cook safely and more efficiently: from lazy Susans to spice racks, pot racks to storage containers. Think about investing some money in new products to help keep your kitchen in order. If you have a kitchen with little counter space, purchase a center island or work island on casters that can be pulled out when cooking, then rolled away into a pantry or closet after use.

- ✔ Pull-down cookbook holders
- ✔ Pull-down knife racks
- ✔ Door organizers for cans and bottles
- ✔ Lazy Susans for large, deep cupboards
- ✔ Pot racks and hangers
- ✔ Under-cabinet lighting
- ✔ Nested storage containers
- ✔ Over-the-door racks and organizers
- ✔ Baker's racks
- ✔ Bread boxes
- ✔ Cutting boards
- ✔ Dish drainers
- ✔ Tiered shelves
- ✔ Drawer organizers
- ✔ Microwave carts
- ✔ Salad spinners
- ✔ Spice racks
- ✔ Timers
- ✔ Instant-read thermometers
- ✔ Silicon hot pads and gloves

Menus

When planning menus, think about using foods that have contrasting flavors, textures, temperatures, and colors. "Taste" the menu in your mind as you plan it. If you think it will be good, it will!

Dinner for the Boss
Parmesan Wafers with Apricots
Pesto Steaks
Duchess Potatoes
Green Beans with Red Peppers
Wilted Lettuce Salad
Toasted Garlic Bread
Raspberry Trifle

Lunch on the Porch
Melon Ginger Punch
Chicken Salad with Nectarines
Smoked Turkey Fruit Salad
Mini Popovers
Oatmeal Cookie Parfaits

Christmas Dinner
Berry Filo Shells
Poached Salmon with Alfredo Sauce
Herbed Baby Potatoes
Sugared Almond Green Salad
Braised Carrots
Parmesan Crescents
Chocolate Toffee Torte

Alternative Thanksgiving Dinner
Garlic Stuffed Cherry Tomatoes
Ham and Sweet Potatoes
Smashed Potatoes
Crispy Broccoli Casserole
Apple and Greens Salad
Cheese Breadsticks
Fudgesicle Pie
Simple Cheesecake

Child's Birthday Celebration
Lemonade
Sausage Rolls
Dill Dip with Crudités
Coconut Fruit Dip with Fruit
Raspberry Continental
M&M's Cookies

Fiftieth-Birthday Celebration
Crab Cakes
Greek Tenderloin Steak
Roasted Sugar Snap Peas
Smashed Potatoes
Simple Spinach Salad
Melty Cheese Bread
Lemon Angel Cake

Sunday Brunch
French Toast
Caramel Rolls
Scrambled Eggs with Pesto
Fruit and Cheese Salad
Raspberry Fool

Entertaining Friends
Cheese Puffs with Champagne
Tomato Bisque
Pressure-Cooker Sausage Risotto
Greens with Basil Dressing
Honey Orange Carrots
Peanut Cakes with Ice Cream

Breakfast on the Run
Orange Glazed Blueberry Muffins
Oat Scones
Grape and Melon Salad in Lettuce Leaves

Cookout Celebration
Pesto Dip with Crudités
Grilled Chicken Packets
Grilled Asparagus
Grilled Peaches
Ice Cream with Mix-Ins

Picnic in the Park
Shrimp Sandwiches
Muffuletta
Fruit and Cheese Salad
Marshmallow Treats
Graham Fudge Squares

Tex-Mex Fiesta
Spicy Mixed Nuts
Guacamole with Tortilla Chips
Green Chile Chicken Burritos
Southern Corn Bread Salad
Ambrosia
Layered Brownies

Appetizer Party
Sparkling Punch
Melon and Avocado Cocktail
Spicy Meatballs
Marinated Olives
Parmesan Cups with Cheesy Filling
Streusel Grape Bars
Chocolate Cream Peppermints
Berry Cheese Cakes

Dessert Party
Melon Ginger Punch
Brown Sugar Bars
Coconut Drops
Chocolate Raspberry Pie
Mini Fruit Tarts
Strawberries with Sour Cream
Chocolate Peanut Butter Pie

Index

THE EVERYTHING SERIES!

BUSINESS & PERSONAL FINANCE

Everything® Accounting Book
Everything® Budgeting Book
Everything® Business Planning Book
Everything® Coaching and Mentoring Book
Everything® Fundraising Book
Everything® Get Out of Debt Book
Everything® Grant Writing Book
Everything® Home-Based Business Book, 2nd Ed.
Everything® Homebuying Book, 2nd Ed.
Everything® Homeselling Book, 2nd Ed.
Everything® Investing Book, 2nd Ed.
Everything® Landlording Book
Everything® Leadership Book
Everything® Managing People Book, 2nd Ed.
Everything® Negotiating Book
Everything® Online Auctions Book
Everything® Online Business Book
Everything® Personal Finance Book
Everything® Personal Finance in Your 20s and 30s Book
Everything® Project Management Book
Everything® Real Estate Investing Book
Everything® Robert's Rules Book, $7.95
Everything® Selling Book
Everything® Start Your Own Business Book, 2nd Ed.
Everything® Wills & Estate Planning Book

COOKING

Everything® Barbecue Cookbook
Everything® Bartender's Book, $9.95
Everything® Chinese Cookbook
Everything® Classic Recipes Book
Everything® Cocktail Parties and Drinks Book
Everything® College Cookbook
Everything® Cooking for Baby and Toddler Book
Everything® Cooking for Two Cookbook
Everything® Diabetes Cookbook
Everything® Easy Gourmet Cookbook
Everything® Fondue Cookbook
Everything® Fondue Party Book
Everything® Gluten-Free Cookbook
Everything® Glycemic Index Cookbook
Everything® Grilling Cookbook

Everything® Healthy Meals in Minutes Cookbook
Everything® Holiday Cookbook
Everything® Indian Cookbook
Everything® Italian Cookbook
Everything® Low-Carb Cookbook
Everything® Low-Fat High-Flavor Cookbook
Everything® Low-Salt Cookbook
Everything® Meals for a Month Cookbook
Everything® Mediterranean Cookbook
Everything® Mexican Cookbook
Everything® One-Pot Cookbook
Everything® Quick and Easy 30-Minute, 5-Ingredient Cookbook
Everything® Quick Meals Cookbook
Everything® Slow Cooker Cookbook
Everything® Slow Cooking for a Crowd Cookbook
Everything® Soup Cookbook
Everything® Tex-Mex Cookbook
Everything® Thai Cookbook
Everything® Vegetarian Cookbook
Everything® Wild Game Cookbook
Everything® Wine Book, 2nd Ed.

GAMES

Everything® 15-Minute Sudoku Book, $9.95
Everything® 30-Minute Sudoku Book, $9.95
Everything® Blackjack Strategy Book
Everything® Brain Strain Book, $9.95
Everything® Bridge Book
Everything® Card Games Book
Everything® Card Tricks Book, $9.95
Everything® Casino Gambling Book, 2nd Ed.
Everything® Chess Basics Book
Everything® Craps Strategy Book
Everything® Crossword and Puzzle Book
Everything® Crossword Challenge Book
Everything® Cryptograms Book, $9.95
Everything® Easy Crosswords Book
Everything® Easy Kakuro Book, $9.95
Everything® Games Book, 2nd Ed.
Everything® Giant Sudoku Book, $9.95
Everything® Kakuro Challenge Book, $9.95
Everything® Large-Print Crossword Challenge Book
Everything® Large-Print Crosswords Book
Everything® Lateral Thinking Puzzles Book, $9.95
Everything® Mazes Book

Everything® Pencil Puzzles Book, $9.95
Everything® Poker Strategy Book
Everything® Pool & Billiards Book
Everything® Test Your IQ Book, $9.95
Everything® Texas Hold 'Em Book, $9.95
Everything® Travel Crosswords Book, $9.95
Everything® Word Games Challenge Book
Everything® Word Search Book

HEALTH

Everything® Alzheimer's Book
Everything® Diabetes Book
Everything® Health Guide to Adult Bipolar Disorder
Everything® Health Guide to Controlling Anxiety
Everything® Health Guide to Fibromyalgia
Everything® Health Guide to Thyroid Disease
Everything® Hypnosis Book
Everything® Low Cholesterol Book
Everything® Massage Book
Everything® Menopause Book
Everything® Nutrition Book
Everything® Reflexology Book
Everything® Stress Management Book

HISTORY

Everything® American Government Book
Everything® American History Book
Everything® Civil War Book
Everything® Freemasons Book
Everything® Irish History & Heritage Book
Everything® Middle East Book

HOBBIES

Everything® Candlemaking Book
Everything® Cartooning Book
Everything® Coin Collecting Book
Everything® Drawing Book
Everything® Family Tree Book, 2nd Ed.
Everything® Knitting Book
Everything® Knots Book
Everything® Photography Book
Everything® Quilting Book
Everything® Scrapbooking Book
Everything® Sewing Book
Everything® Woodworking Book

Bolded titles are new additions to the series.
All Everything® books are priced at $12.95 or $14.95, unless otherwise stated. Prices subject to change without notice.

HOME IMPROVEMENT

Everything® Feng Shui Book
Everything® Feng Shui Decluttering Book, $9.95
Everything® Fix-It Book
Everything® Home Decorating Book
Everything® Home Storage Solutions Book
Everything® Homebuilding Book
Everything® Lawn Care Book
Everything® Organize Your Home Book

KIDS' BOOKS

All titles are $7.95

Everything® Kids' Animal Puzzle & Activity Book
Everything® Kids' Baseball Book, 4th Ed.
Everything® Kids' Bible Trivia Book
Everything® Kids' Bugs Book
**Everything® Kids' Cars and Trucks Puzzle
& Activity Book**
Everything® Kids' Christmas Puzzle
& Activity Book
Everything® Kids' Cookbook
Everything® Kids' Crazy Puzzles Book
Everything® Kids' Dinosaurs Book
**Everything® Kids' First Spanish Puzzle and
Activity Book**
Everything® Kids' Gross Hidden Pictures Book
Everything® Kids' Gross Jokes Book
Everything® Kids' Gross Mazes Book
Everything® Kids' Gross Puzzle and
Activity Book
Everything® Kids' Halloween Puzzle
& Activity Book
Everything® Kids' Hidden Pictures Book
Everything® Kids' Horses Book
Everything® Kids' Joke Book
Everything® Kids' Knock Knock Book
Everything® Kids' Learning Spanish Book
Everything® Kids' Math Puzzles Book
Everything® Kids' Mazes Book
Everything® Kids' Money Book
Everything® Kids' Nature Book
Everything® Kids' Pirates Puzzle and Activity
Book
**Everything® Kids' Princess Puzzle and
Activity Book**
Everything® Kids' Puzzle Book
Everything® Kids' Riddles & Brain Teasers Book
Everything® Kids' Science Experiments Book
Everything® Kids' Sharks Book
Everything® Kids' Soccer Book
Everything® Kids' Travel Activity Book

KIDS' STORY BOOKS

Everything® Fairy Tales Book

LANGUAGE

**Everything® Conversational Chinese Book
with CD, $19.95**
Everything® Conversational Japanese Book
with CD, $19.95
Everything® French Grammar Book
Everything® French Phrase Book, $9.95
Everything® French Verb Book, $9.95
Everything® German Practice Book with CD,
$19.95
Everything® Inglés Book
Everything® Learning French Book
Everything® Learning German Book
Everything® Learning Italian Book
Everything® Learning Latin Book
Everything® Learning Spanish Book
**Everything® Russian Practice Book with CD,
$19.95**
Everything® Sign Language Book
Everything® Spanish Grammar Book
Everything® Spanish Phrase Book, $9.95
Everything® Spanish Practice Book
with CD, $19.95
Everything® Spanish Verb Book, $9.95

MUSIC

Everything® Drums Book with CD, $19.95
Everything® Guitar Book
Everything® Guitar Chords Book with CD,
$19.95
Everything® Home Recording Book
**Everything® Music Theory Book with CD,
$19.95**
Everything® Reading Music Book with CD,
$19.95
Everything® Rock & Blues Guitar Book
(with CD), $19.95
Everything® Songwriting Book

NEW AGE

Everything® Astrology Book, 2nd Ed.
Everything® Birthday Personology Book
Everything® Dreams Book, 2nd Ed.
Everything® Love Signs Book, $9.95
Everything® Numerology Book
Everything® Paganism Book
Everything® Palmistry Book
Everything® Psychic Book
Everything® Reiki Book
Everything® Sex Signs Book, $9.95
Everything® Tarot Book, 2nd Ed.
Everything® Wicca and Witchcraft Book

PARENTING

Everything® Baby Names Book, 2nd Ed.
Everything® Baby Shower Book
Everything® Baby's First Food Book
Everything® Baby's First Year Book
Everything® Birthing Book
Everything® Breastfeeding Book
Everything® Father-to-Be Book
Everything® Father's First Year Book
Everything® Get Ready for Baby Book
Everything® Get Your Baby to Sleep Book, $9.95
Everything® Getting Pregnant Book
**Everything® Guide to Raising a
One-Year-Old**
**Everything® Guide to Raising a
Two-Year-Old**
Everything® Homeschooling Book
Everything® Mother's First Year Book
Everything® Parent's Guide to Children
and Divorce
Everything® Parent's Guide to Children
with ADD/ADHD
Everything® Parent's Guide to Children
with Asperger's Syndrome
Everything® Parent's Guide to Children
with Autism
Everything® Parent's Guide to Children with
Bipolar Disorder
Everything® Parent's Guide to Children
with Dyslexia
Everything® Parent's Guide to Positive Discipline
Everything® Parent's Guide to Raising a
Successful Child
Everything® Parent's Guide to Raising Boys
Everything® Parent's Guide to Raising Siblings
**Everything® Parent's Guide to Sensory
Integration Disorder**
Everything® Parent's Guide to Tantrums
Everything® Parent's Guide to the Overweight
Child
Everything® Parent's Guide to the Strong-Willed
Child
Everything® Parenting a Teenager Book
Everything® Potty Training Book, $9.95
Everything® Pregnancy Book, 2nd Ed.
Everything® Pregnancy Fitness Book
Everything® Pregnancy Nutrition Book
**Everything® Pregnancy Organizer, 2nd Ed.,
$16.95**
Everything® Toddler Activities Book
Everything® Toddler Book
Everything® Tween Book
Everything® Twins, Triplets, and More Book

PETS

Everything® **Aquarium Book**
Everything® Boxer Book
Everything® Cat Book, 2nd Ed.
Everything® Chihuahua Book
Everything® Dachshund Book
Everything® Dog Book
Everything® Dog Health Book
Everything® **Dog Owner's Organizer,** **$16.95**
Everything® Dog Training and Tricks Book
Everything® German Shepherd Book
Everything® Golden Retriever Book
Everything® Horse Book
Everything® Horse Care Book
Everything® Horseback Riding Book
Everything® Labrador Retriever Book
Everything® Poodle Book
Everything® Pug Book
Everything® Puppy Book
Everything® Rottweiler Book
Everything® Small Dogs Book
Everything® Tropical Fish Book
Everything® Yorkshire Terrier Book

REFERENCE

Everything® Blogging Book
Everything® **Build Your Vocabulary Book**
Everything® Car Care Book
Everything® Classical Mythology Book
Everything® Da Vinci Book
Everything® Divorce Book
Everything® Einstein Book
Everything® Etiquette Book, 2nd Ed.
Everything® Inventions and Patents Book
Everything® Mafia Book
Everything® Philosophy Book
Everything® Psychology Book
Everything® Shakespeare Book

RELIGION

Everything® Angels Book
Everything® Bible Book
Everything® Buddhism Book
Everything® Catholicism Book
Everything® Christianity Book
Everything® History of the Bible Book
Everything® **Jesus Book**
Everything® Jewish History & Heritage Book
Everything® Judaism Book
Everything® Kabbalah Book
Everything® Koran Book
Everything® **Mary Book**

Everything® Mary Magdalene Book
Everything® Prayer Book
Everything® Saints Book
Everything® Torah Book
Everything® Understanding Islam Book
Everything® World's Religions Book
Everything® Zen Book

SCHOOL & CAREERS

Everything® Alternative Careers Book
Everything® **Career Tests Book**
Everything® College Major Test Book
Everything® College Survival Book, 2nd Ed.
Everything® Cover Letter Book, 2nd Ed.
Everything® **Filmmaking Book**
Everything® Get-a-Job Book
Everything® Guide to Being a Paralegal
Everything® Guide to Being a Real Estate Agent
Everything® **Guide to Being a Sales Rep**
Everything® **Guide to Careers in Health Care**
Everything® **Guide to Careers in Law Enforcement**
Everything® **Guide to Government Jobs**
Everything® Guide to Starting and Running a Restaurant
Everything® Job Interview Book
Everything® New Nurse Book
Everything® New Teacher Book
Everything® Paying for College Book
Everything® Practice Interview Book
Everything® Resume Book, 2nd Ed.
Everything® Study Book

SELF-HELP

Everything® Dating Book, 2nd Ed.
Everything® Great Sex Book
Everything® Kama Sutra Book
Everything® Self-Esteem Book

SPORTS & FITNESS

Everything® **Easy Fitness Book**
Everything® Fishing Book
Everything® Golf Instruction Book
Everything® Pilates Book
Everything® Running Book
Everything® Weight Training Book
Everything® Yoga Book

TRAVEL

Everything® Family Guide to Cruise Vacations
Everything® Family Guide to Hawaii

Everything® Family Guide to Las Vegas, 2nd Ed.
Everything® **Family Guide to Mexico**
Everything® Family Guide to New York City, 2nd Ed.
Everything® Family Guide to RV Travel & Campgrounds
Everything® Family Guide to the Caribbean
Everything® Family Guide to the Walt Disney World Resort®, Universal Studios®, and Greater Orlando, 4th Ed.
Everything® **Family Guide to Timeshares**
Everything® Family Guide to Washington D.C., 2nd Ed.
Everything® Guide to New England

WEDDINGS

Everything® Bachelorette Party Book, $9.95
Everything® Bridesmaid Book, $9.95
Everything® **Destination Wedding Book**
Everything® Elopement Book, $9.95
Everything® Father of the Bride Book, $9.95
Everything® Groom Book, $9.95
Everything® Mother of the Bride Book, $9.95
Everything® Outdoor Wedding Book
Everything® Wedding Book, 3rd Ed.
Everything® Wedding Checklist, $9.95
Everything® Wedding Etiquette Book, $9.95
Everything® **Wedding Organizer, 2nd Ed.,** **$16.95**
Everything® Wedding Shower Book, $9.95
Everything® Wedding Vows Book, $9.95
Everything® **Wedding Workout Book**
Everything® Weddings on a Budget Book, $9.95

WRITING

Everything® Creative Writing Book
Everything® Get Published Book, 2nd Ed.
Everything® Grammar and Style Book
Everything® Guide to Writing a Book Proposal
Everything® Guide to Writing a Novel
Everything® Guide to Writing Children's Books
Everything® Guide to Writing Research Papers
Everything® Screenwriting Book
Everything® Writing Poetry Book
Everything® Writing Well Book